GAME ON!

How Women's Basketball Took Seattle By Storm

Jayda Evans

SASQUATCH BOOKS
SEATTLE

to my favorite looney tune

Printed in the United States of America
Published by Sasquatch Books
Distributed by Publishers Group West
15 14 13 12 11 10 09 08 07 06   9 8 7 6 5 4 3 2 1

Cover design: Stewart A. Williams
Interior design and composition: Stewart A. Williams
Cover photograph: Jeff Reinking/NBAE via Getty Images
Interior photographs:
    Page 20: Courtesy of Val Ackerman
    Pages 64 and 74: ©2006 NBA Entertainment. Photos by Jeff Reinking/Getty Images
    Page 175: Courtesy of Betty Lennox
    Page 224: Courtesy of Lauren Jackson
    All other photographs ©2006 Latrena Smith Photography

Library of Congress Cataloging-in-Publication Data

Evans, Jayda.
    Game on! : how women's basketball took Seattle by storm / Jayda Evans.
        p. cm.
    ISBN 1-57061-477-6
        1. Seattle Storm (Basketball team). 2. Basketball for women--Washington
    (State)--Seattle. I. Title.

GV885.52.S295E93 2006
796.323'6409772--dc22

                                                2005057948

Sasquatch Books
119 South Main Street, Suite 400
Seattle, WA 98104
(206) 467-4300
www.sasquatchbooks.com
custserv@sasquatchbooks.com

Contents

Foreword

By Slick Watts

Hello Sports World! In 2005, I had a conversation with Jayda Evans while watching the Seattle Storm–New York Liberty game. We talked about her father's team and we discussed the years that her dad recruited for Lute Olson's Arizona National Champion Team. I was very surprised to find that our world had so much in common, as her dad had recruited my son, Donald Watts. As our discussion continued, it led to discussion of this book, which months later led to this foreword.

My first reaction to being asked to write this foreword was "why me?" But after thinking about it, I said "why not me?" After all, I have been discriminated against, I have been overlooked in my life, and I have been around Seattle for 30 years now. In that time I have witnessed every possible sporting event. I was there for the opening of the Kingdome; I was also there for the destruction of the Kingdome. I witnessed the first pass from Jim Zorn to Steve Largent. I witnessed Ken Griffey Jr. scoring from first base to win the big playoff game for the Mariners in 1996. I was here in 1979 when Wally Walker, Fred Brown, Jack Sikma, John Johnson, and Gus Williams paraded downtown as the NBA champs. I watched the Huskies come within one basket of making it to the final eight in the NCAA Tournament, and I witnessed Rip Hamilton of UConn shooting while lying on his back to score the final basket with no time left after my son, Donald, had just hit a three-pointer to put the Huskies ahead with four seconds left. That truly ripped my heart out! Yes, I have seen it all and shared the joy and the pain of this city.

Thirty-four years and I thought I had witnessed every sporting event in this town, yet the most uplifting and rewarding of them all happened in the year 2000, when Mrs. Barry Ackerly went to her husband and persuaded him to bring a WNBA team to Seattle. What a special day! Man, my grandmother, I know, must have turned over in her grave. Just think—women can now compete and improve their skills in high school, continue to college, and live out their dreams of playing professional basketball in a viable league. I know my mom and my sisters feel they are owed restitution because 20 years ago they had to give up their dreams of becoming professional basketball players, leaving it up to the men in the family because they had no options.

We Seattleites should thank those women and men who fought for the women's game, leading to the development of the WNBA, as well as the Storm for bringing WNBA greatness to our city. Jayda's book offers a history of how it all happened, and how this city is better off because of these women pioneers. Some basketball fans may dismiss the women's game as being too different from or lesser than the men's game, but if you look closely there are many similarities. The women's game is more fundamental, featuring active ball movement and below-the-rim play, and yet, contrary to some peoples' beliefs, it's extremely exciting. Each possession in the game seems to mean more.

I love the game of basketball for so many reasons, and I love what the women's game brings to the sport. The team concept that women bring to the game is something we can all learn from. Be there, because I will.

—Seattle Slick

Introduction

There's this goofy thing I do when driving north on Sixth Avenue in downtown Seattle. At Pike Street I always peer up so I can catch a glimpse of Sue Bird, captured mid-dribble with a beguiling glare on a massive Nike billboard.

It's the coolest thing. But every time I take that route to the training facility for practice or to KeyArena for Sonics or Storm basketball games, I have this feeling that I need to make sure it's still there. That's the problem with women's sports. At any moment, for whatever reason, it can disappear.

Uncertainty in athletics is an odd feeling for me. I grew up in the male half of the basketball sphere as my father, Jessie Evans, inched his way up from assistant coach at schools such as the University of Minnesota to become the head coach at the University of San Francisco. Basketball has always been my first love. In fact, I can remember the first time I knew I belonged in a gym with thumping basketballs providing the collective heartbeat of a passionate crowd. I was a junior in high school, and some crush asked me to a baseball game at the University of Arizona because he was a high school pitcher. Only, directly across the street behind the baseball stands at McKale Center, the Wildcats were playing Duke. My dad, then an assistant coach under Lute Olson, was stunned I'd miss the game for baseball. Duke coach Mike Krzyzewski's photo from some Sprite ad was part of a collage on my bedroom wall. I cried when Duke lost to University of Nevada, Las Vegas for the 1990 NCAA championship, and Coach K even brought me autographed T-shirts because the Blue Devils were my second favorite team. But I didn't go to the game. Sitting in the blazing sun with my crush, I broke out into hives. You could hear McKale blowing its lid as the Wildcats took the Blue Devils into double overtime before winning 103-96. And I missed it! Never again.

You never have to worry with most men's athletics. Their basketball calendar always rotates with the consistency of the seasons. There's always another game and another level for the guys to reach. But when women try to enter the family business, you quickly learn things aren't the same. People don't even see that they're unjustly discriminating against women, questioning why they go to such lengths as playing overseas or making financial sacrifices to start up American professional leagues just to play. Bird had this conversation with former college teammate Diana Taurasi in Moscow, Russia, of all places. They'd played on the same team abroad, trying to rake in the cash and stay fit for the 2006 WNBA season while taking in a new culture. But friends still wondered why they had to travel so far when the league's eight-month off-season is enough time to work full-time at home as a teacher or even a coach, like Olympian Dawn Staley does for Temple University. "Diana hit the nail on the head when she said, 'Do people say that to dentists? Do people say that to doctors? Oh, you have a couple weeks off, why don't you get another job?'" Bird told me in a telephone conversation during her brief holiday break stateside. "This is our job. We're basketball players! I'm going to go play basketball!"

Bird and her peers' determination to make it in the male-dominated pro ranks is what makes covering women completely different. For me, sportswriting was a natural progression after a lifetime of cheering on my dad and his players, from Kevin McHale (Minnesota) and Michael Cage (San Diego State) to Fennis Dembo (Wyoming) and Damon Stoudamire (Arizona). But I never really thought about the women's professional game until *Seattle Times* sports editor Cathy Henkel asked me to cover the WNBA. There's still the politicking and backstabbing, and basketball is basketball, but watching the women achieve the same recognition as the men is refreshing. The women spend as much time as the men working out in gyms, sacrificing their bodies to numerous injuries that can nag them throughout their entire careers. And the game, while not as athletically gifted as the men's with its soaring dunks, has a much clearer attention to team basketball. Given how today's men's game is so focused on individual play and money, witnessing such a reflection of a more innocent time in basketball kept me from feeling like I was pigeonholed. Who cares if they're women? They can ball. And too often their stories are left untold, mainly for the ridiculous reason that they are women.

As when I reported on the NBA, covering the sister league allowed me to break away from my Dad's shadow. More importantly, it allowed me to bring some of the same understanding to the women's game. In addition, there are so many more social aspects to cover than in the men's game, which currently circles around race. You can't talk about women's basketball without mentioning Title IX, homophobia, and attendance. But the players involved in the WNBA are more than issues and stereotypes. As with many male players, they have unbelievable talent and artistry to their game and personal stories that inspire.

The women live in a parallel universe as their basketball culture is still laced in hip-hop where mostly everyone wants to sport ice (diamonds), drive flashy cars, and listen to heavy bass blare from arena speakers. Yet the players know they're not the NBA. They're not even trying to be the NBA in terms of exorbitant salaries, so there's no need to continue to point out that fact. They're creating their own definition of a professional woman athlete; there are plenty of fans in support of them doing so, and it's fascinating to watch each wave of pioneers at work. Growing up, I could only rattle on with guys about innocuous basketball statistics regarding male players. Now I can do the same with women and men about the WNBA, freely commenting on a hairstyle and shooting form in the same sentence.

It's a welcome change.

I was assigned to the WNBA beat when the Seattle franchise had no identity at all. The *Times* was looking for ways to diversify the sports section in the predictable baseball-filled summer months and decided to treat the Storm equally with every other professional beat we staffed. Women playing ball added a little spice to the section, plus the *Times* went all out, having me travel to every road game, creating stories within stories. (At the time only a handful of papers, including the *Seattle Post-Intelligencer*, sent reporters on the road, mainly to regional games.) The newspaper's effort brought new readers to the section—readers that relished the insights the *Times* provided because they were just as fanatical as baseball, football, or soccer fans in the area.

The Storm was so awful in the beginning it was amazing I continued to follow them. At least I was getting paid to be there. If it weren't for the *P-I* putting Meredith Bagley on the beat full-time, I would have ripped my hair out writing 26 losing-game stories that first season without anyone to kick back and drink a cold one with afterward. Yet the team's popularity and talent grew. Gradually players had to weave past a few autograph seekers, not just in Seattle but also outside their hotels, in order to board chartered buses in Phoenix or Houston. Bird had to use a pseudonym in some cities, and forward Lauren Jackson could no longer go out without becoming gossip fodder. Everything became an Internet chat—from her weight gain after surgery prior to the 2005 season to whether she and former teammate Sheri Sam were dating.

Parts of Seattle began to identify with the team as the players became headstrong role models. The connection is unique, however. The WNBA still scratches its head over why certain cities embrace their women's basketball teams (like Sacramento and Washington, D.C.) while others don't (like Minneapolis or Charlotte). In 10 years of existence, though, the league has become a visual for all women seeking the independence and freedom to make a living within their passion and be accepted for who they are, not what society dictates they should be. There was a time when that wasn't the case. When Storm assistant coach Jessie Kenlaw played professionally in 1979, the emphasis was on femininity and appealing to a conservative audience that was rowdy at games but wanted the women to be women. "It [the players' perceived femininity] was a lot more significant during that particular era because of lack of exposure," Kenlaw told me during an interview. "Now, I'm not so sure if it's a necessity. We have some players in the [WNBA] who couldn't care less what you think of them. They're not trying to prove who they are to the public. There were so many question marks around what was acceptable and what wasn't. Now, it is a lot more acceptable, so players can kind of pick and choose if they want to cater to a particular marketing style."

I've been told many times that I should write a book, whether it be about my father or about being a female in a male locker room or about the WNBA. It was the persistence of Terence Maikels, an acquisitions editor at Sasquatch Books, that brought this story to publication. He believed there was a story about Seattle and its connection with women's basketball worth telling and approached me with the support of the press behind him. Since I spent six seasons covering the Storm, continuing to travel while all the other papers pulled their reporters from the road, I wanted to step back and look at the team and what it meant to all the people involved. There are the fans, like New York Knicks guard Jamal Crawford, a Storm season ticket holder and Rainier Beach High School alum, who travels to several road games every summer, while other fans gather at places like the Theater Off Jackson in Seattle's International

District to watch the team on TV together. They all feel the highs and lows just like the players. There are the coaches, like Lin Dunn, who gave her entire life to the game, and players like Betty Lennox, who probably wouldn't have grown as much as a person if it weren't for her experiences in basketball. And there are reporters like me, who enjoy seeing the sport in a different light beyond the court. It's a different world that's just starting to carve its beginnings. I hope, for basketball's sake, it doesn't disappear.

CHAPTER ONE

Pioneering for a Women's Game

Honesty spilled from Lauren Jackson over coffee as she reflected on an upsetting 2005 season where the Storm lost to Houston in the first round of the WNBA playoffs. Jackson twisted her mouth, then her body, as she admitted she had needed to "grow up and be more mature" during the season as a fifth-year veteran returning to a team of six new faces, five of them rookies. She had also become a bigger part of the business side, returning early from her native Australia to rehabilitate her surgically reconstructed right ankle, but making time for appearances and filming commercials for the team.

The setting of the WNBA can fool a young player into thinking she's arrived. Especially one like Jackson, 25, who is regarded as an Aussie celebrity. She's gossiped about like a movie star and able to afford designer labels—if she ever decides to step out of her preferred comfy sweatpants that dip below her navel and baby T-shirts that give peek-a-boo looks at her colorful tattoos. She is the only player in her country who can genuinely call herself a professional women's basketball player without having to play in Europe or get a second job

Storm guard Sue Bird's billboard was erected downtown in 2003. She replaced former Sonics guard Gary Payton. (LATRENA SMITH PHOTOGRAPHY)

to remain financially stable while playing in the Australian Women's National Basketball League (WNBL).

She was supposed to be the second generation. Her mother, Maree, played for a pittance, missing the Olympics and the chance to play professionally once the WNBL was initiated, in order to have children, marrying the man "with the beautiful jump shot," that is, Gary, Lauren's father. He played for the Australian national team, too, helping give Lauren the remarkable basketball genes that led her to MVP honors in the WNBA and WNBL, being named the WNBL's top player in its 25 years of existence, and more.

But Lauren Jackson slowly started to realize the path is still being paved. "My mom used to say, 'We were the pioneers in this sport; you've got so much fortune, now you're playing in the world's best league.' But I really think *we're* the pioneers, you know. Many years ago it was the same with the NBA; they were struggling to stay on their feet."

Evidence of today's pioneering can be seen in downtown Seattle, where a 30-foot photo of Storm teammate Sue Bird—the game's third-most-popular player based on 2005 All-Star balloting—hangs over the entrance of the Niketown store. The picture looks so glamorous. Her shiny brown hair frames an oval face accented with freckles, soft lips, and warm brown eyes. Lighting highlights an arm defined by muscles as she palms a basketball with the opposite hand. Out of 3,000 votes cast by store customers during the Storm's 2003 season, the point guard from the University of Connecticut edged recent NBA SuperSonics acquisition Ray Allen, cycling legend Lance Armstrong, soccer star Mia Hamm, and track sensation Marion Jones to replace Sonics guard Gary Payton atop the billboard.

Much like that store's arrival in Seattle in the mid-1990s, Bird being the first woman to soar above the front doors marked a change in the city and its sports. Niketown was the first corporate entity to break through Seattle's independent nature. Bird, with her girl-next-door appeal, personified how women athletes can be marketable and entertaining in their sport. At the time she had lucrative contract deals with Nike, American Express, and Minute Maid. Her "Number 10!" credit card commercial was on constant loops with league promos and ads for the Storm. At the unveiling of her billboard she proclaimed to the *Seattle Times*, "As time goes on, you're going to see more and more female athletes up on billboards. This is another step toward that." And it was. Race car driver Danica Patrick's likeness sells watches on a billboard off of Denny Way in Seattle. Hamm and WNBA center Lisa Leslie have been on Nike billboards, while WNBA stars Rebecca Lobo and Dawn Staley have their images etched on massive walls in their home states. Jackson is even captured in a funky mural decorating the Steel Pig Barbecue restaurant just north of Green Lake in Seattle.

As Jackson and Bird, also 25, bop around in their silver Jeep and desert-sand Hummer H2, respectively, knowing what they experience in Seattle is rare. Living in the spotlight of women's athletics casts a large shadow. Sometimes it's hard to tell if they're the tip of something big or the final stop at all that will be. In a microwave society, people want big results in a flash, and sports, especially new concepts and leagues, can't produce in an instant.

World Wrestling Entertainment (WWE) chairman Vince McMahon tried. He promised smash-mouth football with his testosterone-injected Xtreme Football League (XFL). The eight-team league launched in 2001 as a spectacle featuring cameras everywhere, altered rules, a return to gaudy touchdown celebrations, and microphones on players and coaches, who were given the liberty to curse, holler, and answer reporters' questions while playing. Though McMahon's crotch-grabbing WWE generates hundreds of millions of dollars from the 15- to 24-year-old male demographic, his attempt to strip football raw for the same group was received as a juvenile interpretation of a storied game, leading to a quick demise after just one season.

Mia Hamm and her peers met a similar fate with their Women's United Soccer Association (WUSA). Clinging to the final strands of ecstasy from the 1999 World Cup victory that filled the Rose Bowl to its capacity (90,000), the star-studded league started in 2001 with a $40 million budget for eight teams. By season's end, WUSA had

Storm forward Lauren Jackson (right) is part of a mural at Seattle's Steel Pig Barbeque alongside boxing legend Muhammad Ali and Mariners outfielder Ichiro Suzuki.

(LATRENA SMITH PHOTOGRAPHY)

spent $60 million. Slashing rosters and athletes taking pay cuts did nothing to slow the decline in attendance, sponsorship support, and television ratings. Days before the 2004 World Cup, the league folded, but started research on a better marketing strategy to revive itself by 2006.

You just don't develop deep-rooted rivalries overnight, a player can't enthrall an entire arena to chant her name with one spectacular play, and hype can't be a substitute for talent. It takes repetition and patience, virtues hardly allowed women athletes. Many would rather see women pop up like Hamm did every four years on the Olympic platform with her throng of screaming little girl fans chanting "MEE-AH!" Score a few hundred goals. Win a few gold medals. Then, when it's time to retire, make a victory lap as she did in her final game with her husband's name, MLB shortstop Nomar Garciaparra, replacing hers on the back of her jersey, jogging out of the spotlight to start a family and leave everyone with their memories.

The young 'uns won't accept that.

Drift back to when Jackson and Bird were born in the 1980s and the sports scene wasn't the cash cow it is perceived to be today. The NFL was supposedly too violent. Heck, back in the day NASCAR was a redneck sport relegated to the South. And the NBA was faced with a similar dilemma as the WNBA is today of trying to gain popularity. A poll at the time proclaimed American sports enthusiasts didn't want to watch a league full of black basketball players. Prior to 1985, the NBA couldn't go five years without a team relocating to a new city. But the league kept reshaping its game. Athletes, regardless of gender, continued to play and intuitive businessmen knew there was money in the game somewhere, they just had to find it.

In 1967's Seattle, Sonics basketball joined hockey and hydroplanes as professional sports in a city happy to be tucked far off the beaten path. With the NBA battling its rival, the American Basketball Association (ABA), for marketing and players, basketball had more of a club feel. Nosebleed seats felt like mountaintops, looking down on a stinky cloud of smoke that hovered over the court. Fans smoked cigars and guzzled beer in the stands while watching Bob Rule, Lenny Wilkens, or Spencer Haywood dazzle on the court. Practices were casual and players were approachable, willing to strike a pose in snazzy suits with Afros in perfect round puffs. Attendance was modest, with an average of 5,840 fans drawn to 36 home games at the Coliseum during the Sonics' second season, where the team finished 30-52. The team played before several crowds of barely 2,000, and it took seven seasons for the organization to steadily average more than 10,000 fans. Thirty years to record three consecutive seasons of sold-out games.

The Storm, by comparison, is in line with its brethren. In its worst season, 2002, the team drew 6,986 for 16 home games. By 2005 the team had increased its average by about 2,000 and has the fastest growing attendance in the league. But the focus is always on the empty seats as a way to discredit the WNBA. And it's an easy justification. With NBA players averaging $5-million salaries and riding around in private planes to display their high-flying game, it's easy to look at the women's traditional below-the-rim team game, which a $12 million subsidy from the brother league keeps afloat, and yawn. There's still progress to be made.

"It's a modest investment," said NBA commissioner David Stern. "If one looked at the NBA as a league, we're losing money. If you looked at hockey as a league, they're losing money. If you looked at baseball as a league, they're losing money. It's only because it's a woman's league that someone says, 'Well, how long are you gonna keep losing money?' The amount of money is very, very small. The amount of promotion is very, very large. So, I'm not spinning euphemisms in saying this is a very good investment. This is not altruism."

Glimpses of the future would twinkle before the WNBA's eyes. As crowds swelled to KeyArena capacity (17,072) on October 12, 2004, it seemed Seattle was just catching the wave of women's sports:

a diversion from the commonplace belief that people are only interested in women athletically if they're competing against men.

That October night was a contrast to one five years earlier that began the steady breakthrough of headlining women's sports in the city. On October 8, 1999, it was the dreary kind of evening famed Seattle columnist Emmett Watson described for his "Lesser Seattle" fables, intended to keep tourists from relocating to the city in the 1990s. One where wicked taboos lurked in the shadows while thick rain prickled the streets.

On this night, a red heat rushed through the veins of sports enthusiasts, making the cool temperature feel warm. This crowd was amped to see the crimson flow of fresh blood. Fists clenched as mouths spoke of the forbidden event about to unfold. After months of court filings, governing body rulings, and public debates, the city more known for Boeing jets than sporting bets prepared to host the first sanctioned "Male vs Female" boxing match in the bowels of Mercer Arena. Packs of twenty-somethings paid $15 to $60 to enter the building and bear witness to a different type of history. Some carried posters proclaiming woman power, linking the event to tennis legend Billie Jean King vs Bobby Riggs circa 1973 or Ann Meyers, the heralded Olympic guard, trying out for the NBA's Indiana Pacers in 1979. Others snarled in disgust because the event conjured images of domestic violence or disrespect for the sport, but still took their seats, unable to turn away, as if the match were some roadside accident.

Media from London to Lynnwood descended upon Seattle with paparazzi camera crews snapping photos that darkened the depth of the night's shadows with every flash of the bulb. The buzz, stirring stronger than the city's notorious coffee, made Loi Chow edgier. He was a hack horse jockey from Vancouver, B.C., not a boxer equipped to fight. Chow, 34, was training the real intended man for the bout, Hector Morales, when the pressure swallowed Morales whole and regurgitated a shell of a boxer unable to picture himself throwing a fist at anyone, particularly a woman. Chow tried to keep him tucked away from the critical eye of mainstream America by not even having Morales leave Canada until shortly before the scheduled fight, but the whispers of judgment—What kind of man would do this? What kind of credible boxer would enter this circus?—whooshed their way up Interstate 5 anyway. Chow was the last resort. And hours before the fight he tried to make a mad dash too, according to event organizer Bob Jarvis, not wanting to be *the one.*

Across the corridor was Margaret MacGregor's camp. The rare woman who had practically begged for the fight. MacGregor went so far as to tell reporters she'd egg Chow on if he refused to throw a punch. Minutes before the match, she bounced about, shadowboxing with her Dorothy Hamill–styled sandy-blond hair soaking up the sweat beading on her forehead.

MacGregor, a 36-year-old part-time landscaper from Bremerton, simply wanted to box. She was 3-0 since turning professional in April 1999 and 8-0-1 in kickboxing. According to her trainer, Vern Miller, no one wanted to enter the ring with MacGregor, who was nicknamed "Tiger" and often fought like the savage beast. She had spent 50 months in prison for selling about a gram of meth to an undercover officer, but learned to box after an ex-husband hit her, vowing no man would ever beat her again "unless I let him." The night's four-round fight was supposed to bring her some attention in her junior lightweight class, possibly unearthing some potential competition, but Jarvis had originally planned the guaranteed publicity stunt to promote Martin O'Malley, a proven pro with a 10-0 record who was scheduled to box Tito Tovar of Denver. O'Malley fumed at the proposition backfiring, answering more questions about MacGregor-Chow than his own bout.

MacGregor tried to disregard her role in the scene. In a red and gold satin robe, she exited her dressing room strategically late to "ice" Chow. A determined look gleamed in her almond-shaped brown eyes. All she wanted was to be taken seriously. It's all any woman athlete wants. But pundits within the boxing realm, such as *Fight Game* magazine editor Bert Sugar, called the spectacle "a sideshow, an old carnival act updated for the 1990s." The Association of Boxing Commissions (ABC) lashed out at Washington state for having sanctioned the fight, refusing to recognize it in their official records as anything more than an exhibition. In a press release ABC stated their reasoning was that "professional boxing is readily available to women [and there are] the very real health and safety concerns that most certainly will occur in a male vs female match-up." The Women's Sports Foundation responded in their own release that "as long as competing athletes are matched by ability, muscle mass and other standardized physical variables critical to success in the sport, competition between males and females should be permitted." Others just laughed at the physical makeup of the fight—MacGregor was 5-foot-5, about three inches taller than Chow, and he was winless in the two matches he'd fought against men, the last occurring in 1996.

Chow puffed his chest at first, but appeared to quiver in his corner after the first round and whined to the referee while waiting for the ding signaling the end of each round. MacGregor threw combinations his way, demanding he fight back. He didn't. Chow threw soft, single punches, connecting once. MacGregor connected a jab that landed on his head. Crimson blood broke through his skin and trickled down his face. The sold-out crowd of 2,768 roared like Romans in an ancient Colosseum once she was pronounced the winner by decision after four rounds. They both earned $1,500 for the bout, generating $75,705 at the gate, the second-largest indoor boxing show in Northwest history.

Coupled with Muhammad Ali's daughter Laila's fight against April Fowler in New York the night before, MacGregor's match sparked a growth and acceptance of women's boxing that had made its debut six years earlier in Washington. Today, casino managers across the country claim if there isn't a woman's fight on the card, fans are pissed.

In Seattle, they wouldn't display the kind of bloodcurdling passion for a woman athlete that warms the body on a brisk October night until the Storm stirred up interest again. And this time the women fighting would be taken seriously.

Five years later, it was the Storm's fifth season and a pint-sized guard named Betty Lennox had displayed enough heroics during the season to stir the crowd into chanting her first name in unison, usually as she stepped to the free-throw line at the end of another win. Rippling muscles tattooed with the Tasmanian Devil cartoon character protruded from her jersey, which was emblazoned with the number 22. Her naturally curly dark brown hair was tightly braided into intricate lines of cornrows, and her piercing, determined brown eyes looked almost as deadly as her jump shot.

Lennox converted on a picturesque fadeaway jumper while being fouled by Connecticut Sun guard Lindsay Whalen and responded by flinging her right fist in the air, shouting to the crowd, "That's what I'm talkin' 'bout!" The collective screams at the sold-out KeyArena notched 114 decibels on the noise meter, one click higher than when Gary Payton was introduced in Game 7 of the 1996 Western Conference finals held in the same facility.

Over the airwaves, ESPN broadcasters Greg Anthony, a former Sonics guard; Ann Meyers, a Hall of Fame player; and Terry Gannon, who played for North Carolina State's 1983 NCAA championship team, would boast about the championship just as baritone broadcaster Bob Blackburn had done when the Sonics clinched in one 1979. The Storm's WNBA title was the first major professional championship Seattle had experienced since then, ending a drought of 25 years, the longest of any city with at least three professional teams.

"I liked the way they promoted it in Seattle," said Charmin Smith, a Storm original guard. "It didn't matter that it was a WNBA championship. It was, 'They're bringing a championship to Seattle.' It wasn't lower. It was the same as the SuperSonics. It'd be the same with the Mariners winning the World Series. It was like that significant. I thought that was really special."

Seattleites embraced the post-championship euphoria. When the clock struck noon on October 15, a misty Friday, businessmen and businesswomen in stuffy suits converged in downtown's Westlake Center with freshly face-painted kids and diehard fans wearing green Storm championship gear still creased with the folds from the printing plant. The players cruised to the celebration atop donated convertible Saabs. Coach Anne Donovan rode up front beside Jackson, who wouldn't let go of the silver trophy. Wearing designer Gucci shades, a Storm shirt, jeans, and her blond locks wrapped in a messy bun, Jackson had dreamed of winning a WNBA championship since she first caught a 1997 WNBA game televised back home in Canberra, her country's capital.

The concept of women playing professional basketball wasn't novel to her. Australia had formed a professional league in 1980, and Jackson shined there for four years prior to former Storm coach Lin Dunn selecting her with the No. 1 pick in 2001. Australian stars Michele Timms, who played in the WNBA, Robyn Maher, and Shelley Sandie were among Jackson's idols, behind her mom, of course, who had played for the national team wearing jersey No. 15.

"I was an ornery little shit," Jackson joked of her not-so-distant childhood when she started wearing No. 15 in honor of her mother. "Nobody was ever too good for me because of the athlete my Mum was. They [my parents] were good, they were the best, and so was I."

Americans like to think of themselves at the forefront of everything, but we are far behind in terms of equality for women in professional sports. Archaic beliefs that fragile women need to be bound in corsets and placed beneath the shade of a tree, never to move unless to give birth or cook a meal, overwhelmed advancement of the American female athlete. While Australia, for example, was forming a league in hopes the extended training would help their national team rise to Olympic prominence, America steadily slammed its own attempts, with most sportswriters focusing more on who was a lesbian or who was attractive than who could play ball. That's if they bothered to watch a game at all. Sponsors also focused on femininity rather than productivity, not believing female athletes could push a product. And given the U.S. national team's dominance since women ballers were allowed to compete in the 1976 Olympics, it was understandable why the argument that a home-based league would help develop talent fell on uninterested ears. Americans, led by names such as Sheryl Swoopes and Teresa Edwards, have won five of the eight possible Olympic gold medals.

Few people got it. Not just that women's basketball could be good for little girls in terms of building self-esteem and strength and learning the benefits of teamwork. But also that it's an entertaining brand of game. Women are different than men. You don't need aptly named planets to visualize that theory. And women basketball players bring a different spice to the court. They have an odd way of joining opponents for a glass of red wine or a beer over dinner to share tales the night before clawing at each other for an intense 40 minutes in competitive games. Sometimes best friends will scream audible curse words, collecting a record four technical fouls like Jackson against Sheri Sam when the latter played for the defunct Miami Sol. And instead of acting entitled or alienating their unabashed following with brushes with the law for anything from DUIs to bar fights, WNBA players usually care for the communities they spend short stints in as if they were their own, naturally welcoming the responsibility of being role models.

Because of these dueling mentalities of the players—warrior nurturers who genuinely care about how they're perceived yet play with crude aggression—Seattle has been one of those rare cities craving women's basketball. The game offers a visual to many of the population's own personality. It might seem strange to outsiders. NBC's hit TV series *Frasier* and the whole grunge music movement formed the nation's view of Seattle in the 1990s. Then there's the infamous list of serial killers Gary Ridgway, Ted Bundy, and Robert Yates, along with convicted rapist Mary Kay Letourneau, who've

Storm center Janell Burse (left) blocks an opponent's shot. (LATRENA SMITH PHOTOGRAPHY)

tainted the state's reputation. Add the questionably high suicide rate, and how basketball found a place among swanky cafés, rockers in plaid, and the depressed can be perplexing.

Seattle is actually a cliquish town of about a half-million people in the city itself, with several divided worlds from the arts to aviation, rotating within a majestic setting of snowcapped mountain ranges, cobalt waters, and plush green foliage. It's a primarily multicultural society that strays from intermingling, yet is rooted in a liberal mind-set open to new concepts. Microsoft and the Internet boom of the late 1990s brought a drastic change to Seattle's makeup. Suddenly, hip millionaire yuppies jolted the Mayberry setting of the city. The cost of living skyrocketed almost as high as the condominiums thrown up around the Puget Sound. Once dot-coms busted, however, the area was left with clogged traffic, overpriced land, and a shattered image.

People already had a collective low self-esteem. Following the Mariners through 14 consecutive losing seasons in the drab Kingdome will do that to a person. The team has since relocated to the refreshing outdoor setting of Safeco Field. The Seahawks and Sonics (especially when Payton created a fervor in the 1990s, leading the Sonics to the NBA Finals in 1996, and when running back Shaun Alexander won the NFL's MVP award in 2006) experienced scattered success, but true victory was virtually an unimaginable feeling outside of University of Washington football. A failed economy followed by constant news of layoffs from Boeing to teachers drew the need for an entertaining escape. In the summer there were plenty of outdoor activities, but the season only lasts for about 60 days—and that's no spin to keep tourists out.

By winning the 2004 WNBA championship, the Storm ignited the city's hoops passion. In the following months, the University of Washington men's basketball team won a school record 29 games and was awarded its first No. 1 seed in school history in the NCAA tournament. Seattle's urban high school girls basketball teams from Chief Sealth and Garfield won their respective state championships.

And the Sonics defied all prognosticators by winning the inaugural Northwest Division Championship, finishing an improbable season at 52-30, but losing 4-2 in a seven-game series against San Antonio, who advanced to win the NBA championship.

Basketball fans continued to respond locally. About 1,200 new season ticket holders were secured in the Storm off-season, bringing the total to more than 3,400, and the attendance average jumped to 8,868, with five sellouts in 2005. The franchise had lost an average of $1 million in each of the previous five seasons, but broke even at the end of its fiscal year in October 2005.

As a coach in the now-defunct American Basketball League (ABL), Lin Dunn saw the potential in a women's pro league in the late 1990s. She bused her Portland Power team to Seattle for a February 9 game at Mercer Arena in 1997. The Seattle Reign, in the midst of a six-game losing streak to close out their inaugural season, had pleased the league by garnering the fourth-highest ticket revenues in the ABL. There were 4,496 fans present in the 4,509–seating capacity building. Dunn looked around at the crowd proudly wearing maroon and gold and fed off what she saw.

"The place was packed," she said. "It felt like people were hanging from the rafters."

The Power defeated the Reign 79-76 in overtime, and by December 1998, the league would fold, unable to compete with the NBA's marketing dollars. But *BusinessWeek* reported what many in Seattle already knew, that women's basketball attracted "well-educated, family-oriented fans." A jackpot in terms of seeking advertising dollars. The Sonics, whose former general manager, Wally Walker, had had conversations with former Wall Street colleague turned WNBA president, Val Ackerman, about the possibility of a WNBA team in Seattle, were granted a team in June 1999. Establishing a way for Dunn to coach before that ravenous crowd.

Only it was Anne Donovan who in 2004 stepped onto the Storm's green-trimmed parquet court and twirled around in a royal blue pantsuit accented with a crisp white top and gold bow-shaped brooch. She slowly spun around as if counting all 17,072 in attendance to see her young Storm team play in the championship final. She had spoken of winning the title before the season even started. Over lunch in May at Duke's Chowder House along picturesque Lake Union, she poked at a seafood salad as the words weighted in frustration streamed out. Donovan, a three-time Olympian, said winning was the only way women coaches were going to gain respect at the professional level. Unless you count Nancy Lieberman's championship with Dallas in the less-competitive National Women's Basketball League, no woman had won a title in any of the 13 disbanded leagues or the previous seven WNBA Finals.

When the last buzzer sounded, so many barriers were shattered. Donovan couldn't hold back the tears as she pumped her right fist high in the air. She gritted her teeth each time she belted, "yes! Yes! YES!" On that chilly October night, playing in a league first thought of as a sideshow because it didn't begin in basketball's traditional fall setting, Donovan grabbed respect by becoming the first woman coach to win a WNBA championship. It wasn't easy; the road had been paved with many emotional and physical downsides, from family deaths to player injuries. The biggest obstacle of all was instituting a league. "After the game, I remember thinking to myself, 'I'm never going to play again. I can't ever live up to this moment. How am I ever going to step back onto a basketball court?'" said Jackson, who shifted in her seat as she prepared to mimic one of her favorite dramatic actresses. "I had a Greta Garbo moment when I went home—'I just want to be alone.' I was talking about retiring, and my mum was like, don't announce anything until after you rest. It was a tough year."

It was just the beginning. Removed from the excitement of the championship as the WNBA heads into its tenth anniversary season, Jackson finally understood winning had just cracked new ground for her sport only in her adopted region. Women's basketball didn't have to be relegated to glossy billboards that serve more as hopeful aspirations than reality. The feverish pitch in KeyArena and the long afterglow could be extended—it was just going to take more patience than originally thought. It's the tricky thing about glimpses. There's always the lure to see more.

CHAPTER TWO

Opening Doors:
The Passage of Title IX

Sunday mornings at Val Ackerman's Manhattan home were often predictable. Each week was so crammed with Ackerman stuffing "27 hours worth of work into 24-hour days" that she could barely envision a weekend between travel to games, daily logistics meetings, and constant public speeches promoting her new WNBA league. Making dinner often consisted of flipping through a binder of menus from take-out restaurants in her Tribeca neighborhood. Sleep occurred 30,000 feet in the air aboard a plane. And the pouches under her eyes were a running joke in the office.

The pace slowed slightly on Sunday as she thumbed through the *New York Times* to begin another jam-packed week while her husband and their two young daughters buzzed about. But on May 2, 2004, the WNBA's inaugural president had a burst of emotion. Ackerman's pale blue eyes bulged as she casually glanced over page 4 of the "In Person" section. She leaped from her seat, ripped out the article that caught her attention, and searched for her children.

"Look!" she screamed to the two girls with befuddled faces. Ackerman is a warm person willing to share a smile with strangers, but after working in the hard-nosed sports business and management environment, wild, frantic emotion was not as common for her.

Yet that's what childhood idols rekindle in one's soul. And Ackerman flapped it around in the form of a black-and-white square of newsprint.

"You guys thought I was kidding—look!" she shrieked to the kids again.

Her youngest grabbed the newspaper clipping and began to read the article beneath the headline "Sweetheart of Rodeos Past." The flashback was about Sally Starr, former host of the popular children's television program *Popeye Theatre*, which aired from 1950–71 on Philadelphia's WFIL (later WPVI). Sally, a certifiable cowgirl from Kansas City, would strut onto the set riding a palomino horse (aptly named Pal) and give her signature welcome dressed in a fringed costume complete with a 10-gallon Stetson hat and sparkly sequined stars across her chest.

Ackerman, joining the show's legion of baby-boomer fans as a kid in the late 1960s, was mesmerized by Sally. Her family lived on the edge of the station's broadcast radius, 33 miles outside Philly in Pennington, New Jersey. Most weekdays, Ackerman and her brother, George, sat in front of the television right after *American Bandstand* as Sally Starr rode onstage saying, "I hope ya feel as good as ya look to your gal Sal." She'd give a wide smile and look dead into the camera with deep brown eyes. She had guests like Kentucky Fried Chicken's Colonel Harland Sanders and President Richard Nixon drop by to talk to the kids in between showing Popeye cartoons and Three Stooges shorts.

"She was both glamorous in her way and very cheerful and positive," Ackerman remembered nearly 35 years later. "She was always riding a horse around and seemed like she knew what she was doing with it, so I guess I also thought of her as very strong and in control."

Syndicated game shows and soap operas that attracted more advertising dollars than kiddie programs booted Sally Starr's show

Val Ackerman was a three-sport athlete in high school, playing basketball and field hockey as well as running track. She continued to compete in marathons and Iron Woman competitions well after college. (COURTESY OF VAL ACKERMAN)

off the air. She moved to Philly with crooning cowboy husband Jack Rodgers, who would beat her until one night she sneaked into their bedroom while he was sleeping and cracked a wooden chair over his head. Off-camera, Starr smoked, suffered the loss of her second husband, went bankrupt, and suffered a near-fatal heart attack in 1998. Along the way she continued to make appearances for $300 to $500.

"I was the first woman on a daily show, you know," she told the *Asbury Park Press*. Sally Starr was of the era that included TV shows like *Gunsmoke* and *Bonanza*, but no footage remains of her program.

"I opened the doors for all your anchorwomen and your daily talk-show hostesses and all of that stuff. Because due to women's chemicals and the structure of their lives—being mothers and so on—they [television executives] didn't think we could hold down a daily job. But we proved 'em different. We proved that we could be a mommy, a homemaker, a wife, and a personality. And we kept our feet on the ground."

After reading the article, Ackerman's youngest daughter looked up at her mom with the same expression that had caused Ackerman to adorn the newborn with her childhood idol's name. Formally, the little girl's name is Sarah Elisabeth Rappaport, "but she's never gone by it," Val said. "She always goes by 'Sally.' She loves Sally. And I just loved that show and I thought the world of Sally Starr. I don't know, I guess the name just . . . whenever I thought of Sally, I thought of Sally Starr."

Aside from that article, the little girl with summer blond hair hardly knows about the journey women like her mother had to make in sports and media to create the world she lives in. But even the advancements are far behind in terms of equality, with recent studies of 285 newspaper sports editors showing they still believe women are naturally less athletic and less interested in sports than men. Other studies contradict the editors' beliefs, showing that women account for 50 percent of both the NFL viewing audience and purchases of NBA merchandise.

Raised in the rural town about five miles from where George Washington crossed the Delaware, Ackerman didn't have many organized sports opportunities, even though she came from a family of local athletic royalty. Her paternal grandfather, George, was an athletic director and coach at Trenton State College, and her father, Randy, was athletic director of Northern Burlington, a small high school in South Jersey, during her childhood, accepting the same position at Val's high school shortly before she attended.

"We never went anywhere without being recognized as either George Ackerman's grandkids or Randy Ackerman's children depending on how old the person was that approached us," said Ackerman's younger brother, George, who was named after his grandfather. "The Ackerman side of the family was very, very sports driven. My father to us was a tremendous leadership figure and we were always interested in trying to impress him. But my father was not some sort of lunatic cracking the whip with us. He was always very positive and upbeat in getting and keeping us interested in sports."

Weekends were spent watching Randy Ackerman referee basketball games and attending football games or wrestling matches. At family gatherings the Ackermans played football on the front lawn or competitive softball, Val's parents teaming up against her and George.

If the Boston Celtics were on television, the extended family would huddle around the set to catch the game while debating the careers of basketball legends Bill Russell, John Havlicek, and others. Most evenings were spent playing in their driveway with many lights scattered in the dogwood trees as Val and George shot hoops on the balding grass driveway with Dad.

"There was never a distinction like, 'This is boys' stuff, this is girls' stuff,' you know what I mean?" said Val's mother, Barbara, who worked in politics as the executive assistant to the secretary of state in Trenton until retiring in 1995. Sports were infused into Val's soul. By junior high she was known as a jock, but the only athletic activity available for girls was cheerleading. Everyone in the small town tried out—or was labeled an outcast. Ackerman could tell she didn't quite fit in: She was awkward with the blue and gold pom-poms and more profound than peppy during the Saturday morning tryouts at the school. So, the panel of teacher/judges cut her.

"It was so depressing. It changed my life," said Ackerman of the early Timberlane Junior High experience. "Any girl who had an ounce of athletic ability tried out for the cheerleading team, and I got cut. It was devastating. It was humiliating because I was sort of this big jock. In fact, I was a good basketball player and people knew about me. Everybody was pushing me to try out for the boy's basketball team, but I was too cowardly to do that.

"It was just, you know, the girls who made it were real cheerleader-type girls. They were bubbly and spunky, and I look back and think my heart wasn't really in it at the tryout because I was just sort of not into being a cheerleader. Frankly, the thought of being on the sideline cheering for the boys was not my idea of my life's dream. But that's what you did. The pressure . . . I would have been a freak among my friends if I hadn't tried out."

When Ackerman enrolled in high school, Title IX was beginning to take shape. This historic legislation, signed by President Richard Nixon in 1972, stated that "no person in the United States shall, on the basis of sex, be excluded from participation in, be denied the benefits of, or be subjected to discrimination under any educational program or activity receiving Federal assistance."

Title IX helped Ackerman compete in field hockey, basketball, and track and field while attending Hopewell Valley High. She also swam competitively through a summer recreational program, setting numerous records in the butterfly and diving events. But as a sophomore she came home in tears when the school started its own swim team during the winter basketball season.

"Why would they have two of the sports I love the most at the same time?" she sobbed to her mother, distraught at not being able to letter on both teams.

Ackerman stuck with basketball, becoming one of the 817,073 girls involved in high school sports in 1973, only a year after the law's passage. Just eight states sponsored state basketball tournaments for high schools that year. By 1977, only New York hadn't caught on.

Basketball was easiest to initiate because of preexisting gymnasiums and balls from boys' programs. In fact, girls not part of the tea-and-crumpet upper society were already playing, finding basketball a fun, youthful sport. In booming suburbia, however, stereotypes continued to circulate about the stay-at-home mother who raised her family with the traditional standards of boys playing sports and girls playing with dolls.

"Fortunately, times have changed," Ackerman says.

At that time, most states were of the Victorian theory that warned if women exercised while menstruating, their uterus could enlarge and displace. Plus, women athletes were believed to be unattractive and unnatural "muscle molls," according to sportswriters who covered legendary athletes like Texan Babe Didrikson in the 1940s and '50s.

"They honestly didn't think women had the stamina or strength or endurance to play full court," former Storm coach Lin Dunn remembered of her youth in the 1950s and '60s. "Women were just too weak to play. It would just be too stressful on their bodies to run full court. Come on, gimme a break!

"But even parents discouraged their girls from being involved in sports."

Didrikson, known simply as "Babe" worldwide, was a svelte woman with brown hair and a chiseled facial structure, who competed in every sport imaginable, making her name as an Olympian and a golfer.

During Dunn's preteen days in Tennessee, attitudes about female athletes were only slightly more welcoming. She can recall biking down to the picture show to catch the latest flick. Before the show started, a black-and-white globe spun on the screen and a serious baritone voice boomed from the sound system. A 10-minute segment delivered news nuggets, and Dunn remembers seeing old clips about the sports antics of Babe, whether it was her three Olympic gold medals or 31 LPGA titles won before her death in 1956. At that time, it was the only way Dunn and most other girls in America heard about women athletes, though Dunn at least was able to hear stories from her mother who played a version of basketball in the 1930s—a version that wouldn't allow roving players and dribbling. And if the ball happened to squirt loose, rules restricted the young women from hustling to the court to grab it. The so-called game was as exciting as watching mannequins play.

Secluded in the rugged Pacific Northwest, the blue-collar mentality of Washingtonians had a slightly different view about women's athletics. Rooted in maritime activities, from the Puget Sound–area's rich history with a naval shipyard in Bremerton to the Port of Seattle's global leadership in trade, transportation, and tourism, the region's athletic women weren't as ridiculed as their counterparts in other parts of the country. Since the first residents landed at Alki Beach in the 1800s, women pitched in to establish a life amidst the harsh, rainy terrain. Activities like kayaking, skiing, hiking, and sailing weren't restricted to men since some began as survival in finding food or shelter.

Decades later Canada helped foster an interest in women's hockey in the region, while major professional sports history sprouted with the 1969 Seattle Pilots, a baseball team that lasted one season. Local women played fastpitch softball in the 1950s and '60s, receiving sponsorships from businesses but logging miles on I-5 to find competition from Vancouver, B.C., to Los Angeles, California.

"We received more coverage than the women today," remembered Sis Prentice, a softball notable from the Seattle neighborhood of Queen Anne. Prentice played in an era with future Hall of Famer Margaret Dobson, who held the highest batting average in the ASA Women's Fast Pitch National Championship, hitting .615 in the 1950 title game (8-for-13).

The best tournaments were in Phoenix, Arizona, where Prentice was treated like a star, signing autographs as a spry shortstop for the Seattle Epicures (1949–55), Bellevue Airflytes (1955–60), and Seattle League (1961–62).

Prentice, who had to give up the sport following a ski injury, began playing with a scrappy group of girls at the old Ballard Fieldhouse. "We got into it where we'd beat everybody, so we had to go out of the area," she told reporter Carla Anderson in 1985. "We couldn't find any competition here. Down there [Phoenix], it was big. You were a celebrity."

A former MVP of the Tri-State high school basketball tournament held in Washington, Prentice worked mercilessly like other former female athletes to build athletics programs for girls in Seattle. Title IX helped with funding at local schools and Prentice kept fastpitch alive by coaching and talking about her playing days with friends in local government.

Another notable former softball player key to developing women's sports in the area was Barbara Hedges, who prior to moving to the Northwest had established the women's athletic program at the University of Southern California in the late 1980s during her post there as senior associate director of athletics. Hedges was hired as athletic director for the University of Washington in 1991. During her storied 13 years, she moved to make fastpitch a Husky program in 1993 to comply with Title IX's gender equity rules. Hedges would later spend $40 million to renovate Washington's basketball arena and construct a new football practice facility and stadiums for softball, baseball, and soccer. Her teams won five national and 46 conference titles, making little boys and girls grow up wanting to be Huskies.

Washington started its state girls basketball high school tourney in 1974 with Wapato High, which is located in Eastern Washington's Yakima Valley, defeating Everett High 36-28. Everett, a 30-minute drive north from downtown Seattle, is part of the vast Snohomish County that would birth a key woman player who helped changed the landscape of basketball in the state. While East Coast girls like Val Ackerman dabbled in various types of sports, in the Pacific Northwest the favorites were softball, basketball, and soccer. Washington native Karen Bryant, future Storm chief operating officer, fell in love with basketball, although her high school letterman's jacket rivaled race car drivers' with all the patches from other sports she played.

Everything revolved around hoops. She'd bounce a basketball home in her softball uniform. Her parents would have to pick her up from the neighborhood court a mile from her house so she could eat dinner. And she played her own version of "Combat Nerf Basketball" with her dad and younger brother in the narrow hallway of their parents' split-level home. The trio would drip with sweat as they threw each other against the walls, trying to jam the small Nerf ball into the hoop. Bryant, sporting a raven-tinted curly mop of hair framing an everlasting smile, always won.

It was the early 1980s. Despite numerous opportunities for girls to play sports, there were still mentally damaging labels thrown at the competitors like lawn darts. Bryant, who received support from both parents, was considered a "tomboy" and questioned for her love of basketball. She didn't let it faze her. Taped to her bedroom walls were posters of Julius "Dr. J" Erving, who defied gravity while he wowed fans as a Philadelphia 76er with spinning jump shots and masterful ball-handling skills in the 1970s. And David "Skywalker" Thompson, who seemingly used air as a stairway to the basket, winning the ABA's dunk contest in 1976 before starring with the NBA's Atlanta Hawks and ending his tumultuous career in Seattle and Indiana.

Bryant emulated these players on the court, also keeping an eye on Seattle high school star Joyce Walker, who possessed flair and desire to play. But Walker, and most other women athletes at the time, lacked exposure. President Ronald Reagan then occupied the White House, and although the actor-turned-politician couldn't do anything to erase Title IX's leap toward equality, the staunch conservative did undermine the law with the help of the Supreme Court's 1984 ruling for *Grove City College v. Bell* that Title IX didn't apply to athletics. John Roberts, who was appointed to the Court in 2005, wrote a convincing memo as special assistant to the attorney general in the Reagan administration that argued the legislation should only apply to programs directly receiving federal funding. Athletics didn't receive aid, and in a 6-3 decision, the Supreme Court ruled to negate the terms of Title IX in collegiate sports. Congress reversed the decision with the passing of the Civil Rights Restoration Act in 1988, but it wasn't enough to keep women from begging to survive. Since then, cases have been filed from male sports such as wrestling, claiming reverse discrimination, and stiffer "clarifications" have been passed requiring women to prove their interest in athletics, whereas men aren't required to jump through the same hula hoop. Exposure wouldn't break into the mainstream until the new millennium.

"The first female basketball player's name I remember hearing was Cheryl Miller," said Bryant of the USC star, who was a three-time college player of the year as she led the Women of Troy to an NCAA title and won 1984 Olympic gold. "And I don't even remember when that was. It might have been college [in the 1990s]. It was hard. They weren't marketed. When we'd go to our PE classes, they didn't have posters of Joyce Walker in the locker room. It was NBA and NFL posters. I mean, who made a poster of Cheryl Miller?"

The *Seattle Times* and *Everett Herald* did make a big deal about Bryant, who grew up in Edmonds, a modest port town of about 35,000 people with views of the snow-capped Olympic Mountain range. Born the oldest of three children on December 21, 1967, Bryant was always competitive. She was constantly mentioned in the paper for her athletic exploits, which included being twirled around by coach Bruce Evans on Seattle Center's Mercer Arena court as part of the 1984 Class 2A state championship team.

Woodway High, which is currently Edmonds-Woodway, was caught in a back-and-forth game with top-ranked North Kitsap that ended with a buzzer-beating final score of 54-52. Bryant's team only lost twice in the 27-game season, but her excitement at the win was like witnessing a first victory ever. Bryant's mouth agape, she squealed as she extended her right arm in a powerful fist to celebrate in the middle of disbelieving teammates adorned in cream-colored jerseys with gold and black trim.

The woverflow of bliss was fitting for the sophomore, considering how her sparkling career didn't take the path many onlookers thought it would. By Bryant's senior season, she was seated atop a sterile hospital bed getting an early taste of bureaucracy as she pleaded with doctors to clear her to play in the state tournament with a broken foot. The Warriors were seeded first and expected to win the title. It was an hour before tip-off, leaving Bryant plenty of time to make the 20-minute drive from the doctor's office in Northgate to the arena and finish warming up with her team.

But podiatrist Dr. Stanley Newell and Bryant's father saw past the wants of a desperate teenager, to the long-term effects of downing painkillers like they were sugar tablets and rushing onto the court with an obvious broken bone. Permission was denied, sending Bryant to the first-round game with a dejected look across her normally perky face. Her father, Mike, drove to the back of the arena and Bryant hobbled in through the team entrance on crutches. She could see her teammates warming up, thinking they'd have their star leader in the lineup. Heads dropped in disappointment and empathy as everyone realized she would not play.

"It was so dramatic," she reflected 19 years later. "It's [the foot] still fucked up. They put a little bit of my hipbone in there. I hurt it my last regular-season home game and we were 16-2. It was going to be our senior year, you know, go out on top, nobody was going to beat us. Then it happened."

Bryant was still the focus of the tournament, gracing a page of the *Seattle Times*, holding the X-ray from her left foot, diagnosed as having a stress fracture. The Warriors placed fifth at state without her.

Bryant, considered a talented guard/forward, was recruited by West Coast schools like St. Mary's, the University of Oregon, and Western Washington University, but hadn't signed by her junior season because she dreamed of attending the University of Washington on a four-year ride. "She's the most complete player we've ever had," Bruce Evans told the *Seattle Times* in 1986. "She's got a good variety of offensive moves, good shooting range and provides great leadership."

But Bryant lost her college scholarship offers. Instead she'd have surgery on the foot and bounce from Green River Community College to Seattle University, sitting deep on the bench, trying to regain her reputation and strength. Depression sunk in as Bryant thought about how her playing career skidded off her intended path. Happiness came from relationships she established and the life she built off the court, not from spending hours in a gym shooting hoops or scoring game-winners on the court. Bryant was finally given a chance to play for the Huskies in 1990. Yet UW coach Chris Gobrecht made her walk on to earn it. Bryant did, playing for the 1990–91 team that advanced to the NCAA tournament's Sweet 16 round, losing to Stanford 73-47 in Las Vegas, Nevada. Bryant, 23, dubbed "Grandmama" by teammates because she was older, played four minutes in the game, not logging a stat.

"There are no guarantees," Bryant said. "My career took some weird turns. As a kid, I always knew I was going to play for the Huskies and I was going to be in the record books and I was going to leave this legacy. I wasn't going to go to a junior college. But because I ended up going to three different schools, I'm not in any record books and I didn't leave a legacy. What I took away was all the experience and I think I made an impact, but I miss identifying with one team. I was equally loyal to all of them."

Bryant's scholarship offers were a significant part of the advancement of Title IX. To balance their athletic programs, universities were offering more sports and funding to women, opening up athletics as an option for high school girls as a means to attend college without the financial burden. About a decade earlier, Ackerman received partial "aid," amounting to about $2,000 of the only scholarship available, to play at the University of Virginia. She was a four-year starter, playing from 1978–81 and earning two academic All-American distinctions. Ann Meyers received the first full scholarship to play basketball at UCLA in 1974, earning money for tuition, room, and board.

Staying involved in basketball after college remained sketchy, however. Ackerman had to travel to France in order to continue her playing career, fulfilling a one-year contract, while Bryant left hers unsatisfied due to injuries that depleted her talent and interest. She tried coaching, first as an assistant at her high school alma mater, then as a head coach for three years at Woodinville High School (1993–96), but her passion on the sideline didn't relate to her players.

Bryant kept her face in the basketball community, working for five years in the construction management field. As project manager of her own consulting company, KMB Associates, she worked as a facilitator between the Seattle Center, City of Seattle, and architects renovating KeyArena, host to numerous concerts and home of the SuperSonics. Working onsite put her in contact with everyone from electricians to council members. By the time the project was completed in 1995, she felt like a rock star as she treated her grandfather to the building's inaugural event, a Jose Carreras concert, escorting him in a stretch limo.

"I wanted to make the most of the chances I was given," said Bryant of the opportunity that brought her closer to a return to basketball. "I always wanted to use whatever platform I had to give back and stay true to my sense of community."

Bryant and Ackerman had wiggled their way back to the game, working in cities 3,000 miles apart. Bryant's ticket was through construction and Ackerman's path came through a stint as a lawyer, before mixing her own ambition with her husband's connections to land her desired job. None was happier than her father, who died suddenly two months later from asthma complications at the age of 54.

"I never wanted to coach sports, interestingly, but in the back of my head it seemed I'd always end back up in sports," said Ackerman, who began her position in shock the first two years because of her father's sudden passing. "I really wanted to go to law school, that was a dream, and the ultimate dream job in the end was to combine sports with law."

Not even a decade would pass before Ackerman and Bryant would meet. First as adversaries, grinding away in the opposing ABL and WNBA. Then as allies in one historic league.

CHAPTER THREE

Splitting the Baby:
The Births of the ABL and WNBA

S ix ponytailed fifth-grade girls stood atop concrete steps belting the lyrics to Barney's "I Love You" song off-key—a light payoff for losing an intrateam scrimmage. Val Ackerman and her brother, George, were co-coaches of the team that played in the Trenton area's Police Athletic League. The group included a lineup of George's oldest daughter, Brooke, who lived in the Ackermans' hometown of Pennington, and Val's two girls Emily and Sally, who would make the approximate 64-mile trek via the New Jersey Turnpike on weekends to play. Their 0-7 start was probably why Ackerman, the resident perfectionist in her family, never really wanted to get into coaching.

"We got our backsides kicked a little bit," she said of the 2004–05 schedule.

But the girls were having fun, evident in their smiling faces and bubbly giggles at a season-ending picnic in March, where Ackerman coached the winning intrateam game against her husband, Charles, making him sing with the girls too. For Val Ackerman, the grassroots level of basketball is a reason she forged through her career, often making sacrifices when her daughters were younger to mold a professional women's league. An impressionable mind learning the correct way to dribble or how to be a good sport needed older examples to idolize and that's what the WNBA was to Ackerman: an illustration of strength through adversity and reward through hard work that could trickle down and motivate youths.

When Ackerman was first whispering newborn daughter Sally's name while recovering from her delivery at home, she received a call from NBA deputy commissioner Russ Granik. A lanky self-proclaimed pessimist, Granik was, with Ackerman, a member of the board of directors for USA Basketball during the formation of the first chronicled men's Dream Team that competed at the 1992 Barcelona Olympic Games. Once the women's squad lost in the same Games and at the World Championship in Australia, Ackerman began pitching her idea to look at the men's model to see what kind of results the women could generate if the men's format—a star-studded group training for a year leading into the Olympics—were replicated.

USA Basketball balked at the idea at first. And when the committee finally warmed to legitimately hearing the NBA's proposal, Ackerman couldn't make the board meeting in Colorado Springs, Colorado, because she was giving birth to Sally. On a snowy December afternoon in 1994 she took the telephone receiver from her husband and greeted the voice 1,800 miles away as she held her baby daughter.

"Hey, we're in the women's basketball business," Granik said.

Ackerman, then 34, smiled at hearing the plan she had pushed for since joining the NBA in 1988 was finally materializing. Soon the names of Lisa, Sheryl, and Rebecca would replace Sally, the spitfire cowgirl television host, as symbolic names of beauty and strength in the new millennium.

"The league idea was sort of at the back of our minds," said Ackerman of the formation of the WNBA, which reached its first pinnacle in 2000 with 16 teams. "This [the Olympic team] was the predecessor, the preceding step. We went to USA Basketball, and they initially put up a lot of resistance to the idea. They thought it was, frankly, going to be too expensive. We kept pushing, and they kept coming back to the money. We ended up guaranteeing it [the money]."

The modest Ackerman won't boast outright that she had a strategic plan to start a pro league. "But who else could? She was the perfect person," said her mother, Barbara. "It was a long time coming and no one could have been more prepared than her. She convinced the powers that be that it was the right thing and by golly she was determined to do it."

Ackerman had worked for two years as an associate at the presigious New York City legal firm Simpson Thatcher & Bartlett, where she met her husband Charlie Rappaport, a Brooklyn native and tax lawyer. She was rejected once by the NBA's legal department but finally found an in through her husband's connections, a close friend who recently was hired by the NBA. On a fall day in 1988, Ackerman scurried to a telephone booth in downtown Manhattan, plunked some change into the slot, and dialed her husband's office.

"Got the job! I'm starting tomorrow," she shouted into the receiver as yellow cabs and hordes of people whisked by.

"It was just a real high because it was all sort of coming together in that job," said Ackerman, who also applied for positions with the NFL and Madison Square Garden's legal departments. "That dream of uniting the legal side with the sports side."

The NBA offices were understaffed then. A modest group of about 100 people handled the daily business. Oversights, such as Ackerman receiving two rejection letters when she first applied for a position out of law school, were fairly common. By the 1990s, after Earvin "Magic" Johnson and Larry Bird morphed the NBA Finals into their personal stage of America's cultural war, the NBA offices ballooned to 500 people.

Ackerman, one of the few women in the mix, was busily

working on the players' side with collective bargaining agreement interpretation, salary cap administration, sponsorship agreements, trademark work, and antidrug programs. Granik, NBA commissioner David Stern's right arm, would often pop his head into her office and ask, "Hey, I've got some projects that I need help on. They're not legal, but they might be of interest to you. Do you think you might want to help me out?" And, after one of those queries, Ackerman was off to Spain to help the NBA team with USA Basketball and the formation of the inaugural Dream Team for the Barcelona Olympics.

Six months pregnant with her first daughter, Emily, Ackerman hiked around Spain's hilly countryside for games and appearances wearing paraphernalia such as Michael Jordan and Charles Barkley T-shirts from the Dream Team giveaway stash because she was often out of laundry and maternity fashion hadn't hit the mainstream. Bursting with energy, Ackerman felt like a roadie traipsing after rock stars.

"I was something of an oddity," Ackerman said. "To be a woman in an obviously male-dominated business, pregnant, was not something that people were used to seeing. But everyone was very nice, very respectful, and I was very safe traveling at that time.

"It [the Dream Team] was probably one of the most important things that has happened to the NBA, particularly in terms of spurring its global growth by just having this iconic team that was really kind of a once-in-a-lifetime phenomenon."

The overwhelming response, fans clamoring for photos and crying at the sight of the huge, famous American professional athletes, triggered Ackerman to mimic the men's formula for the struggling women's team no one was paying attention to. Lin Dunn had served as an assistant coach on the highly regarded 1992 women's Olympic team, which included future WNBA stars Cynthia Cooper and Teresa Weatherspoon. They were expected to collect America's third consecutive gold medal, but lost to the Unified Team (from the former Soviet Union) 79-73 in a lackluster semifinals. The American women wound up bringing home the bronze medal instead. Two years later, at the 1994 World Championships in Sydney, the women had to listen to spirited chants of "Viva Brazil!" as they shared a bus ride back to their living quarters with the gold medal–winning Brazilian team. The dejected USA team returned with another bronze honor.

Ackerman knew there was an audience for women's professional basketball. But she believed three components had to align in order for it to succeed: a banner year in college basketball, the grand stage of the Olympic Games preferably in the same year, and sponsor interest. By the mid-1990s, it was all starting to click.

An old friend, Betty Jaynes, who headed the Women's Basketball Coaches Association, needed a sponsor for its annual NCAA Women's Final Four party. Adidas dropped out due to budget cuts, and Jaynes was in a mad scramble to find a replacement for the 1990 event, held in Knoxville, Tennessee. She called Ackerman for help in serving up the ubiquitous beer and pretzels for about 500 people. Ackerman, with the NBA's consent, obliged, and the NBA/WNBA has been a sponsor ever since. After the first Final Four party, about 300 coaches sent thank-you notes on school letterhead to Ackerman's office in New York.

"Dear Val," they started, with colorful teal, orange, or maroon logos adorning the cardstock board trim. "Just wanted to let you know how much we appreciated the NBA supporting our party. If you guys hadn't jumped in, we wouldn't have had one. It was a big deal."

Ackerman stacked the notes into a plain manila folder and walked down the NBA office hall to David Stern's leather-accented quarters. "What is this?" she asked as she softly tossed the folder his way. "Look what we've done."

"I think in the back of his mind he said 'hmm,'" said Ackerman, who became Stern's special assistant to the commissioner 18 months after joining the office. "There's a big community out there. So, fast-forwarding, probably 1993–94, we started kicking things around."

Then, in 1995, the first component fell into place. University of

Connecticut center Rebecca Lobo led the Huskies through their first undefeated championship season (35-0) capturing the imagination of media hounds in New York, the largest market in the country, with her wholesome looks and compelling story. In fact, UConn's 1995 title win at the NCAA Women's Final Four in Minneapolis outdrew the Super Bowl in television ratings in the state of Connecticut, where many big-city marketing-honcho commuters reside. Lobo, a 6-foot-4 Massachusetts native with thick brown hair, tickled the audience with her awkward celebratory dancing after the game. Hers was one of those tearjerker tales, rising to fame as she dealt with the challenge of her mother battling breast cancer.

And, after much haranguing, the NBA coaxed USA Basketball into forming a women's version of the Dream Team, completing Ackerman's three-pronged list of necessities to attempt to launch a league. The 1996 Olympics would be a prime litmus test. Held in Atlanta, it would give women's sports high visibility among potential American sponsors.

Ackerman spearheaded the league's Dream Team efforts, fronting the $3 million proposition to have 12 women sacrifice 10 months in preparation to win Olympic gold in their home country. The players, earning $50,000 apiece, would embark on a glitzy, 52-game global tour, littering the local courts with disposed opponents in a star-spangled-banner presentation of women's basketball dominance. Along the way they'd create a climate for a professional league.

An innovative mind who propelled the NBA from a clingy 1970s reputation of a cocaine-laced cellar to a 1990s primetime seller once he was appointed commissioner in 1984, David Stern always believed women's professional basketball was key to the global growth of the game. Before the WNBA launched in 1996, he even teased that he commissioned the original business plan for the league and tucked it away in his top desk drawer.

"The copyright is somewhere," said Stern, who could be heard playfully ruffling papers through the telephone. "My position is the more young women play basketball then that gives us a tremendous opportunity to tap into them and their families as they become future WNBA basketball players and fans. It expands our product."

As it did research on establishing a WNBA in the states, the NBA, reveling in an enormous profit surplus from increased ticket sales and television ratings, couldn't have predicted they'd have an all-out financial war with the ABL to become the operating body of women's pro ball. Ackerman kept newspaper clippings, library research results, and the business plans of the approximately 13 professional leagues that existed prior to the WNBA in a black folder in her desk drawer.

Jason Frankfort, a New York restaurateur, was the first to establish an organization, announcing a 12-team league in 1976. It collapsed before the first game. In fact, many leagues didn't make it past the press conference. Previous leagues had smacked into similar circumstances—women's college basketball lacking a banner year, insufficient sponsor interest, and the novelty of Title IX—that had kept Ackerman's inquiries to a mere muffle.

A timeline of past leagues shows other ambitious people wouldn't be deterred. Like William "Bill" Bryne Jr., described as a firm businessman. When Title IX was enacted, dollar signs flicked in his brown eyes. The natural evolution to Bryne, especially after witnessing the successful 1977 Association for Intercollegiate Athletics for Women basketball tournament, where Delta State defeated Louisiana State 68-55, was a professional league. And he dreamed it up big-time, cofounding the Women's Professional Basketball League (WBL) with eight charter teams in markets from New York to Iowa.

The Iowa Cornets became the first team to join the league in July 1978, with Cedar Rapids businessman George Nissen paying the $50,000 franchise fee. The New York Stars, New Jersey Gems, Minnesota Fillies, Milwaukee Does, Chicago Hustle, Dayton (Ohio) Rockettes, and Houston Angels soon followed. The league wound up being a periscope into the future world of women's professional basketball.

The WBL made its debut on December 9, 1978, in Milwaukee, with the Does hosting the Chicago Hustle in Milwaukee Arena. About 7,824 people filed into the arena, curious about the spectacle to unfold. Back in the dressing rooms tucked in the corridors of the aging arena were two nervous teams. The players took snapshots and made idle chitchat to pass the time in locker rooms more suited for dancers about to perform *Cats* than basketball players. Antique-framed mirrors hung on the far walls, and chairs facing makeup mirrors became the players' improvised "lockers." Because of the setup and the women being uncomfortable with communal showers and dressing in front of each other, most opted to get ready at home or at their hotels. They'd arrive and depart in their warm-ups, itching to get back to their place to shower and change.

The teams played the traditional professional four quarters, 12 minutes each, with a 24-second shot clock. The Hustle led by three points at halftime. Despite Milwaukee tying the game at 81 points in the fourth quarter, Chicago cruised to a 92-87 win behind forward Debra Waddy-Rossow's 30 points. Teammate Rita Easterling, an imminent All-Star, recorded a WBL single-game record of 21 assists with her 14 points and nine rebounds.

"I had no sense of history," former Dallas Diamonds head coach Greg Williams is quoted as saying on the WBL's Web site. He later coached in the ABL and for the WNBA's Detroit Shock. "Only in retrospect did I look back and think, 'Wow, that league was just so far ahead of its time, it wasn't even funny.'"

About 1,200 miles south of the action in Milwaukee, current Seattle Storm assistant coach Jessie Kenlaw's Houston Angels prepared to make its own mark on history. Kenlaw was working as a physical education and science teacher when the league phoned her to let her know she was drafted in July 1978. Kenlaw was married and living in Savannah, Georgia, while her three siblings stayed within a 5-mile radius of her mother's home in their native Guyton. She thought nothing, however, of jumping into her Toyota Celica and driving the 960 miles to Houston to chase a dream, leaving her husband behind for the first few months. Along the way, she picked up teammate Dollie Mosley, turning the drive into a fun road trip.

"Everybody told me I was crazy, I mean *everybody*," she said. "I left a teaching job. I was teaching physical education, health, and science, but it was a once-in-a-lifetime chance for me and I didn't have to think twice about it. If there was a chance to play . . . I was going to take it. It was something I had to pursue. I was also wanting something a little bit more than I was exposed to and I was a risk taker."

Players were only paid an average of $5,000 to $15,000 for an entire seven-month season, but Kenlaw and the others didn't care. Most players held standard jobs to pay living expenses. Kenlaw worked in the women's retail department at a sporting goods store one season and as a part-time manager at Space City Trophies another year. She'd rise early for the 10 AM practice, then head to her second job until 6 PM. Employers were supportive in rearranging her schedule when her team made road trips to Minnesota or New York.

Kenlaw had had to appeal for her college, Savannah State, to allow the women to play in a collegiate league. She was selected MVP her senior season—when the president of the school finally agreed to form a team. Kenlaw hadn't played competitively for two years when the WBL called, but she still yearned for the game. It was the early years of women finding equality in sports, and unless an aspiring player had a role model who went against the odds, envisioning a future in sports didn't stretch beyond teaching physical education or coaching.

Kenlaw could have had a career overseas. At Savannah State, she was a cleanup player underneath the hoop, averaging 17 rebounds per game. The Tigerettes lacked exposure, however, and no one within her bubble knew enough to tell her about the opportunities in Europe.

"I had no knowledge of going oversees. Had I, I certainly would have gone," Kenlaw said. "I wasn't as polished offensively and had no kind of jump shot. But anything in the paint and all the garbage points, I took care of that for 'em."

Kenlaw stayed fit and was a reserve player with the Angels, watching All-Stars Paula Mayo and Belinda Candler lead the team to a 26-8 record to clinch the Eastern Division. Candler, sporting a curly Afro, had the silky shot, while Mayo was dubbed "Moose" for her aggressive style. The Angels averaged a striking 99.4 points before the installation of the three-point line, which would have ranked them 10th in scoring among the 30 NBA teams in 2005. The Angels allowed 90.5 points, making for high-scoring shootouts on most nights.

In April 1979, Houston, with its superior shooting accuracy, swept New York 2-0 in the first round of the playoffs. The Angels won the first game 97-91 and the second 93-84. They advanced to play the Iowa Cornets, featuring the popular Molly "Machine Gun" Bolin, a perky blond who helped the league grab attention with her conventional good looks and deadly jump shot. The five-game series was tied at two games apiece when the teams returned to Houston for the decisive fifth matchup at Hofheinz Pavilion.

Nearly 6,000 fans paid to witness the championship game, easily topping the crowds of 500 the Angels often played in front of. Kenlaw's heart raced and shivers crawled up her spine at Bolin and Candler going back and forth, displaying their offensive prowess. Kenlaw wouldn't experience a feeling quite like that until 25 years later, when Storm guard Betty Lennox and Connecticut Sun forward Nykesha Sales did the same in the pivotal Game 2 of the WNBA Finals at KeyArena, Sales finishing with a finals record of 32 points.

On this May 1 night in 1979, it was Candler outdazzling Bolin, who averaged 32.8 points, helping Houston defeat Iowa 111-104 for women's professional basketball's first championship. Kenlaw wore her clunky, team-issued diamond- and sapphire-encrusted ring engraved with her last name for a few years after clinching the title. But the Angels wouldn't repeat. They folded after the second season, struggling financially. All of the WBL teams did.

Off the court, the league was better than some television soap operas. One episode was the Milwaukee players walking off the court because they were owed money. Brawls between teams were more regular than at hockey games. And even the officials weren't paid at times, leading them to boycott.

The signing of No. 1 draft pick Ann Meyers in 1979 was an ordeal in itself. She originally balked at joining because of a tryout with the NBA's Indiana Pacers for a $50,000 contract, getting cut during training camp, but was supposed to bring more press to the WBL because of her household name. Except publicity for the entire league was minimal. Unless it was about Bolin's Farrah Fawcett–esque promotional team poster, or former NBA players such as Dean "the Dream" Meminger (New York Knicks) and coaches such as Larry Costello (Milwaukee Bucks), who joined the WBL to lead the women. The WBL team the California Dreams also was a newsmaker when owner Lawrence Kozlicki sent his players to modeling school because he believed they spent so much time playing that they never really learned feminine traits, like putting on makeup and dressing ladylike.

"That was a riot," Dreams player Patti Bucklew is quoted as saying.

Ms. magazine satirized the idea with a cynical cartoon depicting players in skirts allowing their more aggressive opponents to have the ball and pass by with the requisite "please" and "thank-you."

By the time Nancy "Lady Magic" Lieberman and Carol "The Blaze" Blazejowski signed for $100,000 and $50,000, respectively, in 1980, the WBL had pinned all its hopes for survival on the Summer Olympic Games in Moscow. Unfortunately for the league, President Jimmy Carter announced that the United States would boycott the Games unless the Soviet Union withdrew from Afghanistan, which it did not. The WBL, needing the grandeur of the Olympic stage, was unable to secure a major television deal and sponsor and folded after the 1980–81 season. It was the second-longest-running professional women's league, after the WNBA.

"It just wasn't the right time," said Ackerman, who studied clips from the WBL and kept them in her thin folder. "It was just still a little bit before its time."

Kenlaw bounced around three of the bundle of leagues that quickly evaporated after the enticing hype. She played for the Phoenix Flames in the Ladies Professional Basketball Association and returned to Houston for the Women's American Basketball Association's short run. Later leagues included the gimmicky Liberty Basketball Association (1991), which made its debut on television with its skimpy unitard uniforms and lowered hoops, and the Women's World Basketball Association, which began play in 1993 with six teams.

It was all under the radar. While the men's game was growing in popularity with stars like Michael Jordan, Reggie Miller, and Charles Barkley, the women were playing in anonymity. They couldn't even call themselves "professionals" without a weird or stunned look. And even women who were in the field didn't know much about their plights, hearing tidbits well after the fact.

Lin Dunn, then building the women's basketball program at the University of Miami, was one of those people. She prided herself on keeping within the eye of the sport's circle. Meyers, Lieberman, and Blazejowski were players she followed from their high school careers to dominance at UCLA, Old Dominion, and Montclair State, respectively. Once they entered the WBL, it was as if they disappeared.

"It got so little media attention that you couldn't hardly keep up with it," Dunn said. "I didn't ever get to see them play."

The 1970s was the brief Age of Aquarius; liberation was as hip as disco. Corporations, however, have never been hip, always following the profit path. As America headed into the ultracapitalistic, conservative 1980s, women athletes weren't viewed as safe moneymaking marketing tools. The standard still belonged to waifs following Twiggy's 1960s catwalk, not muscular shapes on hardwood courts.

The pioneering aspect kept the women going, however.

Seattle's University of Washington campus was the ninth stop of a 20-game NCAA tour to begin Ackerman's female Dream Team's exhibition play. On a rainy November 28 night in 1995, about 5,741 fans trickled into the barnlike Edmundson Pavilion to watch the Huskies battle the Olympic hopefuls. UW coach Chris Gobrecht, a fiery basketball junkie, knew she was feeding the team to the wolves. In past seasons, her purple-powered squads had handed Lisa Leslie's USC and Katy Steding and Jennifer Azzi's Stanford University teams losses on the same court. But the 1995 Washington team was young. Leslie, the glorified 6-foot-5 center; Steding, a 6-foot forward; and Azzi, a trim 5-foot-8 guard, meanwhile had teamed with seasoned Olympic veterans Teresa Edwards (5-foot-11) and Katrina McClain (6-foot-2) to create the superwoman-esque force complete with uniforms festooned with white stars overlaying the waistline of their USA shorts.

By halftime, Team USA led 56-18 and Washington had missed 16 of their opening 22 shot attempts. Leslie coasted to 21 points before intermission, finishing with 24 and eight rebounds in the 92-47 victory. A freshman guard named Jamie Redd, who would later play for the inaugural Seattle Storm, was the sole bright spot when the Huskies outscored the national team 26-15 in the final 10 minutes behind Redd's 10 points. She finished with 14.

The game wasn't about the game, really. It was about possibility. "This game is about our sport and our country," as Gobrecht said in the *Seattle Times*. Team USA needed to cream its opponents to get the crowd thinking about the advancement of women's ball. Regardless of how obvious it seemed, some people needed a visual to see women players could develop beyond college, a mysterious concept since stars such as Azzi and Edwards spent years in the darkness of overseas play—forgotten by those who watched them rise to collegiate prominence. Leagues in Spain and Italy have thrived for decades, but when the Orlando Miracle moved its franchise to Connecticut in 2003, becoming the first professional team in the state, the common question asked of coach Mike Thiabult was if his team could beat UConn's famed women's team. "What more could a woman athlete do?" some thought. And when players returned to their college campuses for alumni games, fans expected them to have creaky bones at age 24, unable to keep up with the college squad.

Financial supporters needed the real illustration, too, to see how much more marketable their product was if passed out at a Team USA event. At an open practice sponsored by the makers of Jell-O, about 600 little girls were bused into Seattle from Snohomish to Tacoma, materialized a market as they licked pudding spoons and shrieked at the sight of Leslie dunking a basketball.

Blending with the masses wearing purple T-shirts that November night in 1995 was Steve Hams, a former Hewlett Packard executive who had announced in September with Gary Cavalli and Anne Cribbs the inception of the American Basketball League. Cavalli and Cribbs had their own advertising/public relations firm in Northern California at the time and the pro league was initially Cavalli's, following eight years as associate athletic director and sports information director at Stanford, a link that helped him form a relationship with Azzi.

Not knowing of the NBA's plan and receiving mixed messages through newspaper and television reports, Azzi helped champion the idea of the ABL. The new league had already secured verbal agreements from nine of the national team members and said they had $4 million in sponsorship money. By February 1996, they announced the league would tip off in October on the heels of the Atlanta Games with eight teams—the Seattle Reign, Portland Power, San Jose Lasers, Colorado Xplosion, Columbus Quest, Richmond Rage, Atlanta Glory, and New England Blizzard. Overseas, top players could make $100,000 to $200,000, with the average being about $60,000 for perimeter players and $80,000 for posts. The ABL planned to take care of its players first, ranging its salaries from a

Washington native Karen Bryant was the ABL's youngest general manager when hired in 1998. She currently is the Storm's chief operating officer. (LATRENA SMITH PHOTOGRAPHY)

$70,000 average, with a minimum salary of $40,000 and a maximum of $125,000 for playing a seven-month, traditional fall season.

"There has been a tremendous growth in participation by girls, a lot of that having to do with Title IX. And there is a broad-based talent pool developing," Hams told the *Seattle Post-Intelligencer* at the game. "Sponsors now see the women's game as a growing and lucrative market. They see opportunity. They see television ratings strong for the Final Four and good ratings for regular-season games. Besides, sports fans want products that are really closer to what they feel sports is all about."

Legendary UCLA coach John Wooden probably explained that "feeling" best when he was later quoted in sports sections across the country as saying he preferred the women's game because it was more "pure" with the traditional "team" concept. It still emphasized passing the ball, which sometimes passed through the palms of all five players before a shot was attempted. Women rarely looked for one-on-one situations to exploit, instead setting each other up through screens. Players hustled for loose balls in the women's game, and the overall lack of dunks prevented games from looking like a roughly edited highlight reel.

Still, Ackerman and the NBA were hesitant to announce their plans, despite constant questioning and prodding from decorated players such as Nancy Lieberman, who was quoted as saying in 1993 that "only the NBA can make a women's professional basketball league work." Suddenly the "when" will a pro league start twisted to "who" will make it work.

But Team USA hadn't even hit a satisfactory stride by February 1996. The Olympic Games were so far off in the distance, seven months to be exact, that thinking about the WNBA was ridiculous to Ackerman since there was still nothing to gauge. To the NBA, the ABL founders sounded like a trio of women's basketball outsiders trying to make some quick cash on a tired idea. But the players were hooked, especially the veterans who knew the torture and loneliness of playing overseas. Edwards and Azzi wore ABL T-shirts and hats with its catchy "It's a whole new ballgame" slogan to every Olympic press conference and television appearance possible, promoting the league. In eight cities, there was a hectic frenzy to form front offices, find coaches and players, attract sponsors, and create sellable identities for a seemingly mythical tip-off 10 months away.

"We launched and said, 'Boy, we've got to try like hell to get the stuff,'" said Karen Bryant. "He [Cavalli] wanted to be first. That meant we started a league without some of the things we knew—it's not that they didn't think that stuff was important, they knew it was important. But he felt it was more important to get the league launched in the fall. It just meant we sort of, from day one, had our backs against the wall in trying to secure national sponsors and a credible television package."

As a city, Seattle has risen twice from ashes since being founded on November 13, 1851. The first layer of soot derived from the Great

Fire of 1889. According to historical reports, a pot of glue boiled over into a heap of turpentine-soaked wood shavings, igniting a blaze extending 64 acres of city blocks. Chaos emitted as barrels of alcohol were heaved into Elliott Bay in hopes of the cocktail's survival while horses, people, and shackled prisoners from the county jail rushed to escape the whooshing flames, which lasted 12 hours.

The June 6 fire was greeted with cheers from city planners, however, because the previous Seattle land design was a rat-infested mud trap waiting to slip into the Puget Sound. Now the area is a gorgeous, fireproof red-brick historical sight with cobblestoned walkways called Pioneer Square.

The southern tip of downtown as well as the rest of the city was transformed into a black smudge again in 1980 when Mount St. Helens erupted. The top 1,300 feet of the mountain burst from its base, spreading 230 square miles of destruction at about 8:30 AM on May 18. Fifty-seven people died, mostly from suffocation, and survivors are still haunted by the sci-fi sight of plumes of ash jetting into the air, circling the globe.

In many ways, the creation of women's professional basketball felt like the city's third birth from ash to Bryant, a Washington native. A haphazard series of unlikely events, like a loyal fan base derived from virtually no marketing and players willing to pay their own way, led to a crystallized dream. The culmination left an indelible impression in a city's mind that previously thought it only had room for interests in baseball, boating, and other outdoor activities during its cherished drier months. Women's basketball seemed to be a phenomenon happening elsewhere. Teams were sprinkled through the Midwest, the closest being Iowa, and as far as anyone in the Northwest knew, the NBA was uninterested. Commissioner David Stern said so in 1992. Then a "working group" was created to look into proposals for a women's pro league in April 1993, but a month later Ackerman announced the NBA had "no plans to start a women's league"—the NBA would only help promote women's ball. So, when the WNBA was announced in April 1996—eight months after the

ABL made its declaration to erect a league—the sole thing keeping mouths from dropping around the Pacific Northwest was that the closest WNBA team was 577 miles south in Sacramento, California.

The ABL continued its goals regardless of the NBA's announcement. Bryant was steadily working in the construction field when she was tipped off about the ABL placing a team in Seattle. She wanted to help spread the word, but didn't expect anything more. Bryant first contacted Hams, who put her in touch with Cavalli and Cribbs. A week later, Bryant was immersed in volunteer work, calling friends and handing out fliers about the pro league at basketball camps. Noticing her ambition, Bryant was hired by the ABL in May 1996 as director of basketball operations. She was the second person hired to help launch the Seattle Reign, working from Suite 408, which had as much zip as store-brand vanilla ice cream. There was one desk, two chairs, and a few ballpoint pens and No. 2 pencils with bite marks from their former owners. An energetic corporate climber at 29, Bryant had a lot of work before tip-off in six months.

As director of operations, she hired two other people but mostly handled everything except media relations and sponsorship/sales. Bryant's connections in the city as a former high school coach, self-employed businesswoman, and member of the University of Washington's 1991 basketball team put her in the right circle to gather sponsors too, though. And that was the toughest part. Every day her small staff learned a new way to hear the reply "no," growing skin thicker than rawhide. With the NBA already an established basketball league with television relationships and corporate sponsorships, everyone expected the deep-pocket corporate brand names to automatically back the WNBA. The task became harder and harder, yet optimism abounded.

"It was so much of an unknown, people were really cautious about investing money in something they had never seen before," Bryant said. "How do you buy something you've never seen? That's the whole concept of being new and being a pioneer is you're trying to sell a vision. You're trying to sell something that doesn't exist."

The city, from the mayor to the Seattle Center complex where Mercer Arena and the Sonics' KeyArena are located, was hugely supportive, even giving a few cost breaks. What they could see that sponsors were hesitant to put money behind was the benefit of helping women into professional sports. With women on the City Council board and throughout local businesses, doing so spoke to equal rights and empowerment.

Seattle has always prided itself on its ability to be open-minded, diverse, and community-based. A woman's professional league encompassed all three. Plus, basketball was hot in the city. The "Reign Man," "The Glove," and "Big Smooth," or in layman's terms, Shawn Kemp, Gary Payton, and Sam Perkins, had just led the Sonics on a thrilling ride to the NBA Finals, losing a best-of-seven series 4-2 to the Michael Jordan–led Chicago Bulls. Seattle finished the regular season at 64-18, and it seemed everyone was sporting the team's logo: a Space Needle topped with a basketball replacing the *I* in Sonics.

Even the downside of professional men's sports seemed to help the Reign establish itself. If Seattleites weren't interested simply because it was more basketball, they were interested because the women would play for the joy of the game and not megasalaries better reserved for teachers or the underpaid, underappreciated part of society that seemed to find its way to women's hoops.

"It had a real feel-good opportunity to it," Bryant said.

But there was still the looming NBA with its plans, and Bryant didn't even know what cities they were targeting. Sweeping through the college tour undefeated, Team USA steamrolled its way to the Olympic gold medal before 32,987 fans at the Georgia Dome in August, avenging the World Championship loss to Brazil 111-87. The players cried and did cartwheels to display their thrill at accomplishing the difficult goal. And instead of being shuffled back into obscurity, the players were part of the rumbling new era of the women's movement. With 287 female athletes, America had the largest contingent of women at the Olympic Games, and the 3,779 total women competitors, out of 10,440 combined, represented a

26 percent increase from the 1992 Barcelona Olympics. Team USA collected gold in women's soccer and softball, along with gymnastics, crafting images of successful women athletes and creating a thirst in Americans for more opportunities to view women's sports.

Warped from the 10-month experience or advised by agents to be patient before joining a professional league, Lisa Leslie, Rebecca Lobo, Sheryl Swoopes, and Ruthie Bolton wouldn't play in the ABL, though. They were noncommittal from the beginning, but Leslie backed out of a previous oral agreement. Eager fans in Seattle and across the eight-team league didn't care. The remaining Olympians scattered across the nation to jumpstart what would be the 13th attempt at a professional women's league in America.

Venus Lacy, a 6-foot-4 center who averaged 6.6 points and 4.4 rebounds in eight Olympic games, was assigned to the Reign's inaugural roster. Lining up with her were former Husky stars Rhonda Smith (1991–95) and Tara Davis (1990–94).

It was basically a formality later that August when David Stern stepped to the microphone and motioned for Ackerman to join him at the podium, appointing her president of the WNBA. Media gobbled the moment up, rolling cameras, snapping flashbulbs, and quickly bombarding Ackerman with questions about how the WNBA would take "the *other* league" out.

"It wasn't something we expected when we started planning for the WNBA, that there'd be another league and the talent pool could be potentially split," said Ackerman, trying to downplay the WNBA's clear advantage given its financial backing. "I thought it was a way to get press, it wasn't a bad thing. I didn't buy into the rivalry because it was sort of made to seem like one was David and the other was Goliath, when I really felt we were both Davids. I knew how hard it was and so on."

Although the ABL's projected first-year merchandise sales shrunk from $4 million to less than $1 million, the Richmond Rage's uniforms were delayed in arrival, and an ad in Seattle referring to God as "she" backfired, the league tipped off as planned with three games in October 1996. The Reign played puppet to the Colorado Xplosion in Denver, losing 82-75 behind guard Edna Campbell's 22 points, 11 in the final minute of the third quarter. About 5,513 fans, mostly former players and boosters of the University of Colorado's successful Division I program, gathered for the event, falling for the lively Campbell, who stood 5-8 and often displayed her charming dimpled smile. In Hartford, Connecticut, 8,767 watched the New England Blizzard and hometown sweetheart guard Jennifer Rizzotti beat the Richmond Rage and Olympian Jackie Joyner-Kersee 100-73. Meanwhile in San Jose a techno laser show introduction was overshadowed by Azzi's Lasers defeating Edwards's Atlanta Glory 78-70 before 4,550 people packed in the Event Center at San Jose State.

By the time Seattle returned for its home opener, the team was 1-2, and Bryant, her staff, and her sister were still trying to pull together the opening night festivities at 4 AM on October 26. Amid the excitement was news about Olympian Sheryl Swoopes becoming the WNBA's first player to sign a contract on October 23. Ackerman, who stressed for months about who she would find to play in her league, couldn't wait to pull the faxed document from the receiver. She tugged and pulled, and when the document finally released from the chute, she was teary-eyed. Ackerman giddily showed the signed contract to everyone in the NBA/WNBA offices, then promptly framed it and placed it on her desk. The moment also made bigger national headlines than the ABL's debut weekend.

"We knew that we had an uphill battle," Bryant said. "From a local standpoint, we tried to just focus on our opportunities in Seattle and let the league sort of fight it out at the national level. There wasn't a WNBA team in Seattle, there wasn't another WNBA team in the Northwest, and there really weren't any plans to put a WNBA team in the Northwest. They told us they weren't interested [in] going into ABL markets. So, we were like, as long as we solidify our fan base here, maybe the WNBA will help us. It promotes women's professional basketball, and if somebody sees the WNBA and gets excited and lives in Seattle, they're going to come watch the

Reign because that's their only outlet. We tried to put a positive spin, but many of us were really nervous about our future."

Constantly swirling around the ABL were questions regarding its viability. The Friday that it debuted, *USA Today* ran an article picking apart the finer points of the league. Potential sponsors wouldn't return Anne Cribbs's calls. Only two teams had ad agencies and they were working for free. The business plan of paying players exorbitant salaries appeared doomed to fail. And the league was virtually starless in terms of household names.

Inside the ABL arenas, you could feel the fledgling league simply needed time. Time they weren't going to get. Not with the WNBA calculating every misstep and using every NBA marketing tool to its advantage, casting a swanky superhyped shadow over everything the cash-strapped ABL did. Yet players remained optimistic.

"We're going to give America the best women's basketball we can give it," Olympian Teresa Edwards told the *San Jose Mercury News* after the Lasers' opening loss. "For those who aren't going to come out, you're going to miss the party. A lot of people are waiting to see about us, but the fans who came out are already part of the happening. This isn't a wait-and-see thing."

Seattle didn't wait and see. UW's Chris Gobrecht, with her thin lips and shaggy hair accenting her sideline banter, had stirred a passion for women's basketball in the Puget Sound, advancing the Huskies to nine tournament appearances in 11 seasons. The Reign simply road the purple train, even keeping its jersey colors in the purple family with a nice maroon (although it was officially listed as cardinal). The Reign returned to Seattle with a losing record, but you couldn't tell by the fans' reaction to their first glimpse of the team.

Mercer Arena, the Reign's home court, sat on a corner of cultural conversion where different worlds would collide elsewhere. On crisp fall nights, patrons dressed in suits or sequined evening dresses would intermingle with others in jerseys or casual fleece pushing strollers as they dispersed to the theater, a Sonics basketball game, or the mini amusement park. All are still located within the small radius of the Seattle Center, which was originally built for the World's Fair in 1962.

Reign organizers were careful not to schedule matchups on nights when the Sonics played. (The Sonics would sell out all 41 of their home games at KeyArena during the 1996–97 campaign.) The Reign conflicted with their schedule three times, but stayed within their average 3,229 fans in a raggedy building that held 4,509.

The largest crowd was for the opener, when 4,591 people crammed themselves into Mercer Arena. A few chairs were losing their stuffing, and lines for the scarce women's bathrooms were worse than at some local bars, but the facility did showcase new paint, court, locker rooms, and lighting, upgrades made specifically for the Reign. Notables such as Bulls champion James Edwards sat courtside with Eric Goodwin, guard Gary Payton's agent, as the crowd entertained itself with the timely "Macarena" dance or the antics of Triumph, the team's birdlike mascot. Players smacked through massive paper signs as they were introduced and exhibited a physical game, defeating Portland 83-70 on a Sunday afternoon. Kate Paye, a guard who played against the Washington Huskies as a Stanford Cardinal, led the Reign with 19 points, five assists, and four steals.

As Venus Lacy blew kisses to the crowd, they returned the admiration with a standing ovation following the final buzzer. The game, still, wasn't about the game. It was about opportunity for the women and a score for equal rights—themes Seattle could easily back with its liberal community that often protested against cold corporations feasting on struggling independent businesses. It's nothing to see a pack of Seattleites picketing the takeover of a neighborhood grocery store or fight to save a lost baby whale. The Reign, with its grassroots status, played into the city's philosophy. The women hustled, were blue collar, and simply wanted to play. They were also accessible, attending state girls tournaments to sign autographs or participating in causes, such as walking to raise money for abused or abandoned animals. They fit in down to the genuine smiles they wore.

"After the games they were on what we liked to call a 20-minute clock," said Mel Greenberg, a *Philadelphia Inquirer* reporter who covered the league. "No matter how hard fought the game, after 20 minutes both teams would pop out of the locker rooms to sign autographs for every fan left in the building. And they'd do it with a smile. I was always amazed at how they could do that."

Following Seattle's first home victory, the players and coaching staff joined fans at Pike Pub and Brewery on First Avenue, across from where the Kingdome has now been replaced by the Seahawks' Qwest Field and the Mariners' Safeco Field. They chugged beer and snacked on bar food as the two sides—the gritty players and their loyal fans—familiarized themselves with each other, signing autographs whenever requested. At that moment, it didn't matter that the league's projected merchandising sales fell $4 million short of what was anticipated. That the ABL would lose $5 million in expenses the first season. Or that the WNBA was spending $15 million on its new snazzy ad campaign. The pithy slogan featured a nationally broadcast spot of Leslie and Lobo strutting though a tunnel with Swoopes, who had a basketball cupped on her hip. The trio stopped at the edge of the court where men were playing and blurted, "We got next." Compared to the ABL's $1.5 million budget of ads mostly taped to kiosks, there was no contest about who had the capital to to bully their way onto the court.

Yet, at that moment when Paye laughed with teammates Lacy, Tari Phillips, and Rhonda Smith, the women symbolized iconic figures most had never experienced before. They were personifying what many older women in the crowd hadn't dare fantasize due to societal limitations.

The Reign continued to fascinate minds, even though their play didn't dazzle the rest of the league; they finished with records of 17-23 their inaugural season and 15-29 the next. Still, the team was a solid draw, averaging 3,229 fans at Mercer Arena in 1996–97 and 3,321 the next season. But overall the ABL was sinking. New England was basically carrying the league, averaging 8,209 fans the first two seasons combined. Bryant was sending every bit of money she had to the front office.

"I wrote them a check for $100 and sent that off one time," she said with an exasperated tone in her voice.

General manager Allison Hodges of the Chicago Condors, an expansion team for the 1998–99 season, was paying all of her team's expenses out of pocket and recalled several conversations with Gary Cavalli where he stated the league was bankrupt, then financially stable—all within hours of each other. It didn't take a genius to see what was happening. The WNBA secured three-year television contracts with ESPN, NBC, and Lifetime. Its glossy commercials aired constantly during NBA games, and in-house at arenas. Anytime the WNBA hiccuped it was news. It didn't matter that the ritzy league's overall talent couldn't ball with the ABL. Who needs talent when you've got cash?

After the ABL concluded a relatively successful opening season, stars lined the courtside seats of the Great Western Forum to see the Los Angeles Sparks tip off the WNBA against the Houston Comets in June 1997. The game was aired globally on NBC, grabbing a 3.5 Nielsen rating in America, paying off the publicity. The competition was suspect.

"It wasn't a very good game, unfortunately," said Ackerman of New York's 67-57 win. "The players were nervous. It wasn't a well-played game by any stretch of the imagination, but we got our foot in the door. We had to start somewhere and we did. In general, the first season was beyond our expectation in terms of response and turnout."

The WNBA, which played two 20-minute halves, chose the summer for its season due to its less saturated sports landscape and availability of empty arenas during the NBA off-season. It also played a shorter 28-game schedule with a smaller ball and kept player salaries minimal—about $10,000 to $50,000—allowing athletes to play in other leagues to compensate for low pay. The league also provided short-term housing and rental cars for players to share. When Houston won the first championship, the league drew 9,669 fans, easily topping the ABL's average 4,095.

Although Swoopes, Leslie, and Lobo were marketed as the first faces of the league, Swoopes would miss 19 games to give birth to son Jordan. Leslie had a memorable season, leading the league in rebounding (9.5) and Lobo averaged 12.5 points and 9.0 rebounds in the two-game postseason, her Liberty losing to Houston for the inaugural title, but it was a little-known guard by the name of Cynthia Cooper who stole the show. She was the regular-season and championship MVP, averaging 28.0 points in the playoffs for the Comets. Her exuberance on the court, shuffling backward while howling to the rafters, and consistent scoring were perfect for the made-for-TV league.

The contrasts between leagues were easy ammunition for the ABL. Five of the 1996 Olympians played in the ABL. It had 44 of the Kodak All-Americans and six of the last 13 NCAA Women's Final Four MVPs, plus six of the last 15 Naismith and Associated Press college Players of the Year, including the Reign's Kate Starbird, the No. 1 draft pick in 1997. But regardless of what Ackerman believed, the WNBA was a Goliath, and the ABL's stones of athletic superiority were lost in the dense marketing smoke screen.

A continent away, learning the game was 16-year-old Lauren Jackson. She lay on her bed in the dormitory-style rooms at the Australian Institute of Sport, tuning in to the Los Angeles-Houston game later that summer, another advantage of the WNBA's global television viewership. She had played against the Comets' Chinese player Haixia Zheng, whom the Aussies called "Big Huey," mostly because of her 6-foot-8 height. And Lisa Leslie with her bow and girlish run was one of Jackson's sports idols, second to her mother. Looking at women with figures not much different from her own 6-foot-5 stature, Jackson was entranced.

"It looked so cool," she said. "All I remember thinking was, 'I want to play in the WNBA someday.'"

Jackson was the prototype of the young girl the WNBA wanted to captivate for its league. But first, it had to make sure it was the league that survived of the two running in the late 1990s. That meant pouring more money into marketing and the exposure veterans craved. Soon such ABL stars as Nikki McCray and Dawn Staley were ditching the "cause" and going with what was perceived as stability and financial security.

The NBA and David Stern were connected. Nike, despite its alleged verbal agreements with the ABL, wasn't going to sponsor the league when it was clear the WNBA would give it a bigger spotlight among the new sought-after market of mothers. And players, no matter how well intentioned, remain egotistical in wanting to be on television, getting their name out to the public so they can grab individual sponsorship deals themselves. The ABL couldn't hang. It couldn't secure a television deal beyond the modest Black Entertainment Television and Fox Sports. Reebok was a national sponsor for two seasons but had budget problems of its own. And disorganization within the front office led to Cavalli jumping on a routine conference call between general managers one Tuesday afternoon in December to announce the ABL had filed for Chapter 11 bankruptcy. He'd send the teams about $200 each but told them not to expect anything more.

Three days before Christmas, the news spread across the Puget Sound area. It was one sentence aired on KJR, the local sports radio station—the only time the 24-hour sports network would utter a word about the league. The station is part of the Clear Channel corporation owned by Barry Ackerley, a staunch businessman who also owned the Sonics. Coincidence? Reign fans didn't think so. Their ire was squarely directed at the NBA, with local columnists backing the verbal onslaught, thinking most sports outlets were keeping quiet about the underground ABL to aide in its demise. Six months later when Ginger Ackerley, Barry's whimsical wife, sat atop a podium happily announcing the WNBA would replace the city's mourning over the Reign with a team, it was widely received with great animosity by those within the ABL sect. It was just proof of the NBA's meddling to form its own legalized monopoly of the sport.

"It was hard because you really didn't see it coming," said Jessie Kenlaw, then an assistant coach for the Colorado Xplosion. "It was so unexpected in how it happened. I was home for Christmas and heard it over the news. It was painful and there was no clue the league was about to fold. But there was always hope that something would happen and the league would survive. So, you kind of worked hard to stay connected. I always believed in my heart that we would have a league."

The Ackerleys knew they needed people to bridge the widening gap between hurt ABL fans and the still present "cause" of women's basketball in order for a Seattle WNBA team to be successful. So the inaugural team rose from the Reign's ashes. It included Karen Bryant, the ABL team's former general manager; Edna Campbell, the Xplosion guard who had often lit up Mercer Arena with her picturesque jump shot; and Angela Aycock, a laid-back former Reign player. Also on the first roster were point guard Sonja Henning and guard Charmin Smith, who had played for the Portland Power. Then, of course, there was coach Lin Dunn, whose intoxicating southern drawl would subdue any fume. For a while, at least.

When Seattle joined the league, Ackerman had moved to a corner office on the 16th floor of the NBA's Manhattan skyscraper. Her panoramic view was up the famed Fifth Avenue, with glimpses of the tree-lined Central Park and Metropolitan Museum of Art. It was peaceful, regardless of the 16-hour days of operating a fledging league hitting its first zenith with 16 teams. And by October 2004, shortly after the expansion Storm won its first WNBA championship, Ackerman felt her league was stable enough for her to step down from her presidential position to spend time with her family and become the new president of USA Basketball.

The office threw her a gag party complete with gifts ranging from cookbooks (she never had time to cook before) to comfy slippers. Then she packed up 12 boxes of materials and flicked off the light on her era with the league. Four months later, Donna Orender, who had played for the WBL's New York Stars, New Jersey Gems, and Chicago Hustle, was named Ackerman's successor.

"It was a real trip down memory lane, kind of the history of the league," said Ackerman of stuffing her office into cardboard boxes.

CHAPTER FOUR

Lin Dunn

O n a balmy night in July 1999, laughter and thumping musical beats led the way to a party boat docked on New York's strip of the Hudson River. Sweet-scented perfume and cologne mixed with the marine air as WNBA sponsors, players, coaches, friends, and national media—all gathered for the weekend's inaugural All-Star game—boarded the yacht *Princess* for a tour around the harbor. Tina Thompson, a power forward on the championship Houston Comets team, was the last to hop on.

"You comin'?" The striking 6-foot-2 player beckoned down the dock at her date, who was dressed in a sharp camel-colored suit. When he shook his head "no," she returned to talking on her cell phone and walked up the ramp where the party had already started.

Wearing flirty summer dresses or backless tops with crisp pants, the women displayed their chic off-court personalities. The night signified the WNBA's first star-studded festivity, and although many aboard the cruise ship hadn't participated in a professional All-Star game before, the ABL had hosted two in its abbreviated existence. The WNBA had waited three seasons before its midseason showcase, but that didn't mean the league didn't know how to party.

Olympian Lisa Leslie, who had received a contract with the

prestigious Wilhelmina Models Inc. before entering the league in 1997, got funky on the dance floor with her coach, Michael Cooper. Dancing was a regular part of Sparks practice under Cooper, who had made his name as a defensive genius in knee-high socks during an 11-year NBA career.

Comets forward Sheryl Swoopes, the first woman Nike named a basketball shoe after, sauntered between floors to make sure photographers and peers saw her. Adding to the lively atmosphere, Sacramento guard Ticha Penicheiro let a belly laugh loose in a dimly lit corner adjacent to the dance floor. Everything, from the delectable hors d'oeuvres to the fine wine served in delicate stemware, was first-class this evening.

At the bow of the ship, Comets coach Van Chancellor's almond eyes twinkled like one of the stars in the midnight sky.

"I'm just a country boy from Mississippi!" he told an East Coast reporter in his thick southern dialect. "And look at me now!"

Chancellor, who would win the first four WNBA championships, was the Western Conference coach at the All-Star matchup, an honor given to the winning staff that reached the WNBA Finals the previous season. He gazed at New York's "Old World" skyline—the proud-standing Twin Towers symbolizing big-city success in a pre–9/11 period. A humble 55-year-old man who still wore the sports jackets to his 1970s leisure suits and tossed wrapped Brach's candies into the stands at games, Chancellor had to take a moment to absorb the magnitude of the changing face of women's basketball.

Fluttering around the deck was one of his guests, Lin Dunn, who as a consultant helped Chancellor sift through talent during the 1999 April draft. Old chums for decades, Dunn preceded Chancellor at the University of Mississippi in 1977–78, coaching one season before he made Ole Miss a strong Southeastern Conference power. Entering the women's college basketball ranks as a high school coach with a degree in math and a master's in physical education, Chancellor guided Ole Miss to 14 NCAA appearances in 19 seasons.

Chancellor hardly needed to escort Dunn at the party as

she made the rounds with cocktail in hand. After 30 years in the coaching business she knew almost everyone on board, including media invited to cover the weekend's All-Star game.

Near the linen-clothed buffet table stood Carolyn Peck, the Orlando Miracle coach, who had succeeded Dunn at Purdue University in 1996, winning the 1999 NCAA title in a 62-45 decision over Duke University. Dunn had coached Comets guard Cynthia Cooper, who was now spying on the upper deck dance floor, as an assistant for the 1992 Olympic team when Cooper was a scoring sensation corralled from play in Italy. And Brian Agler, who coached the Minnesota Lynx at the time, was out on a lower deck mingling. He knew Dunn from their days coaching in the ABL, which had folded just eight months earlier. Dunn had been named 1997–98 Coach of the Year while Agler, a native Midwesterner, had won both of the ABL's championships with the Columbus Quest.

Dunn could have used a nametag to state her purpose on the ship as it sailed around the harbor, however. She wasn't affiliated with any of the league's 12 current teams and wasn't working with the WNBA in any official capacity either. Yet there she was slinging one-liners, offering cheers, and enjoying the glittery city lights with her sister, Carrie Thompson. It had been a rough winter for Dunn, until Chancellor phoned to ask her to be part of his draft-day staff. The talent pool was a coach's feast with an influx of 42 ABL players merging into the WNBA. The disbanded league's capable player list was so deep that WNBA veterans unionized to restrict teams to three ABL players—five for expansion teams Orlando and Minnesota—so they wouldn't automatically lose all of their hard-won jobs. Deemed a lesser league in nationwide media, the ABL had been regarded as having the more talented athletes. Chancellor wanted to draft wisely and knew Dunn would help.

Chancellor wound up integrating one of Dunn's former players, Stanford alum Sonja Henning, into the starting point guard role for his 1999 championship team. Henning, a Racine, Wisconsin, native who also possessed a law degree from Duke University, was

Lin Dunn shouts directions from the sideline. Her visible passion and colorful personality were the early draw to the Storm as the team struggled to get acclimated in the WNBA. (COURTESY OF JEFF REINKING/NBAE/GETTY IMAGES)

the 24th overall pick in the second round. She had the difficult task of replacing the beloved guard Kim Perrot, who was diagnosed in February with lung cancer that spread to her brain. Perrot underwent what was believed to be successful brain surgery at the University of Texas M.D. Cancer Center, but died in August after a seven-month battle at the age of 32. Henning, a subdued 29-year-old, was part of Dunn's Portland team that began the 1998–99 season at 9-4. Dunn, taking the court with soon-to-be Olympic names like DeLisha Milton-Jones and Natalie Williams, felt she could win the ABL championship. Tucked in her enclave with Teresa Edwards and Taj McWilliams-Franklin, Philadelphia Rage coach Anne Donovan also thought she was guiding a championship team. The Rage was 9-5 before the ABL ceased operations.

Both would have to wait for that elusive professional title in another league and city they'd never thought much of before, however.

"There was no doubt in my mind that we were on track, because we'd got into the playoffs," Dunn said of her Portland Power team.

"The year before we'd gone from worst to first, and I'd really thought, 'OK, we're going to do it this year.' And then for that [the league filing for Chapter 11 bankruptcy] to happen—yikes!

"It was the holidays, it wasn't like you got two weeks' notice and a severance check. It was really sad."

At the time, Dunn was preparing to return to her childhood home in Dresden, Tennessee, to celebrate Christmas with her mother, LaRue, and three younger siblings as she normally had done during the holidays. She hated the trip simply because the flight was too long, about five hours. Dunn had adored the Pacific Northwest from the moment she arrived, however. The colorful bridges, fragrant roses, and lush summer greenery made Portland the most majestic city she'd ever experienced. Until she traveled to Seattle. Suddenly there were even more sparkling blue waters, plus a peculiar contrast of warm sunny skies with a faint backdrop of snowy mountain ranges. Add the friendliness of the people, and Dunn sighed quietly in her apartment as she left, seemingly for good.

Whenever Dunn made the trip back to her hometown (population 2,855), it was headline-worthy in the weekly newspaper, the *Dresden Enterprise*, with "Dresden's Dunn" in bold print. She'd throw together homemade soup from whatever ingredients she could find in the fridge, and neighbors would stop by with spoons ready to dig in.

One stoplight and a few stop signs directed traffic in town, where Dunn's grandfather, Cayce Pentecost, built the courthouse and served as its county judge. He also was a Baptist preacher, "marryin' 'em and buryin' 'em," Dunn liked to say. A recently built McDonald's off the bypass of Highway 22 is the nearest fast-food chain. Folks usually drive 10 miles to Martin or 20 miles to Paris for restaurant dining. Unless the Coffee Cup in town is open for breakfast or lunch, that is. *USA Today* doesn't even make it to Dresden.

"We're just too far out in the boonies," Dunn said.

In the split-level house that used to belong to her grandparents, Dunn hooked up DirecTV in her room to catch every women's basketball game possible and keep up with national news.

Basketball and her parents' divorce were the reasons she had moved back to the town originally in the mid-1960s. Before the divorce, her father, a Ralston Purina salesman, had moved the family to Florence, Alabama, where it was illegal for girls to play basketball.

Born May 10, 1947, Dunn grew up before Title IX was passed. The swelling wave of civil rights for minorities and women was spreading to the sports culture in the 1960s. Couple the movement with Dunn's father urging her and younger brother Bud to compete in everything from football to track in the pseudo sports-plex in their Alabama backyard, and the athletic love was nurtured in Lin. The threesome combed the neighborhood for sawdust to build their own pole-vaulting pit. The basketball court was simply gravel ground and a basket made from a milk crate nailed to a severed telephone pole about nine feet high. Lin and Bud would play forever. Or at least Lin would play while Bud tried to wrestle the basketball from his ballhog sister.

Dunn's parents' separation as she prepared to enter high school would have been difficult if it hadn't been for basketball. The sport was legal for women to play in Tennessee. So, when her mother moved with three kids in tow back to her parents' home, located in the western part of the state, Dunn didn't feel like her world was crumbling.

"I'm thankful that my parents got separated," said Dunn with an uneasy laugh. "I know that sounds terrible but it's true."

Her focused blue eyes and bouncy brown ponytail became a fixture at the high school's rickety gym from 1965 to '66. Dunn, playing the forward position, would shoot the lights out to everyone's delight. In one game where the Lions won 56-42, Dunn scored 52 of her school's points. Still, after two years of winning enough acclaim in sports to turn her grandparents' home into a virtual shrine, the basketball heroics were over. At the University of Tennessee-Martin, where Dunn attended and played competitively on the volleyball, badminton, and tennis teams, women's basketball was considered strictly an intramural sport.

She became one of the biggest advocates of Title IX, having missed the chance to play competitive college basketball. Like many who wanted to stick with sports, she started coaching and discovered another outlet for her gift of gab, personable approach, and endless energy.

Dunn's career started at Austin Peay in Clarksville, where she was paid $7,000 as the 23-year-old coach of the established volleyball and tennis teams and the start-up basketball program, and teacher of eight physical education classes. She was given another $500 stipend to chaperone the cheerleading squad to football games and other events.

The basketball team borrowed the men's practice uniforms and used athletic tape to make numbers on the back of the jerseys. Practices were whenever Dunn could swindle court time, often early morning or late at night. Yet just because she was a new coach, there were only seven games, and the team had 11 players, it didn't mean competition wasn't fierce. Travel to road games was in Dunn's red 1966 Chevrolet Impala, which could squeeze in five starters, two bench players, and Dunn.

"You better have a good week of practice," Dunn would holler out to her players, reminding them the trip was in her car; and since everyone didn't fit, the week's session regulated dibs on who rode.

Circumstances and Dunn made the team close. They slept on the host team's cold gymnasium floor because the athletic department didn't budget per diem for hotel rooms or meals. They'd sing her favorite Patsy Cline songs on the three-hour drives to Vanderbilt or Tennessee Tech to keep Dunn awake and confide in one another while dealing with the inequities in their desire to play.

The experience embedded a drive for equality in Dunn, but frustration built inside her. She snapped one season, telling the athletic director if she wasn't paid to coach the teams, she'd quit.

"Fine, quit," was his response.

Not sensing a change in the athletic department's attitude, Dunn did. She moved on to start programs at Mississippi and the University of Miami before compiling a 75.2 winning percentage from 1987 to '96 at Purdue University. In fact, Dunn was so admired in West Lafayette, one of her wild print sports jackets was enshrined in the Indiana Hall of Fame. Dunn constantly carried Title IX pamphlets with her to educate young girls and would speak anywhere about the benefits of women competing in sports. With a salt-and-pepper bouffant hairdo, wardrobe of fashion faux pas sweaters and blazers (including a polka-dotted sport coat), and big wire-rimmed glasses, she became a colorful character in the women's game.

"Oh Lordy! I was always teased with my fashion," said Dunn, whose sport was concerned with feminine appearances early on, leading many who didn't feel comfortable in frilly clothes to miss the mark on fashion. "Back in the '70s, you were expected to wear dresses and skirts. I remember wearing one dress—it was black and gold and had a big bow on it. It was down on the side. You know, sometimes when I hook up with coaches at the [NCAA] Final Fours, we always get to reminiscing, so we're always kidding about stuff. I'm guessing it was early 1990s before we started wearing pantsuits. It was kind of an evolution."

All Dunn wanted was for her gender to have a fair chance to play sports. If that meant sacrificing herself, she was game. And it almost didn't matter how many times she was derailed from her efforts. Dunn would dust herself off and try harder the next time, just like she did as a kid playing in the backyard with her younger brother and sisters.

Image mattered in professional sports as leagues tried to sell themselves to million-dollar sponsors, but the pioneering of a new concept spoke to Dunn when she first heard about the ABL forming. At first, she was comfortable with the stability of her college position at Purdue, especially with a highly regarded recruiting class entering that upcoming fall season. Except following her seventh NCAA appearance in nine seasons, she was the eighth lowest paid coach ($65,000) in a conference she dominated. Dunn began grumbling about her salary, but ruffled the wrong feathers and was fired, with the university saying it "would be best served under new leadership." After Dunn's ousting, she was linked to numerous offenses. She was rumored to have violated recruiting guidelines, although in 1995 she was reprimanded for secondary infractions and had her recruiting time reduced. It was also rumored that she may have illegally given money to athletes, altered drug tests under her leadership, and conducted shoe-contract improprieties. In November 1996, after Dunn's March firing, prized recruit Ukari Figgs, a 5-foot-9 guard, was suspended for one game for exchanging school-issued shoes at an athletic store for more valuable athletic items. And gossip swirled about a personal relationship between Dunn and assistant MaChelle Joseph, one account involving Joseph being tied to a tree and left in a forest.

"People said wild things, just wild things," Dunn told the *Seattle Times*. "That was the thing I was most concerned about in my loss was the perception, because of the way it was handled."

Dunn demanded answers for the abrupt dismissal following a 20-11 season. However, she settled out of court for $100,000, with the stipulation that the university, Joseph, and Dunn would not comment on details regarding the charges. Purdue lost six players because of the saga. Dunn's tattoo of the 1994 Final Four appearance, a deal made with her players if they reached the illustrious game, was a stinging prick all over again.

There wasn't any of that in the ABL. No 300-page NCAA bible of rules that seemingly grew every year. No wooing of indecisive 17-year-old girls. No homophobic scare tactics from opposing coaches used to sour possible recruits from Dunn's program. No concerns with pregnancies, academic eligibility, or having to be a surrogate mother, although Dunn enjoyed supporting her players.

As she recharged in her Dresden home during the summer of 1996, she knew a change in her approach was needed after the Purdue fiasco. But no one was calling to offer the opportunity. The WNBA and ABL had already started their respective preparations for their upcoming seasons with assistant coaches and staff trickling into place. Dunn felt as if she were quarantined with the plague, the way she was rejected when she reached out to share her services in any capacity.

Finally, when ABL cofounder Gary Cavalli contacted Dunn about replacing Portland Power coach Greg Bruce, who had compiled a 5-17 record and numerous feuds with his players, Dunn felt she could focus on what she does best—coach. The turnaround was fast: She accepted the position over the phone and was told to pack while getting ready to coach as soon as she arrived. She had stayed prepared, though, with stacks of videotape and scouting notes on players scribbled on yellow legal pads. On January 2, 1997, Lin popped off the plane, dumped her stuff at the hotel, and took a cab over to Memorial Coliseum located in downtown Portland to begin implementing her style on the talent-laden team at a morning shootaround.

"I walked into the locker room and couldn't believe who was there," said Dunn, who had a vague knowledge of every team, but was still surprised at the saddened faces.

Staring back at her were pouty looks from Olympian Katy Steding, a forward with a smooth three-point shot; former UCLA standout Natalie Williams, a 6-foot-2 forward with talent in volleyball and basketball; the "ponytailed princess of hoop" Michelle Marciniak, the 1996 NCAA Final Four Most Outstanding Player, whom Tennessee coach Pat Summitt was recruiting when the coach went into labor; and the studious Coquese Washington, a meticulous 5-foot-6 point guard. They had talent but were poorly directed and losing confidence with every passing loss. "It was dismal," their new coach recalled.

In typical Dunn fashion, she started her introductions by teasing the players about how they led the league in infamous categories, such as most points given up, and they snorted. How they had a perfect losing record in November—"O-fer-November"—and the athletes replaced wanted tears with uncontrollable chuckles. They were going to be OK.

After the midmorning session, Dunn rushed back to the hotel to gather herself for her professional debut. She laid her clothes out on the bed and dressed after a short nap and shower.

As she strolled onto the court, absorbing her new atmosphere, she looked down and noticed something terrifying. Immediately, she hustled over to Power general manager Linda Weston.

"Linda, I want you to look down and see if you notice anything," Dunn said, her blue eyes bulging with a never-seen-before fear.

"Oh, my God!" Weston screeched. Dunn was wearing similar pumps, only one was navy and the other was black.

"I don't have time to go home; I'm going to act like . . . nothing," said Dunn as she waltzed away with her little fashion secret. And her new Power team defeated Richmond 79-63.

"I'll never forget it as long as I live," Dunn said with a laugh. "I guess I was a little nervous even though I didn't think I was."

Portland would finish the season 9-9 under Dunn's guidance, with a 79-76 overtime win at the Seattle Reign's sold-out Mercer Arena, marking the turnaround in Dunn's opinion. The scene in Seattle also captured her imagination. Portland was beautiful with all of its water and bridges and roses. A young-feeling city, it was even supportive of the ABL team, averaging 5,064 fans.

But there was something about Seattle. Especially during that February 1997 game. The Pacific Northwest has such a remote feeling; the people create their own world. While New York hums about being where the world meets, the Pacific Northwest revels in not having the Big Apple media eye shining on it, ruining its natural beauty with unwanted, intrusive attention. The area is free to craft its own vibe, often staying ahead of the pack with its uniqueness, and building rivalries within the region. None runs bigger than the one between Oregon and Washington. Especially when it comes to sports.

During college football season, contests are held to find the best jabs between University of Oregon Ducks and Washington Huskies, such as Dawgs fans' repeated claims that Oregonians are a bunch of inbred people with little intelligence. Ducks fans retaliate with "Huck the Fuskies" T-shirts at football games.

The instilled animosity carried to the ABL. The Seattle Reign's best crowds were when Portland rolled into town. About 4,500 people jammed inside Mercer Arena when Dunn made her debut as a professional coach in the region. She can remember two things: the crowd and the fact that her team won.

"It was a great, great atmosphere," Dunn said. "It was good for us to be able to go up there in that environment and win."

In a small, windowless office back in Portland, Dunn was optimistic about the future of women's basketball, having witnessed a dozen other leagues fold before they even got rolling. With a full training camp and additions like guard Sylvia Crawley and DeLisha Milton-Jones, Dunn finished the following season 27-17 to win the Western Conference. Williams was named the MVP, averaging a league-best 21.9 points. But the Power lost 0-2 to the Long Beach StingRays in the playoffs. On December 20, 1998, on Fox Sports Net, Dunn coached her last victory in the league. It was a 94-85 win against the San Jose Lasers in California.

"This is a great way to go into Christmas," Williams bubbled to the media afterward.

Dunn awoke Tuesday morning, December 22, 1998, stretched, and flicked on the television, looking for the motivation to pack for her six-day holiday trip back to Dresden. It was a mundane routine with all the travel in the ABL. The plan was to ease out of bed, eat breakfast, finish tidying up around the apartment, and pack. Then she'd be off. Clicking the channel to CNN, it wasn't a game that caught Dunn's eye, however. Crawling across the bottom of her screen was the glaring news that the ABL had filed for Chapter 11 bankruptcy. Suddenly, her phone was ringing off the hook. The news started to spread like a cold virus. Dunn was out of a job. Again.

"We all knew the ABL was struggling," Dunn said. Players owned stock in the league and knew their escalating salaries, now ranging from $40,000 to $150,000 in the third season to compete with the WNBA's lure, couldn't possibly be substantiated if a major television and sponsorship deal continued to blow off their inquires. "We all knew that it [the ABL] really had some tough challenges. But we really believed it would make it through the season. I don't think we realized it could just fold at any second. And once it did, they weren't able to get in touch with all of the teams, it just happened so fast. We started calling everybody and I was like, 'whoa!' [It was] extremely disheartening trying to find people, trying to tell everybody. It was just sad that it hadn't worked, because so many people had invested so much of their time and effort and money in this cause, to try to make this work.

"With the ABL, it just seemed that the players were a little more invested at that particular time, in the late 1990s, in trying to make the league work. It was less of a business and more of a cause."

Some would say that was part of the problem. Rage coach Anne Donovan wasn't surprised when the league folded because she visibly saw the threaded string the league was hanging by every day. She had accepted the position by phone and even though she had credible players, she had no front office support, and at times 50 people would be in the stands at games.

"It was a nightmare in Philadelphia," said Donovan, who still thought fondly of the league. "It was not a team that should have been up and running. My demise was a phone interview. If I'd gone up there to see the organization and meet the people, I would have known. We had a very good roster. It's easy as a coach, you don't care about anything else. But there wasn't any aspect of it, other than some really good people that were trying to keep it afloat, that was solid."

The official notice about the ABL broke rather nonchalantly on a weekly telephone conference call between general managers. They were casually discussing schedules and marketing, and sharing information about ticket sales when Cavalli interrupted the chatter with news that the league was done—displacing 90 players, 10

Dunn (center) designs a play for her team during a huddle. An avid reader, she used books about sibling rivalries, astrology, and coaches' memoirs to experiment on different ways to communicate with her players. (COURTESY OF JEFF REINKING/NBAE/GETTY IMAGES)

coaches, numerous front office personnel, and thousands of fans. While lawsuits accusing WNBA were filed, claiming it had sabotaged the ABL by scooping up major sponsors, preventing the fledgling league from securing a national television contract, Dunn was devastated.

The WNBA had constantly set itself up for criticism with its questionable timing. Announcements, such as the launching of the league and player signings, seemed to snare the spotlight from the ABL. Attempts to market both leagues with an All-Star game, as proposed by Cavalli, who was willing to pay and organize the game, received a succinct response from Ackerman. "It's a one-time publicity stunt that in the end isn't good for women's basketball," she stated in a press release. And of the debate that the ABL had better players, Ackerman's mantra to the media was, "I think the whole story line is tiresome."

After the ABL folded in 1998, the WNBA jumped on the void in June, revealing goals to expand in four cities, two that were smack dab in the middle of ABL cities. WNBA president Val Ackerman gleamed at her league's rapid growth, a smile that looked more like the Grinch's to hardened ABL fans in the Pacific Northwest. The quick expansion was a result of a collective bargaining agreement reached by the players and the league in April, plus desire by 14 NBA owners to seize the potential influx of talent.

It would seem difficult for anyone associated with the grassroots ABL to immediately leap in to the WNBA—even with its nationally televised games on ESPN2, major sponsors such as Nike, and play in posh NBA arenas.

Still, seven months after having her future tangled in Chapter 11 documents, Dunn picked up the phone from her Dresden home again and listened to Karen Bryant, Seattle's new senior director of WNBA operations. Bryant knew of Dunn because she was the general manager for the Seattle Reign during Dunn's tenure in Portland. That itch to see the growth of women's basketball continue motivated Dunn to agree to fly to the Emerald City for an interview.

"She had name recognition in the Northwest," said Bryant, who had been the organization's first hire for the new franchise. "I knew Lin Dunn well enough to know that she was going to roll up her sleeves and get out there and campaign with me. That's really what we were doing, running a campaign. I knew Lin would do the dog-and-pony show all over town and that her personality would draw people to our product."

Dunn hadn't been to the city since her defunct Power lost 70-61 to the Seattle Reign at Mercer Arena on December 4, 1998.

"I never knew for a fact that the WNBA willingly and knowingly and intentionally did anything to put the ABL out of business—I don't know that for a fact," Dunn said. "Did I hear those rumors? Sure. But at the end of the day, my number-one priority is women's basketball. Women's professional basketball, now, and the growth. I've been a pioneer in the game my whole life—college, now professional. So, I'm going to support whoever is supporting women's basketball.

"It wasn't any problem at all for me to move on. We have women's professional basketball, it's the WNBA. I got to know these people and I've always felt from the very beginning of my connection to the WNBA that all the people I've ever come in contact with—Val Ackerman, David Stern, [WNBA director of player personnel] Reneé Brown—they were genuinely committed to women's professional basketball and were good people. I've never had thoughts that they were the bad evil people that tried to put the ABL out."

On the surface, Lin Dunn shouldn't have fit in in Seattle. She sips Folgers coffee and wears Italian-designed sweaters in 80-degree heat, claiming she's ice cold. Then there's that southern drawl that immediately pegs her Tennessee roots. The twang wraps listeners into her molasses charm and they're hooked. Suddenly, Dunn is a one-woman show giving tummy exercises with hearty belly laughs. That's what her first interview with Bryant would portray. The two immediately bonded. Even Sonics owners Barry and Ginger Ackerley, who purchased the WNBA team, succumbed to Dunn's charms as she toured their high-rise offices in downtown Seattle.

Aside from her sense of humor, there was Dunn's basketball knowledge, which stems from three decades immersed in the game.

Bryant knew from the beginning that she wanted Dunn as Seattle's inaugural coach, keeping the interviewee list to three potential candidates, including former Reign coach Tammy Holder, although it was really just Dunn's job to reject. Bryant was one of the working suits among the average 4,000 fans present as Lin's Power assembled an 13-2 record against the Reign. "I just knew I didn't want to coach against her," Bryant said at the press conference announcing Dunn as the coach.

"I had beaten their butts in Portland," Dunn retorts. "So, it was kind of a combination. It was a good fit."

Dunn was able to quash any ill feelings about the WNBA in pursuit of the overall picture of women's basketball, but some in the city couldn't tread through the pain of the emotional loss as quickly. And there was little time to alter perceptions. Bryant and Dunn had to work fast. Of the four expansion teams—Seattle, Miami, Indiana, and Portland—Dunn was the first coach hired, on July 22, 1999. But the league had mandated that all potential expansion teams had to secure 5,500 season ticket deposits valued at $50 each by October 15, 1999, in order to officially be awarded a team. The new franchises also had to ink television contracts for a minimum of six games, set up staff specifically for the WNBA team, and make a financial commitment for promotion and advertising.

"Lin's just got that charisma. You don't have to be with her long to know that's a strength," Bryant said. "I remember taking Lin to the meeting, and Ginger was like, 'Wow, where did this lady come from?' They hit it off right away. I think Ginger was really excited about partnering with us. I think the three of us thought we all brought something different to the table, and collectively we were going to make sure this thing got off the ground in a huge way."

CHAPTER FIVE

Whose Ball? The WNBA Fights for Court Time in Seattle

Darkness tiptoed over Seattle. By December 1998, the entire Puget Sound area was soaking in 91 consecutive days of precipitation, adding to the gloom of losing its hard-won professional women's team.

Spalding basketballs, gym shoes, athletic shorts, and T-shirts returned to the trunks of cars, waiting for their turn to substitute for business suits, pantyhose, briefcases, and high heels after work. Former Reign players like Naomi Mulitauaopele and Kate Starbird joined the traditional workforce after bankruptcy eroded their ability to utilize their natural talent to play basketball.

Mulitauaopele, a 6-foot-4 center from Chief Sealth High in West Seattle, was supposed to have been entering her rookie season in the ABL. The sweet-mannered Samoan, whose jet-black curly locks hung like Rapunzel's, worked the night shift at Airborne Express while caring for her 16-year-old niece, who had dropped out of school and run away from home. Squeezed into the unexpected full-time mommy duties were workouts to stay in basketball shape.

Starbird, who had used her silky three-point shot to become

Washington's leading scorer while attending Lakes High School in Tacoma, had to grit her teeth once the ABL folded and admit a momentary truth her father used to tell her as a teenager.

"You can't make a living off basketball," the stern military veteran used to tell young Starbird, who'd rush through her homework to make time for playing. A brilliant mind, she had attended Stanford and started her own animation company, 3HC, with a college friend, plus she'd worked at Microsoft. Suddenly, her technology skills were the ones paying the bills for the 1997 No. 1 draft pick.

Starbird, a 6-foot-2 guard, still needed that basketball fix, though. She'd drive to the cracked white community recreational building at Green Lake, a homogenously populated neighborhood in Seattle, or to the University of Washington recreational gym to play pick-up ball. Some nights or weekend mornings it was a virtual who's who of local basketball stars. Former Huskies, Sonics rookies, native Washington NBA players, and ex-ABLers would descend on the courts to play. Other times there were just unknown faces, women sparked by the Reign's brief presence in town, who wanted to see if they still had it.

Joyce Walker wondered if she still had it as the ABL was getting started in May 1996. There was an open tryout in Atlanta, and Walker attended along with 600 other hopefuls, spending three days in a sticky gym surrounded by younger players constantly letting her know her time had past.

"That's the great thing about having a professional league, is that there's another place if you don't want to go to Europe," Walker said. "Those youngsters just had a few more years on me. It was fun, I had a great time, but I had put too many miles on the body. It was somebody else's turn. But I saw colleagues I hadn't seen for a while, I talked to some friends that I grew up with playing that were doing some coaching, and that really began to spur my interest. Just kind of seeing how you could possibly transfer."

The second woman to join the Harlem Globetrotters, that traveling team of glitz and skill, was the closest Walker had come to playing in a professional league in America. She left her mark in the various gyms in Seattle, a playground legend you won't see in a soda commercial because, simply, she's a woman.

"Guys . . . man, you didn't want to play against Joyce because she would embarrass you," said Rick DuPree, who grew up with Walker and went on to star in football at the University of Washington. "She was bad."

That's not bad meaning bad, but bad meaning good. A fervent beat was taking over a different part of Seattle, the predominately black Central District and Rainier Valley. Musical legends from Quincy Jones to Jimi Hendrix laid a foundation of flavor to the area rich in a soulful culture.

It seems like a distant time now as tufts of green grass poke through a faded tennis court's concrete cracks on the Rainier Valley Community Center's campus. Bustling life zooms by on a cheery blossom-lined street just over a hilly embankment. But this is where the concept of women playing a comparable version of basketball that men set as a standard was nourished.

Before demolition crews toppled the area, a small gym housed the space where some of the hottest games in Seattle were played. Outside the four walls, the city was going through an identity crisis, not knowing if it was New York Alki (a name almost given to the city by its original pioneers who wanted it to be a reflection of the East Coast metropolis) or the Great Northwest. Inside the steamy gym, character was spotted before duffel bags could hit the court.

"Shooter!" a deep voice would yell, and adjustments were made to squeeze the newcomer with game onto the next team. It was pick-up basketball with playground rules. No chalkboard was needed to keep track of who had next, just a boisterous mouth capable of seizing opportunity. The muggy gym, with an unforgettable odor of rotten sneakers, stale alcohol, and funk, was where names were made.

Walker lived for the environment. Oh, she had to earn her way onto the court, but it didn't take long for her to be recognized as a true baller. She had the ill jumpshot and the quick wits to keep her team on the court for hours. She was always picked to play, opening men's eyes to what a woman could bring to the game. Walker, then a teenager who had moved to Seattle from Los Angeles when she was 10, would travel her game around the city, playing on courts with names like "Wonder Bread," "Rotary," or "Mini."

It was the late 1970s, and the women's game was just beginning to get notice in the town. The Sonics won the NBA championship in 1979 behind the play of blond center Jack "The Banger" Sikma and "Downtown" Freddy Brown, the high-scoring sharpshooter.

"Joyce could shoot," DuPree said. "She was like a 'Downtown' Freddy Brown where she could hit the 15-, 18-foot jumper, and Joyce was tough. She could take you off the dribble and she was just so physical. I remember my ninth grade year my team was 6-foot-5, 6-foot-3, and then the guards. We were down at Seattle U [University] during a summer program, and Joyce was down there. We played two-on-two. It was me and the 6-foot-5 guy, and Joyce was with someone else. It didn't matter. It didn't matter because she just killed us. I was guarding Joyce, and it was embarrassing. We couldn't stop her at all."

Seattle was deep in basketball fever. Especially the south end, where the old community center sat. Walker remembers about 200 people cramming their way into the dilapidated facility, hoping they might see action on the court. Of course, if you were hoping, you didn't have game.

On the waxed floor, Walker worked her magic. She looked like a baller with the shorts, baggy T-shirt, and crooked, kinky 'fro that was some semblance of a Jheri Curl on a good day.

"Back then, we didn't care what we looked like," Walker said of the pioneering women athletes. "Not like today where the women look much more feminine."

Then, it was all about basketball. And this was where lessons were learned, against the guys who dominated the game. If a woman could hold her stance against them, she could thrive against her own gender.

That was Walker. Running her mouth with jabs like, "You better get somebody who can guard me," or her favorite, "You can't touch this." But when she lined up against women, she left all of that at the playground. There was no need to trash talk when her game was already burying opponents in a barrage of jumpers, layups, fadeaways, and defense.

By 1977, as a brash freshman, she led her Garfield High team to a second-place finish at the Washington state tournament. By her senior season in 1980, Walker busted out with a state-record 40-point game en route to clinching the Bulldogs' first Class 4A state title. Walker averaged 38 points in three games—besting her season average of 35.5—and poured in 35 of Garfield's winning 59 in a one-point win over Lincoln High School. Guys even transferred from Garfield, not wanting to be the second-best player at the school.

Walker relocated her fiery play to Louisiana State University, leaving behind the courts that groomed her game. She set a Southeastern Conference scoring record of 2,906 points (24.8 average) that stood until Tennessee's Chamique Holdsclaw broke it in 1999. Later, Walker was inducted into the state of Louisiana's Hall of Fame. Although she often forgot basketball, drifting to a crowd that preferred to drink or get high off marijuana and cocaine rather than hoops, Walker was one of the lucky ones. She was invited to the Olympic training facilities in Colorado Springs as one of the top high school players in the country. She met legends like Michael Jordan, Sam Perkins, and James Worthy in between sessions playing against some of the nation's brightest talent. Walker had natural ability that carried her to the fame of six-figure salaries and worldwide travel.

She was a spark. But there were others. And the playground wasn't going to get them the correct training or exposure for scarce college scholarships. Seattle native Jim Webster knew it and started an elite level of training for young girls called the Seattle Magic. The multitiered program was through the Amateur Athletic Union (AAU) and traveled the state as well as the country.

Both Starbird and Mulitauaopele played AAU basketball,

Mulitauaopele with the Magic, and many look at the emergence of club league as the foundation of what has helped grow women's basketball. In Washington, there was just an abundance of talent. Four of the national top-50 girls' high school programs in 2005 were from Washington, and schools were regularly signing local players to Division I college scholarships.

Although AAU helped garner some technical training for the girls, the University of Washington helped build exposure. Athletic director Barbara Hedges was hired in 1991, becoming the second woman to oversee an athletic department. Under her tenure, the school raised $100 million toward creating an athletic campus many schools across the nation would envy. She also placed importance on women's athletics on her campus, hiring quality coaches, like softball coach Teresa Wilson, and attempting to divvy funds equally. But one of the best hires came before Hedges's time—Chris Gobrecht in 1985.

Gobrecht, a bright basketball mind, quickly molded a team Seattle embraced. Her Husky program had the most-attended women's collegiate games in a major city, and in 10 of her 11 seasons, they won at least 17 games. Gobrecht is a thin woman with cropped sandy blond hair, whose voice ranges from a soft whisper to an octave surely heard atop Mount Rainier. Rivalries ran as deep as the Husky purple with her; she would tell fans she hated Stanford well after she stopped coaching in the Pac-10 in 2004, accepting a position at Yale. She reached the NCAA regionals four times and made stars of names like center Rhonda Smith-Banchero and forward Tara Davis, making the women's games an event on par with Husky football.

"They would have 6,000 plus at those games," said Walker of the UW program, the only spot for sports the city knew until the hydroplane races came along in the 1960s and the Sonics in 1967. "You had some good local talent staying home. I really believe that a by-product of building up something in the city is knowing that the girls in the Seattle area or surrounding area go to a major college. And that's what happened [with Gobrecht]. You could identify with them because you knew their history. You've seen them grow."

Seeing the players grow also formed an attachment that was practically unbreakable. Smith, who averaged 15.5 points in 116 games, and Davis, who averaged 10.1 in 113, played in the ABL for the Reign. Yet neither was as talented as in their younger college days, playing junk minutes and the role of ticket grabbers as recognizable names in the community. Still, their faces helped open hearts to others like Mississippian Niesa Johnson, a 5-foot-9 Reign guard, and Texan Shalonda Enis, a 6-foot-1 forward. Fans weren't just watching familiar players Starbird and Mulitauaopele, they were watching an extension of women's basketball players' careers. An aspect they missed with Walker's game, unless they happened to travel to Italy or bought a ticket to a Globetrotters game to see her play.

The flick *Love & Basketball*, released in 2000, tried to depict the realities of playing overseas: A coach screaming in another language. Tending to your own injuries. Making friends with former enemies because you're desperate to have a conversation in English. Truthfully, players never knew what to expect overseas. Anne Donovan, who left Old Dominion in 1983 as the nation's noted shot blocker (801), was treated supremely when she visited Japan for a pseudo-recruiting trip. Everyone had smiles and the Japanese coach for the team Shizuoka was welcoming. The only problems were the food and language barrier.

When she arrived to play, however, the first week of practice was an eye-opener. The 6-foot-8 American had to position her lithe body in front of her coach, who was punching a teammate in the face. One of his closed fists landed on the teammate's nose and blood gushed onto the court, the only thing stopping the altercation.

"All of the negative situations I'd heard about were in Europe," said Donovan, who had a no-abuse clause in her contract. "It was in there and I didn't know what it meant. Just like any recruiting trip, you never show a recruit anything negative. The contract seemed outrageous, it had to be a translation issue. Little did I know . . . "

Still, in Asian countries, payday for the teams was like clockwork, and players could make more money for an approximate four-month season than in eight months in Europe. Centers and power forwards were paid more because of their size, and foreign perimeter players had to be special to garner any time or real money because sponsors could get by paying the domestic players a pittance. Americans were often more talented and skilled in the sport, attracting the crowds. Domestic players were liked by fans, but often not as much as the more-talented, flashy Americans. The natives accepted the discrepancy in pay, too. They worked second jobs if not in school and viewed the Americans as good competition to prepare for play at American universities or possibly in the WNBA.

Walker was one of those special players with broad appeal. She took her game overseas and immediately attracted followers because she could shoot. Even men loved her game as she shook off defenders and faded back for uncontested jumpers. Looking around at all of the international women's teams playing in modest conditions, but still playing past college, many wondered why it couldn't work in America. Names like Cynthia Cooper and Teresa Edwards were making Japan and Italy known for their basketball, giving ideas to young European girls about the joy of sport, while American girls played with the sole idea that basketball is a means to get a scholarship to get an education to get a career. The ABL brought more than that simplistic progress when it arrived in Seattle.

"When I was young, I used to always watch the Reign and thought, 'Well, maybe I can play,'" said Seattle native Sheila Lambert, 25, who plays for the Detroit Shock. "These girls [players] come out here and compete. Seattle likes to see that other than to see guys. With guys it's a dunk fest, but just to see some basketball, period, these girls bring them out."

It had been a while since Seattle had dealt with the loss of a sports franchise. So long that hardly any of the people remembered when the Seattle Pilots were moved to Milwaukee in 1969, and therefore they didn't know how to mourn. Not that many mourned the Pilots because the baseball team returned in 1977. The Reign's impact was deep and needed a release. Sometimes it would happen in the frozen food aisle between the peas and vegetable medley at the Wallingford QFC, a grocery store located in Seattle's quaint north Lake Union neighborhood. Karen Bryant would roll her squeaky cart, bypassing the rows of greenery, and a voice would chill her bones icier than the artificial air pumped through the freezer case. "I never got my money back!"

The familiar sentence regarding lost deposits for Reign season tickets had been firmly stated so many times, the faces became a blur to Bryant, then the general manager. Some were close friends. Some were volunteers who spent hours stuffing envelopes or passing out fliers to let the city know about the basketball team. But all of them lost money, about $300 on average, when the ABL completed its paperwork for bankruptcy on New Year's Day 1999, accumulating $25 million in debt.

Bryant's instructions were specific once word came in December. Pack up the modest office of computers, desks, chairs, notepads—everything—load it on a truck, and place it in a storage unit. Through sobbing tears, Bryant and her staff did so, sending the key to a bankruptcy attorney in California. While they packed, the phone rang with season ticket holders feeling sorry and frustrated, but also wondering what happened to their money.

"I'm telling them, 'I don't know, we're no longer an organization, so I can't—we're basically indebted to this bankruptcy company,'" Bryant said. "It was awful. There are people in this community that still hang on to that, and I can't say that I blame them. The closest thing that I can relate it to is being part of a political cause, helping to raise money, investing your own personal money, and then the initiative just dies."

The past doesn't easily die in Seattle. People hold on to memories. And independent Seattle felt spurned by the commercial NBA that to some shut down the ABL. Tempers needed to be soothed, and a void needed to be filled. The UW was on the decline under coach June Daugherty, placing fifth in the Pac-10 Conference in back-to-back seasons after the ABL folded.

The resurgence was coming at the grassroots level. Inspired by televised WNBA and college games and the Reign, high school girls were taking basketball seriously, searching for better competition and coaching. By the 1999–2000 school year, 10,026 girls played in Washington state.

Walker, who had been working her own summer camps, Hoop Sense, to give students sound minds and fundamentals, accepted a position to coach her amateur Garfield High Bulldogs in 2000. Her enthusiasm to return her school to glory, along with other committed coaches across the state, were part of the reason the WNBA began tinkering with the idea of putting a team in the Northwest. Walker had been sober for a decade, but still needed to learn how to make herself, with her dyed blond hair and gold teeth, approachable to the girls on her team. It took a season, but the personalities blended and the WNBA was in the shadow as an aspiration for the team.

"A lot of girls emulate the WNBA players," Walker said of her basketball team and campers. "I hear it in my players. [Senior guard] Malia [O'Neal] don't talk a lot about them when she likes them. When she likes them, she'll say little quiet things. Like Sue Bird is somebody that she likes in terms of how she runs the floor. She really likes the way that Lisa [Leslie] has come around. She likes the little [Connecticut Sun Lindsay] Whalen kid, but she doesn't always do a bunch of talking about stuff. She just thinks [Diana] Taurasi's got big cajones, believes that she can get it done.

"When you're in the locker room you hear them talk about

players. So they know, they know names now because of the exposure. I think that's what's huge."

No matter how many benefits Seattleites could see in having another professional team, the pain hadn't dispersed by the time Lin Dunn had accepted the coaching position. In that sense Dunn was ideal for the job, and Bryant ideal in the front office. They were the first faces of the WNBA team. In fact, of the coaches hired elsewhere—Linda Hargrove in Portland or Ron Rothstein, a former NBA coach hired in Miami—none had the traits needed to change bitter attitudes. Hargrove, a country girl herself, was too conservative to whip up fried chicken for sports radio personalities like Dunn did, adding hot sauce to the batter for her own personal touch. And Rothstein, an equally impressive basketball mind as Dunn with years of NBA experience, wasn't quirky enough to dribble through downtown streets for 5.5 miles to collect season ticket deposits. With a September drizzle slicking the Seattle city streets, Dunn, then a stout 52-year-old, used her effervescent personality to introduce curious strangers to the league while bouncing its signature oatmeal-and-orange ball on the hilly sidewalks with Bryant. A camera crew and local media documented the comical moment. By the WNBA's mandated October 15, 1999, deadline, Seattle had secured 7,176 deposits, enough to be granted a team. While it was great that the franchise had secured fans, the inaugural season was eight months away, and the team didn't have players, uniforms . . . shoot, it didn't have a name. And that was probably the trickiest part.

Sports have long been used to develop masculinity. Through playing games, little boys are taught how to lose with dignity, build confidence, and receive the splendid payoff that usually comes with hard work, perseverance, and patience. Women who've dared to compete have long been harassed with sexist or homophobic labels, like being called a "dyke" or "lesbo," to keep them off the playing field—as if allowing them to learn the same values while developing healthy bodies would destroy the world as we know it. To counter this, women's teams either overtly feminized themselves and their

Los Angeles center Lisa Leslie (9) drives past Storm center Simone Edwards (4). Edwards was allotted to the team during its inaugural season in 2000. (LATRENA SMITH PHOTOGRAPHY)

team names to appeal to marketers, or wore makeup so their more "desired" heterosexual identities were strongly emphasized in promotions or by the media. Basketball, with its blue-collar roots, is a prime example of men's difficulty in envisioning women playing ball. Their stance is colorfully portrayed in their nicknames of squads. In the past, there were the Houston Angels and the Philly Foxes, with buxom caricatures of the mascots used as the logo. When the WNBA announced its formation in 1996, chauvinistic sportswriters and fans offered supposedly witty nicknames for the league. In the beginning the league spun its brethren NBA team's monikers to identify the women, hence the Houston Comets (Rockets) or Sacramento Monarchs (Kings). But when Detroit was named as an expansion team in 1998, submitted names playing off the "Pistons" ranged from "Headlights" to "Bumpers."

Seattle was more covert with its underbelly, ditching the SuperSonics nickname as a base, offering "Amazons" and "Boom" instead. Those suggestions could have paid tribute to successful online company Amazon.com and the city's history in airline flight too, but the juvenile snickering could be heard around the water cooler as the team was discussed. Ultimately at a party on January 6, 2000, the new millennium women's team was dubbed the "Storm."

While entertaining about 1,500 fans at a logo-unveiling event on January 23, 2000, at KeyArena, Dunn's mind was on another continent. Her freshly named team's college/international draft was in April, and from Dunn's personal research with expansion teams in football and baseball and consulting for Houston coach Van Chancellor, Dunn knew she'd have to build from the draft. She needed a formidable post to establish the burgeoning Storm. Dunn had already picked up five solid veterans. But those were the unprotected players from the 12 established WNBA teams that were allowed to protect eight on their roster. Guard Sonja Henning had won a championship as Houston's starting point guard in 1999, and Edna Campbell had started in Phoenix, but Charmin Smith had only played 13 games in Minnesota and Angela Aycock essentially was drafted as a familiar face to sell tickets.

To Dunn's vexation, the WNBA didn't award the four expansion teams the top picks in the college/international draft, folding them into the order instead. Dunn fretted impatiently in a paper-laden draft room adjacent to her team's practice facility and waited out the top eight selections. With her ninth overall pick she chose Kamila Vodichkova, a Czech Republic native who had played professionally for BK Gambrinus the past two years. ESPN announcers Ann Myers, Matt Devlin, and Doris Burke froze midbroadcast. Who in the name of women's basketball was Kamila Vodichkova?

"Ah, I hope we're going to receive some information on her here," Myers said to fill the dead air.

Dunn was sly, if anything. She'd moan about hurt knees, aging limbs, and a blind right eye before a "friendly" game of tennis, then transform her racket into a whip as she lashed winners all over the court with the power of Serena Williams. Her basketball mind was no different. In fact, one of the toughest things for sportswriters about covering Dunn was her unwillingness to tip her hand—under any circumstance. You may have wondered what she was doing, but Dunn always knew. Her staff never saw Vodichkova play in person, scouring instead over tapes sent by her agent. On the jumpy film the 6-foot-5 center wore her signature stoic face as she planted her body like a tree stump under the basket for rebounds and spun around for baby hook shots with fluidity. Dunn, also the Storm's general manager, had waffled between selecting Vodichkova and an American, Summer Erb, a thick 6-foot-6 center Dunn had recruited to Purdue before being fired. Erb opted to attend North Carolina State.

"That was the most important pick that we would ever make," Dunn said. "We needed that person to come in and really help this team. Not just then, but for a couple of years. It couldn't be a bust."

Dunn snatched other teams' unprotected players, dug deep for an obscure "steal" in the draft, and formed a team close to her vision when hired in July. Training camp seemed more like bitty basketball camp as players practiced defensive drills, figured out the correct hand to use for layups, and learned what would become their daily routine of warm-up shooting, running, and dribbling drills.

The players were hypersensitive. At the four corners of the training facility court located on the Seattle Center grounds in the shadow of the Space Needle were chilled cans of Diet Pepsi, Dunn's favorite beverage. She'd pace the court like a ringmaster, lashing her critiques at the players, taking sips from whatever can was closest in between statements. In the pocket of her nylon sweatpants was a cellular phone that seemingly never stopped ringing.

"We were all paranoid that season," Smith said. "Coach Dunn was always on her cell talking about trades. One time in shootaround the phone rang and she answered it. We were like, 'You know, we're practicing!'"

The Storm was in Charlotte at the time, running through offensive and defensive setups for the following night's game against the Sting. The Eastern Conference team featured Olympian Dawn Staley, regarded as one of the best guards in the game's history, and forwards Andrea Stinson and Allison Feaster, whose deceptively small size hid uncanny strength and outside shooting power. But the Sting, a charter team then coached by T. R. Dunn, didn't have the right mix inside. They finished the 1999 season with a losing record and began the 2000 season winless in the Sting's three games prior to playing Seattle.

Lin Dunn's Storm wasn't doing well, either. The inaugural season opened May 31 on the road, where the Sacramento Monarchs, with former ABL MVP Yolanda Griffith, whupped on the Storm like a beater on fresh eggs. Campbell needed to bathe in ice, she had so many aches from trying to speed past the Monarch's convoluted defense. Australian guard Katrina Hibbert, who scored the franchise's historic first points on a putback off her own miss, looked exasperated after the game. And Vodichkova had bruises on her arms and a cut above her eye—postgame mementos she'd become accustomed to in six seasons playing in the WNBA.

By the home opener on June 1, Dunn had cemented her infamous line about the expansion Storm. "We're just a baby. A 1-year-old competing against 4-year-olds," she squawked repeatedly like a well-trained parakeet.

Houston was the home opening opponent at KeyArena. The Comets' prestigious stature as winners of the first three WNBA championships added glitziness to the already showy event. But in the visitor's locker room, coach Van Chancellor fumed at being part of the otherwise electric atmosphere.

"I'll tell y'all what I'm tired of, every time we get an expansion team, we've got to open their season," he told reporters. "It's tough. They get all pumped up to play us."

Firecrackers whizzed from the arena tiles and 10,840 fans filled the KeyArena lower bowl. While Dunn had scrambled to create a team, Bryant had scrambled to find fans. But the WNBA, averaging 2 million a season, still didn't have an exact target audience for its niche sport. Female high school players were an obvious choice, parents with daughters, and basketball fans. But Sonics season ticket holders weren't even a fraction of the makeup of the Storm's audience. And about a third of the Reign's fans wouldn't cross over because of the WNBA link.

Bryant had one advantage—a budget. She went from the ABL's word-of-mouth and cheeky fliers to print ads and radio spots, plus the league had national stock TV commercials. Bryant was finding an audience that, when converted from the deposits, became a base of 5,000 season ticket holders—a conversion of about 70 percent. And it was a rare bunch that didn't budge opening night, even when Houston led 58-31 at one time during a 30-point blowout. "A Sonic crowd would have been long gone, but this crowd cheered through the carnage," *Seattle Times* columnist Steve Kelley wrote the following day.

After the national anthem, the arena was pitch black. It was time for the players' introductions. They were ushered to strategic tunnels scattered atop the lower bowl, and as each name was called, a spotlight descended upon them, following them down the steps while they carried the trademark WNBA ball. The players slapped high-fives to fans and were directed to hand off the basketball to a little girl waiting on the court, symbolizing their role as sports figures for youths. It's a tradition upheld across the league today.

Tears streamed down the cheeks of older women in the crowd as the evening unfolded. Most had paths like Dunn, playing an insulting version of the game because it wasn't proper for a young lady to sweat. Or being shoved out of experiencing sports at all because of being called hurtful names by homophobic peers and adults as impressionable children. Or playing in a time when there wasn't a higher plateau than college. For those women, it was overwhelming to see the players in their crisp white jerseys with "Storm" emblazoned across the chest and the supportive crowd that wildly cheered every play. The gimmicks used to intensify the experience weren't the hokey metal sheets shaken by volunteers for sound effects like at Reign games, and players didn't run through a paper poster, as if they were a high school team. Even though it had nothing to do with the game, you could see the money put behind the league from the media guide to the sound system. And looking around at all the fans eager to see them play was a sight many hadn't seen since college.

"I was almost in tears because I was starting," Smith said. "Coming down the stairs, I was like, 'Don't fall, don't fall.' You can't really see where you're going. But when I was standing there getting ready for the jump ball, tears came to my eyes because I was so excited. That's all I wanted: to play basketball. And I'm lined up with, like, Sheryl Swoopes! I was like, 'Alright, I'm guarding Sheryl Swoopes in the inaugural home game of the Seattle Storm!' I got chills. I got that rush."

The women's movement aspect of the game was the driving force of the first season, however. Once the ball was tossed up, the Storm was smoked like a slab of Texan ribs. Comets players Swoopes, forward Tina Thompson, and guards Cynthia Cooper and Janeth Arcain had played together for three full seasons, plus Cooper and Arcain, a Brazilian Olympian, had vast experience playing professionally overseas. The Storm on the other hand was still learning how to pronounce everyone's name.

Houston easily defeated Seattle 77-47. The Storm also lost its next two games, to the expansion Portland Fire and on the road to the Phoenix Mercury by 33 points. When the team landed in Charlotte, Dunn put the hustle on getting someone, anyone, in to help the team offensively.

Midway through practice the night before the June 9 game, Dunn stopped midsentence to answer her cell. After a few minutes that felt like an eternity to the team, she returned to the session.

"My fault, y'all. I thought that was about the trade," she quipped, oozing her southern drawl to soften the edges of the harsh implications. But her players still stared back mortified.

"We're all like, 'Oh God!'" Smith said. "Sure enough, we got Stacey."

Stacey Lovelace was signed on June 8 after Dunn waived Angela Aycock and Tajama Abraham, players she wasn't getting desired production from. Lovelace was a floating free agent who Dunn knew from her Purdue days, where she'd coached the 6-foot-4 forward to the 1994 NCAA Final Four. Lovelace also had played in the ABL and overseas.

Recently waived by the Indiana Fever, the Detroit native was finishing a workout in her Atlanta home and planned to meet friends for a barbecue dinner. When her agent called to notify her she'd been signed by the Storm, the evening's plans changed to throwing a few items into a duffel bag. Flying to Charlotte. And after briefly meeting her new team at the hotel, being pulled aside by Smith to cram a handwritten copy of the Storm's playbook into her mind.

The next morning Smith and Lovelace reviewed everything on the chartered bus to shootaround and again on the way to the game that night. Lovelace's mind raced, but being the new player not included in the Sting's scouting reports, she was able to sneak around the offense as a decoy to score 13 points and grab a team-high nine rebounds in the Storm's first victory, 67-62.

"I had no idea what to expect," a stunned Lovelace told the *Seattle Times* after the win. "I didn't even know if I'd play at all. I'm still in the process of trying to get it together. I mean, yesterday I was just at home and now I'm a part of history for this franchise."

The Storm rained on the beach party theme night at Charlotte Coliseum. A paltry 3,946 fans gathered to see the game at an antiquated rural arena that seated 30,000. Some fans played in the sand set up behind the hoop closest to the visitor's bench. Others batted around colorful beach balls in the stands as the game progressed. Everyone was given commemorative white terry-cloth towels picturing the Sting's bumblebee mascot, date, and names of the two teams. Joyous over the win, after giving a postgame interview to the team's traveling radio station, Dunn grabbed one of the towels and twirled it about, almost dancing a giddy jig back to the locker room.

The only problem with the win was Storm fans in Seattle couldn't see it. All of the games were broadcast on the local sports station, KJR (950 AM), but ratings weren't high for the new team. When the Storm returned home later in the week, fans were able to experience that winning feeling that made you want to dance a two-step in the aisles. It was unexpected, though. Los Angeles was the opponent lined up along the visitors bench, moving in unison during its warm-ups and looking every bit as intimidating as its 4-2 record, which ranked second in the Western Conference. Dunn had picked up another player, trading the rights to Serbian center Nina Bjedov to Cleveland for shooting guard Michelle Edwards, a former star at the University of Iowa in 1988. Edwards, 34, had spent more time on the Rockers bench than the fabric covering the seats at the time and was happy to be traded, even if it was for a player who never reported to play that season.

"I might as well have been on IR [injured reserve]," the freckle-faced Edwards joked to the *Seattle Times*. "My role was best cheerleader and my best cheer was 'Come on, let's go!'"

Edwards blended nicely with Lovelace, however, freeing team leader Campbell to score 22 points in a 69-59 overtime victory at KeyArena. Edwards added 12 points, and 6-foot-4 bookend centers Simone Edwards and Quacy Barnes rotated to contain Olympian posts DeLisha Milton and Lisa Leslie, who fouled out after scoring eight points.

Sparks guard Ukari Figgs sent the game into overtime tied at 55 points apiece, hitting a pair of free throws. Campbell promptly regained control of the game, nailing a three-pointer that sent the crowd into a frenzy. She scored seven of Seattle's points in overtime as the Storm outscored the Sparks 14-4 to win its first home game. Los Angeles coach Michael Cooper fumed at the loss, cursing his players and promising changes in the starting rotation after the game.

"That was pathetic," he told reporters. "We let an expansion team take it to us in every aspect of basketball."

It was the biggest win of the Storm's inaugural season, but Seattle would only win once in its following 15 games. The Storm was 2-5 against the other three expansion teams, finishing the season with a league-worst 6-26 record utilizing 17 different starting lineups.

Seattle's worst performances in the Western Conference were against the Houston Comets, which won its fourth WNBA championship in August. The Comets swept the Storm in a three-game series, holding the expansion team to an average 50 points per game while scoring 78.7 themselves. A tweaked excerpt from rap artist Tag Team's 1993 hit "Whoomp! (There it is)" changed to "Swoopes! (There it is)" was belted out by the crowd after her every basket and rang in the Storm players' heads after two road losses in Houston. The All-Star forward, who'd win the regular-season MVP and Defensive Player of the Year titles that summer, averaged 18.7 points on 61.1 percent shooting from the field against the Storm.

Dunn, once a ball of fire on the sideline as she whirled around, giving directions to multiple people simultaneously, simply sat on the bench by season's end. Exasperated, there was nothing left to pull from her team. She blew up once—in a loss at Indiana—but eventually caved to her team's doomed fate.

"I hate to lose," she told the *Seattle Times* in August as her players still displayed smiles while practicing or tending to various injuries. "It's been a hard season, so yeah, I'm not as intense, but I've got to know when to give them a kick in the butt or a pat on the back. Lately it's been two pats instead of a kick."

CHAPTER SIX

The "L" Word

The Westin hotel connected to The Galleria shopping mall is where the Storm usually stays when it travels to Houston to play the Comets. The sprawling labyrinth of 300 luxurious brand-name stores was a treat for the players, most of whom are seasoned shoppers. In between shootaround and games or after practice, if the Storm arrived early enough, you could spot the team cruising the window fronts for deals, blending with travelers from across the globe who descended upon the nation's fourth-largest city to spend, spend, spend.

Lone Star state flags wave proudly from light poles and the windows of mammoth trucks bulldozing their way on the freeways and streets. Men adorned in Stetson hats, handlebar mustaches, and snakeskin cowboy boots pepper the population. And a portrait of the state's former governor, President George Bush, hangs above Jesus in some Mexican cantinas. The illusion is of a staunch Republican society entrenched in proud conservative family values of life, love, and liberty.

Drive five minutes toward downtown on Westheimer Road and a different flag waves just as proudly among an approximate six-block radius—the rainbow flag symbolizing homosexual pride.

In 2001, "homosexual sodomy" was still deemed a criminal
act in Texas, not erased from the books until a 6-3 decision by the
U.S. Supreme Court in 2003 (*Lawrence v. Texas*). In the gay mid-
town community of Houston, however, clubs such as South Beach
thumped music and provided sculpted male go-go dancers for the
jubilant gays getting sweaty on the dance floor, while the barnlike
lesbian bar Chances offered hip-hop and karaoke nights for its
clientele. Before Comets games, the most popular event for local
lesbians, Café Adobe, would be packed with predominately black
lesbians dressed in red Comets jerseys and sipping the Mexican
restaurant's delicious array of margaritas.

The mere image—beautiful women sharing laughs over enchilada
dishes—incenses more than just homophobia in conservative
Texans, who'd rather their daughters be whores than dykes. When
the September 11 terrorist attacks changed the landscape of New
York forever, southern preacher Jerry Falwell actually said America
was responsible by not abiding by God's wishes, linking homosexuals
to the terror. (After Hurricane Katrina took more than 1,300 lives
throughout the Gulf Coast and destroyed New Orleans, conservatives
again pointed at homosexuals because of the Southern Decadence
parade, an annual gay celebration.)

As people across the nation grieved at the horrendous image
of airplanes crashing into the Twin Towers, toppling both buildings
on a workday morning, sports leagues fell silent. Male athletes who
flaunted their riches were suddenly reevaluating their place in a new
society along with other Americans. A unification occurred, with
impromptu vigils and patriotic displays of American flags on cars
popping up across the country.

In Houston, however, Comets All-Star Sheryl Swoopes was
actually starting to feel more detached from mainstream society. Her
divorce from husband Eric Jackson was finalized in the spring of
2000, ending their four-year marriage. The two have a son, Jordan,
who was named after the famed basketball player. After so much
heartache, Swoopes expected the 2001 season to be another pinnacle

in her career. Instead, she was the fashionably dressed player on the sideline, suffering a season-ending torn anterior cruciate ligament as well as a lateral meniscus tear in her left knee five weeks before the WNBA kicked-off its historic fifth season.

Marketing analysts peg the fifth season as significant for any new endeavor. Much attention is paid to the league's obnoxious hype machine, but ads don't keep the WNBA afloat, repeat customers do. And president Val Ackerman trumpeted throughout the season that her-once mythical dream was "involved in a real-life game of *Survivor*, where the fans are the ones casting the votes." The past two seasons, Swoopes was the top vote-getter for the league's All-Star game, continuing to attract fans after she first grabbed the spotlight while scoring 47 points to help Texas Tech University win the 1993 NCAA title in a 84-82 decision over Ohio State University. She was the bare-bellied picture of heterosexuality, exposing her pregnant self on the cover of *Sports Illustrated for Women* in 1997.

"She's more like a legend; she had been playing for a long time," said Sonics forward Rashard Lewis, who was deep in Comets fever along with his classmates when he attended Alief Elsik High School in the Houston suburbs (graduating in 1998). "She wasn't one of the youngest players that came out of college and was playing. I wanna say she was more like an old G [gangsta]. Everybody knew her by playing in the Olympics, playing overseas, and now she had the chance to play in the WNBA. We was excited for her and felt like the Comets was the best team."

Lewis, who was selected by the Sonics in the second round of the 1998 draft, was among the cluster of NBA wannabes, college stars, Houston Rockets, and WNBA ballers and wannabes that would hoop for hours at the secluded Westside Tennis Club. Lewis and Swoopes would give each other the standard head nod acknowledging the other's presence, but never formally met. It was just common ground to get a solid workout during the off-season. At least that was Swoopes' plan when she and teammate Coquese Washington arrived at the facility on Monday night, April 23, 2001.

Finally getting on the court for a coed pickup game, Swoopes caught the basketball and intended to drive to the basket for an easy layup. She never left the court. Swoopes planted her left leg and felt a pop before crashing to the court, writhing in pain. Doctors say that 75 percent of knee injuries in women happen the same way. It was the first major injury of Swoopes's career. She underwent successful surgery in May. Basketball was definitely her livelihood; she earned an estimated $1 million combined from the WNBA and sponsorship deals with Nike, which was manufacturing the sixth edition of her namesake shoe. Raising a child and staring at bankruptcy due to the divorce and mismanagement of her finances, Swoopes couldn't afford the setback of the injury.

Internally, however, Swoopes was battling a different struggle.

Jackson, who's three years younger than Swoopes, was her high school sweetheart. He was her biggest fan, traveling the globe with her during the tour leading to the 1996 Olympics, shagging her rebounds and sitting in specific seats so when she looked up from the court, she could easily find him in the stands as he motioned directions about her play. Marriage became rough, however; Swoopes can't be described as Miss Congeniality. Fans refer to her as "Her Majesty" and the word "Diva" marks her space in the Comets locker room. There were disagreements, travel strained their relationship, and Swoopes told a reporter she had matured faster than her husband. Helping her through the difficult period was Comets assistant coach Alisa Scott, a former player of Van Chancellor's at the University of Mississippi. Somewhere in between sobbing about Jackson, talking about basketball, and sharing each other's secrets, a spark was ignited.

Swoopes was in love with a woman.

These feelings are practically incomprehensible in the black family. Swoopes, born in 1971, was raised in Brownfield, Texas, by her mother, Louise, a single parent of four children. They lived in a postage stamp–sized three-bedroom home. Louise was a religious woman, firmly believing boys roughhoused and girls played peacefully with dolls. Basketball didn't fit into the equation

Houston forward Sheryl Swoopes (22) drives past Storm guard Betty Lennox. Swoopes is the first high-caliber athlete to state publicly during their playing career that they are homosexual. (LATRENA SMITH PHOTOGRAPHY)

and neither did homosexuality, preached as an abomination in the church. In fact, when Swoopes left home to attend the University of Texas in 1989, she promptly moved back home claiming there were too many lesbians in the program. Louise told the *Austin American-Statesman* that two lesbians made sexual advances toward Sheryl.

A majority of black families even consider homosexuality a "white thing," as if being queer is race-specific. Overbearing religious beliefs in the black community have prevented discussions about safe sex and AIDS—even though two-thirds of its sufferers are black women—believing premarital sex is a sin. But not all women diagnosed with HIV were promiscuous. And issues regarding homosexual feelings are quickly disregarded as sins. Pray and it'll go away was the response. It wasn't leaving Swoopes. Not when she glanced at Scott's warm dimpled smile and commanding stance that exuded a certain coolness, which made Swoopes feel safe. She wanted to shout to the world that she was in love, but society's anti-gay climate made her keep her feelings buried inside. People suspected, however. Hundreds within the basketball circle already knew.

"I . . . in a way, I knew growing up in Houston," said Lewis, who still returns home during the off-season. "You heard rumors around the area, but I feel like it's her life and it's her responsibility. If she decides she wants to come out with it, then I don't think people should criticize because she's the one that has to worry about what she has to face. Not us."

Swoopes dropped hints of her courtship over the years. She referred to "Scotty" in her acceptance speeches for awards. She made the rounds at parties during the 2003 NCAA Final Four in Atlanta with Scott by her side. And Jordan, who continues to travel with Mommy during the summer, would run to Scott and collapse in her arms as lovingly as he would Swoopes's. By the summer of 2005, after being introduced at a black lesbian conference in Dallas that spring with Scott, Swoopes had had enough of the secrecy. But she still feared saying anything.

"I've been through a lot of pain and dealing with a lot of

emotions," she said after a Comets shootaround prior to playing the Storm, making the team bus wait while she spoke to a reporter. "It took a long time for me to come to terms with being a lesbian. I feel I've lost a lot of sponsorship deals because of my lifestyle and haven't been marketed the same way because of who I choose to love."

The stigma of what a woman should be doing after a certain age still holds the progress of women's team sports back. Along with sexuality. Sixty percent of the television viewing audience is male, which traps the WNBA between marketing talent and sex. Ackerman had the NBA's marketing clout at her disposal, getting 13 major companies from Coca-Cola to General Motors to spend a reported $10 million in sponsorship and advertising to support the inaugural eight-team league. Over the years came more control of what the image should be as the WNBA discovered what its fan base was and whom it still needed to target.

Spotting lesbians in a crowd or a so-called mannish-looking player has always given men credence to unfairly call the sport "full of lesbians." It's not until a Sue Bird or Swin Cash comes along, a white and black version of charming looks with basketball skills that'll leave a guy on his tush in a game of one-on-one, that men sit up and take notice. And although women comprise 80 percent of household purchasing power, according to marketing surveys, the television ratings, where men dominate and sponsors can hawk their product, make the WNBA kowtow to whatever that demographic wants.

The Los Angeles Sparks has held functions at Girl Bar, a lesbian hotspot. The Minnesota Lynx advertises in *Lavender*, the largest gay publication in the Midwest. The Storm has heavily marketed lesbians since its inception. As a league, however, the WNBA hasn't been public about its homosexual contingent.

"They better not touch that topic; I don't think it's any of their business," said Garfield High coach Joyce Walker of the WNBA headlining for homosexual rights. "I think it's their business to take care of the people that work for them that might have issues that come up to really address and making sure they're OK, health-wise. But I don't know that it's an issue for them to address with women being gay or not being gay. I don't think you sweep it under the rug, but I don't think it's a format where you have to have some big topics of discussion. I think you need to honor your workers, regardless of what their preferences are or what their choices are."

Walker has been with her partner for seven years and both work at the high school. Hanging in her office is a basic white sheet of paper listing unacceptable behavior; homophobia is highlighted in yellow. Except, as she led the Bulldogs to the Class 4A Washington state championship in 2005, it wasn't an issue with her players, many of whom dress in baggy sweatpants with hair braided in intricate cornrows, not concerned with looking overtly feminine as young girls did in the past. Walker's door is always open, but she tells her players relationship issues are "not welcome in this locker room. When you show up you need to be focused on what we're trying to do. I don't want to hear about you over here with such and such."

Karen Bryant said the WNBA is evolving toward a similar stance. She held a commitment ceremony with her partner on a gorgeous sunny day on the shoreline of Kitsap Peninsula; many WNBA and Storm front office people attended. She flashes her diamond ring with pride as she whisks past the KeyArena press row and labels herself an "out" lesbian, not seeing the issue as a "pink elephant in the room." She simply separates her private and work lifestyles.

"There's a percentage of the population that I don't deal with much that is still so very narrow-minded, and my hesitation is never wanting to hurt the Storm or the WNBA because of my lifestyle," Bryant said. "I'm not in it for that. I don't want in anybody's mind to create any room for any negative perception about the league. I care too much about the brand, what we're trying to do, what we stand for to make my lifestyle a part of the Storm."

Swoopes couldn't stifle the words any longer, however. The Comets, which missed the playoffs for the first time in history in 2004, finishing 13-21, had placed her on the trading block. A move that stunned opponents, but there weren't any takers for the demanding 33-year-old who boasted a high salary. It was her worst season since returning after the birth of her son in 1997 to average 7.1 points in nine games. In 2004, she averaged 14.8 on 42.2 percent shooting from the field, returning from the Olympics drained as the Comets won just one of its eight games in September to drop from contention. Livid, Swoopes returned in 2005 to average 18.6 points on 44.7 percent shooting from the field to win the regular-season scoring title and top Storm forward Lauren Jackson for MVP. Swoopes also won the All-Star game MVP award, choking back tears as she thanked Scotty for her support. Scott was backstage trailing behind the forward as she swiftly moved from photo shoots with sponsors to media interviews to a postgame party at Michael Jordan's restaurant at the Mohegan Sun Casino Connecticut, where the game was held.

The Comets defeated the Storm 2-1 in the first round of the playoffs, Houston's first postseason series win since 2000. Swoopes averaged 18.4 points, 5.6 rebounds, and 3.8 assists. Her team went on to lose to Sacramento in the Western Conference finals, but Swoopes was feeling vindicated and confident. By October, after planning a lesbian cruise vacation with Scott and being offered a lucrative spokeswoman deal with Olivia cruise line, Swoopes was ready to come out. She did so in a first-person article in *ESPN The Magazine*. Coincidentally, the news broke the same week civil rights icon Rosa Parks died.

"I'm tired of being miserable. Not being free to be who I am, not being okay with other people knowing who I am," Swoopes stated in the article. "It has been miserable. And it hurts. I'm an affectionate person. Going to the movies or dinner, seeing so-called normal couples show affection in public and knowing that I can't hurts. It's frustrating to hold everything inside and not be who I want to be.

I'm sure life is not going to be easier for me just because I'm coming out. But at least I'll be free."

Storm coach Anne Donovan wasn't surprised at Swoopes's public announcement. It caused a wave of news in papers and on television shows. Swoopes was pimped on every major network discussing her sexuality, and the Internet boomed with discussions about her disclosure. The league and Comets headquarters were bombarded with feedback, the majority of it positive—fans fell in love with Swoopes all over again.

"Swoopes is who she is, I have to say that," said Donovan, who served as an assistant coach on the 2000 Olympic team. "And I will say that it hasn't always worked in her favor. She does [things] on her own terms."

The news even swirled overseas, where an all-time high of 62 percent of WNBA players were in the midst of off-season competition. Players text-messaged each other, but were mostly blasé about Swoopes's announcement, according to Bird. "We already knew and were aware of it and in support of it . . . and, to be honest, didn't really care," she said. "So, when the news broke, it was like a blip—not a big deal."

Each year, the new season's hopeful women will descend upon Seattle from lands as distant as Russia or as close as California, some slightly tired from playing in eight-month leagues overseas, but still amped about what could unwrap in the upcoming four months. The majority of the players will unpack pictures of family, dogs, and homes in their team-issued apartments at the base of Queen Anne. Sue Bird, like Jackson, simply dusts off the mantel and furniture at her town home, also located in the quaint neighborhood not too far north from their home facility, KeyArena.

Seattle takes on a different feel in the summer. Although the stretch between October 2004 and May 2005 was among the area's driest, causing newly elected governor Christine Gregoire to warn of a summer drought, the period was still cold with sporadic chilly rain. Jackson experienced the indecisive temperature for the first time then. While making a whirlwind "Stormin' the Sound" tour similar to those of former players Charmin Smith, Jaime Redd, Kate Starbird, and Michelle Marciniak have made, Jackson experienced firsts like seeing cheerleaders at high school girls games ("I thought they were a myth," she said) and a few Sonics matchups at KeyArena. Snuggled beneath a three-quarter-length black leather coat and fleece Sonics blanket, Jackson had to answer earnestly when asked by a Fox Sports Net reporter what she thought of the NBA atmosphere.

"Our fans are so much more enthusiastic," she said. "We had 18,000 people here for the finals and this place was rocking. We have the best fans in the world."

When the WNBA originated in 1997, it took a lot of heat for playing in the summer. The season is synonymous with the crack of a bat, cannonballs in cool waters, or the tart smell of engines screaming around asphalt tracks. Basketball was invented for the wintertime, when indoor activities in snowy climates were a necessity.

But when the NBA owners moved ahead with the women's league, it was to fill their cavernous facilities during their players' off-season while conveniently placing a new product in the less cluttered sports time period. It made sense, but selling the idea became the immediate focus.

The NBA's marketing strategy seemed to play along with the need to introduce fans to the idea of pro ball in the summer; their WNBA "We Got Next" ad was plastered everywhere. But every promotion up until 2005's "This is Our Game" campaign has been oversexed and hardly athletic.

The WNBA could not be hotter in any other season than the summer. There's a different culture in the league that's the essence of that period in the calendar year. It's when the women come out.

While the players return with toned bodies and a unified "in-it-to-win-it" tint in their eyes, their audience comes out too, sun-kissed highlights in their hair, wearing colorful tank tops and shorts or frilly skirts baring tattooed legs. The WNBA reported 65 percent of its in-arena audience is female. And it doesn't take long for a fan to figure out that the majority of that audience are lesbians.

But one campaign you'll most likely never see? "WNBA: It's a lesbian summer."

"There's nothing to be ashamed of or to hide about it," Bryant said. "But the league has to be careful in walking that line. Does the league value, embrace our gay and lesbian fans? Absolutely. Is it going to take a political position on gay marriage? No. What we're trying to do to be successful is try to be as inclusive as possible. We can't afford to divide our audience, it's that simple. It's not homophobia, we talk very openly about our lesbian fan base at our meetings, but we can't do it at the price of alienating another part of our fan base. And it's not our issue. It's a societal issue. We're sports, we're entertainment."

Tears were shed at the closing of Phoenix's restaurant A League of Their Own in 2004. The Storm lost 84-76 to the Mercury in a close game, and afterward fans drove to the lesbian-owned joint for dining and drinking and socializing on the patio in 87-degree night air or inside the cool art deco, piano-lounge interior. Red wine and beer flowed as tables full of lesbian, gay, and straight Mercury fans wearing the team's chartreuse gear rehashed the game with pockets of Storm fans clad in green and gold, who also identify with the same diverse background. Undoubtedly the conversation turned to who's who in the WNBA—as in who's family, a sister, a lesbian. The mere speculation makes some players' skin tingle with fright and frustration.

"We don't go to their job and guess what they do in the bedroom, [so] why is it a topic with us?" said Jackson about automatically being assumed a lesbian because she plays basketball. She declares herself single.

Silence steaming from societal ignorance and fear only ignites the speculation. Rosters become equal play cards for heterosexuals and homosexuals, and some pass time or pique curiosities by guessing what the players won't willingly tell publicly. New York Liberty teammates Vickie Johnson and Crystal Robinson had no problem circulating glossy flyers for an All-Star game after-party in July 2004 at Caché, a club in the heart of Times Square. The function was co-presented by Girl Club Productions, noted lesbian party planners, and the colorful handout even stated that "the first 75 women receive free drink coolers." Once the $25 general admission fee was paid, a short trip down a dark staircase opened partygoers to a packed dance floor of multiracial women grooving to the beat with other women.

Popping her booty in heels and an elegant cocktail dress like she was posting up an opponent in the paint was first-time All-Star Adrian Williams, who played for the Phoenix Mercury. By the bar was Teresa Weatherspoon in shades and a crisp linen suit. And surveying the dance floor were Johnson and Robinson, making sure everyone had a good time. Yet, despite the obvious public outing from the fliers to the locale at the gay-friendly establishment, the players don't talk openly about their orientation. For most players, the issue should be strictly basketball.

"Being in the WNBA, that's the hard part for a lot of women is that you are judged by people," said Betty Lennox, who has heard more negativity from men than women. "It's a bad critic out there because we want to be successful and they think . . . it's just sexist. They want us to play like women. How is a woman supposed to play? That's what I want to know. Just because men play and maybe we can do the things men can do, that doesn't necessarily mean that we're trying to be like men. We're just out there getting our ball on just like they're getting their ball on. If the men don't know how to play, are we going to say that they're gay?"

Actually, that's exactly what does happen. In NBA locker rooms, the term "faggot" or "fag" is freely used in teasing each other and if someone isn't playing right or not acting like a so-called "man," the term "girlish" is tossed about. Sonics players insist that the way the culture is, a male athlete couldn't possibly come out of the closet like Swoopes and survive.

In fact, of the three major male professional sports—baseball, basketball, and football—only MLB and NFL players have come out, but well after their respective careers ended. The most notable figures were infielder Billy Bean, who came out in 1999 after playing in MLB from 1987–95, and former UW running back Dave Kobay, who played for five NFL teams, retiring in 1973, and becoming the first out male athlete in 1975. But despite an estimated one in ten persons in the U.S. being homosexual, none have come out in the NBA.

"It's best they keep that to themselves; I don't want to know about it," Lewis said. Boston Celtic forward Paul Pierce claimed their locker room is too small, just 15 players, and they all need to be on the same page. That means hanging out with each other at five-star restaurants after games and flirting with women.

But the men contradict themselves. First, there are an equal number of WNBA players on a team as NBA players. Second, if they're truly confident in their sexuality, why should it still matter?

"I know I love women and if there was somebody gay in the locker room, it wouldn't bother me at all," said Sonics All-Star guard Ray Allen. "I wouldn't treat them any different; he's still a teammate. But I think eventually guys like that [gay] work themselves out of the league because they gradually become alienated from their teammates because they're not like the rest. Men, we go out, even when we have relationships back home, and have fun. That's what you do being a team, you have fun together. Whatever your sexual preferences are, you still have to be able to be a part of the team and if you don't because of your sexual preferences, it pushes you away a little bit."

What attracts lesbian fans to the WNBA is exactly what incenses lesbians about the WNBA. Since women's basketball's inception in 1892 with gymnastics instructor Senda Berenson Abbott adapting

James Naismith's rules for her Smith College women, the sport has been encircled by the women's movement. Equal rights, opportunity, and accepted beauty of all types of women have been enshrouded in the bouncing basketball. As the longest-lasting professional women's team league, the WNBA provides a visual representation of what women can accomplish. Myths that women are catty, feeble, and can't work together to achieve a common goal are dispelled as soon as Jackson and Lennox step on the court with their Storm teammates. They huddle around each other, swaying back and forth to the hip-hop chant "We ready!" as they pump themselves up in a private moment before tip-off. Then, the athletes harmonize their individual styles to execute a game plan designed by Anne Donovan.

Their interpretation of sportsmanship isn't unknown to any woman who has pledged a sorority or joined a support group. But the public display before a raucous crowd of 17,072, showing their acceptance through cheers and handmade signs, leaves an indelible impression for the little girls and boys who also are jumping around euphoric. From that moment on, anyone who snips to that young mind that women or girls can't put aside personal agendas to work as a cohesive unit is immediately brushed off. That mind has seen it, felt it, through the WNBA players.

"It's so awesome to me to get a fan letter in the mail [from] kids that see this is a possibility for themselves or their sisters, just this newfound respect that women can be athletes, too," Donovan said. "They can be strong and passionate about the same thing that men can. Those kids really get it. They're getting that this is something significant and that these women are powerful."

The women are role models for adoring little fans. Unlike popular television shows such as UPN's "America's Next Top Model," the WB's "The Starlet," or any other reality television show, the league demonstrates through each nationally televised game that competition between women does not always have to come down to beauty and that aggression is just as feminine as grace. Brawn is just as sexy as brains.

The WNBA pushes its teams to make games a family environment, offering activities for kids during timeouts, autograph signings after games, and plenty of giveaways targeted at youths. (LATRENA SMITH PHOTOGRAPHY)

Today, youths are filled with modern images of what women can be. "Athlete" is added to the traditional list of "teacher," "nurse," or "parent." It's a thought many older fans in the audience could not even fathom. The self-esteem boost for girls has helped produce some of sports' proudest statistics—female athletes are less likely to experience teenage pregnancy and 80 percent of women executives were once "tomboys." Plus, sports makes women more self-reliant.

Still, what's completely lopped off while the league posts heterosexual players' newlywed photos and baby pictures on its Web site is how much impact lesbian players could make. You know the lesbian players are there. Stay long enough at games, and players will leave with their partners. At Seattle's Lesbian and Gay Film Festival, the chatter at one of the movie's after-parties was whether some of the Storm players would be at the Pioneer Square club the Catwalk because they've been known to go there in the past. This time, however, the players took on megastatus in the community, having won the WNBA championship. One woman thought she might faint if a player walked through the club doors.

In addition to Swoopes, only former New York Liberty forward Sue Wicks and current Minnesota Lynx center Michele Van Gorp have publicly stated they are lesbians while still playing in the WNBA, Van Gorp doing so in local magazines that cater to the gay-lesbian-bisexual-transgender (GLBT) community. The stories, primarily personality profiles treating lesbianism as an equal part of the players' physical makeup, created mini stirs in mainstream media in Wicks's case. Van Gorp's was hardly a blip across the wires. She's celebrating the fifth year of her civil union with her partner, Kyleen, and happily lives in Vermont during the off-season.

To Van Gorp, being a lesbian is not news. For years, one of the entries underneath her bio in the Lynx's media guide is she "lives with her spouse in Vermont," and the two have frequented many Lynx functions together. Even New York Liberty general manager Carol Blazejowski states in her media guide write-up that she "resides in Nutley, New Jersey, with her family: Joyce, Lainey, and Luke."

The four out lesbians say their reasoning is to acknowledge the family that has supported them, but none wants to be labeled a lesbian activist. In fact, WNBA player contracts specifically stipulate that players cannot say or do anything that could be considered "detrimental" to the league, and what is detrimental is conveniently defined by the league. If a player (like Swoopes) were to come out and audience attendance at games declined soon thereafter, the league could technically dismiss her, regardless of whether or not her coming out had anything to do with the decline.

In a sense, WNBA players are not allowed to be complete people. Bird loves to joke about her first glass of wine at a public restaurant after having been anointed the favorite "girl-next-door" by everyone, including the media. "I was stared at," she said with a slight chuckle. "Yes, I'm 21 and I like to have a glass of wine with my dinner sometimes, there's nothing abnormal about that."

"Sometimes as a celebrity or a professional athlete, I don't think you're allowed to be human," said Swoopes, whose Nike contract, an 11-year relationship, remains intact. "That can hurt you, but everybody is different. I think there's enough endorsements out there for everybody. And I think everybody in the WNBA represents lots of different things besides sports, but I don't think a lot of players in the league have been given that opportunity. It's unfortunate because you have to change who you are to fight for the sponsorships, to fight for the endorsements, but that's life. That's the way it is."

By contrast, male athletes can flat-out show their ass, saying and doing anything, and be sympathized with or crawl their way back from societal disgust with a pithy press release or press conference. In the NBA, for example, Jason Kidd abused his wife, Vin Baker abused alcohol, and Kobe Bryant had what he described as "consensual sex" with a 19-year-old hotel employee, resulting in a rape trial that was nullified after his accuser dropped the charges.

Because of incidents like these, the NBA had become a dribbling blemish for the refined commissioner David Stern. Cable ratings declined 35 percent since Michael Jordan retired. Ten players named to the All-Star team skipped college to join the league. An attempted racial brawl between Marcus Camby (New York) and Danny Ferry (San Antonio) occurred on the Martin Luther King Jr. holiday. Three starters on the Phoenix Suns roster were arrested in separate incidents. Olden Polynice (Utah) was arrested for impersonating a police officer. Sonics forward Ruben Patterson was suspended after pleading guilty to a misdemeanor assault charge. And wiry guard Allen Iverson, who would win the All-Star and regular-season MVP honors, eclipsed his own rap sheet with violent, degrading lyrics on the track "40 Bars"; he opted not to release his CD only after the urging of Stern. The music still circulates on the Internet, however, featuring verses such as "Come to me wit faggot tendencies/You'll be sleeping where the maggots be."

Players' assumed egotistical attitudes—laced in enough diamonds to keep De Beers in business—just put Stern on the defensive. He didn't want to apologize for a small segment overshadowing the whole, instead telling Chris Matthews on the show *Hardball*, "Not only are we a slice of life, we may be the few people with the ability to change it [life]."

Major League Baseball even returned to record fan attendance under the veil of steroid abuse, while in the NFL, Ray Lewis played after a suspected murder rap and Deion Sanders ditched cocaine charges and became a minister. Even NASCAR had its dark moment when a driver cursed in the winner's circle, and as long as he apologized the following day, which he did, he was forgiven. They're human after all.

Until they're female.

The dirt swept underneath the WNBA's rug forms more speed bumps than a residential street in front of an elementary school. Former Los Angeles Sparks forward Latasha Beyers was accused of raping another player in the league with a sex toy along with four male junior college basketball players and snapping photos on her cellular phone. Coincidentally, the incident happened within the time frame of Kobe Bryant's charge. But unlike Bryant, who was not only retained but supported by the organization throughout his ordeal, Beyers was promptly kicked out of the WNBA. She has since claimed that she's been blackballed from the league because she's a lesbian.

"You can't make that comparison. It's plain and simply economics," former Storm original Edna Campbell said of Beyers. "That organization [Los Angeles] is going to stand behind Kobe because he brings in multi-millions of dollars. It's easy to cut off someone that may have a tainted image when they're almost invaluable, so to speak."

Whether just or not, it's not equal treatment. Former Mercury guard Brandi Reed was a notorious malcontent who was impossible to control. Despite talent, she was forced out of the league. Meanwhile, in the NBA, the entire Portland Trail Blazers team has seemingly been given a million second chances for every disobedience from smoking weed to arguing with coach Maurice Cheeks, who was fired. Sparks forward Rhonda Mapp was kicked out of the league for being caught once with marijuana—the harshest substance abuse policy of all the professional leagues.

It seems the WNBA cherry-picks what issues it's willing to help its players through. Campbell, a San Antonio guard, survived breast cancer in 2003 and spent the 2004 season as the league's national spokesperson. Washington Mystics forward Chamique Holdsclaw suffered through depression in silence until she finally had to leave her team in a cloud of darkness. The Mystics organization supported her by saying her abrupt absence was due to a "minor medical condition" in a press release.

In March 2005, Holdsclaw broke her silence about the mental illness, appearing in an exclusive interview on ESPN's SportsCenter. Playing in Spain, she told the station that her "life was on pause . . . I had to stop." And that she felt a pressure in her chest that immobilized her for days.

"To think about tomorrow or the next day gave me a headache," Holdsclaw said, while pointing at her head and letting an unseen-before sincerity exude from her face, framed by streams of black braids.

Mystics president Susan O'Malley said in the piece that her organization believes players deserve "a circle of privacy" regarding certain matters. But Holdsclaw said it was hard for her to see people attack her character, prompting her to disclose she was diagnosed with depression. Immediately, the overwhelming letters thanking her for sharing her struggle flowed in. Holdsclaw read one from a 54-year-old woman saying she, too, suffered from depression and telling the 1999 Rookie of the Year to "take all the time you need" in rejoining the WNBA. Two days after the television interview, Holdsclaw was traded to the Los Angeles Sparks for Olympian DeLisha Milton-Jones and a draft pick, getting her desired "fresh start."

Don't lesbians, who struggle with the same societal battles, deserve a role model who's strong enough to declare her sexuality? Watching Van Gorp, who retired in 2005, sprint from the Lynx bench to ruffle an opponent inside the paint with turnaround jump shots and strong defense, knowing she's a Duke grad, a Julia Roberts fan, and a lesbian in a committed relationship is cool. Just another example of a successful lesbian, like talk-show host Ellen DeGeneres, comedian Rosie O'Donnell, or musician Meshell Ndegeocello.

But the players and the league dance a smooth tango around the issue. Swoopes, though she has every right, even softens her outing by saying she wasn't "born gay." The league says it has no stipulation on its athletes, and they in turn use concerns of losing endorsement deals and bringing unwanted attention onto their team as reasons to keep quiet about their sexual orientation. Lesbians and league officials, who spoke under the condition of remaining anonymous, estimated that approximately 40 percent of the 154 WNBA players could be identified as lesbians.

The league will see what the response is to Swoopes in the summer of 2006. It's already planning a bang-up celebration for its monumental 10th anniversary, and what better way to party than with a big coming out? On its Web site during the off-season, the WNBA posted an action photo of Swoopes and a list of posts from its forum. Leslye of Cleveland, Ohio, wrote: "I applaud Sheryl Swoopes's courage, honesty, and pride! Coming out is certainly not an easy or comfortable thing to do; the alternative, however, is unbearable in the long run. When in the closet, those we love are disrespected (even one's self); the false sense of safety & protection is revealed when one is 'outed' or when one recognizes the closet as a psychological prison. I predict that you will have many many more fans BECAUSE you exhibited your ethics, courage, even heroism by coming out; I know because I have just become one of them! Congratulations on your newly accepted Freedom. Now, tell your sistah-ball-players to follow suit . . ."

Others following in Swoopes's wake are unlikely.

"For some it's uncomfortable because it's [being a professional athlete] a high-profile lifestyle, so when you step out and make that choice to be public with it [being a lesbian], you're really public with it," Donovan said. "It's not Mary and Jane in the stands. These are people that, when they're identified as a lesbian or whatever their stance might be, they're going to be forever tagged with that. In the media, it's going to resurface no matter what team they go to. Look at Sue Wicks [Wicks's coming out appeared in *Time Out New York* in 2002 as the final answer in a long interview about league issues that wasn't picked up nationally until after baseball star Mike Piazza held a press conference stating he was not gay; later, Wicks refused to talk about it, not wanting to be a "lesbian" role model]—I mean my God, it was one piece of one line in an article and she'll forever be tagged. So, I think that it's some that are reluctant to get that tag. It's such a small part of who they might be."

On the one hand, it's hip for the WNBA to market to the lesbian and gay community. The Houston Comets place ads in GLBT publications. The Storm is a member of the GLBT business bureau, makes appearances at the Timberline, a gay bar downtown that closed in September 2005, and has even auctioned off Jackson at a Girl for Girl party, sending her on a date with an out lesbian.

Yet, prior to the 2001 season, when the Davis Dykes wanted their group name on the jumbotron scroll at Sacramento Monarchs games, they were told it would be inappropriate for the "family-friendly" environment. Never mind that many of the lesbians also have families. And the Liberty lesbian fans butted heads with the organization on numerous occasions, demanding to be recognized by standing and kissing during timeouts in protest to not being allowed to wave signs or carry what was deemed "gay paraphernalia." Since the firestorm both of those incidents created, the league has lessened its perceived restrictions on marketing; it's more comfortable for teams to make the obvious link with the homosexual community, although it is not publicized. Plus lesbians, joining white males, have been proven by marketers to have the ever-coveted disposable cash.

Jackson is paraded about, and press releases detailing where she'll be next litter sports department e-mail inboxes like confetti, but the appearances in the homosexual community are omitted. And if a reporter happens to bump into her there, they are subtly asked not to write about it. After all, it's a nonissue. The WNBA can quickly point to Van Gorp to prove that case. There were seven stories following her original "I'm a lesbian" article in *Lavender*. So, no one cares, right? Well, Swoopes generated 284 articles and countless television appearances before leaving to play in Italy, not to mention a running feature on Logo, a new television channel catering to homosexual viewers.

Still, a month prior to Van Gorp's revealing, the *Seattle Times* broke the story about Jackson posing nude in an Australian publication called *Black + White*, which featured 35 Aussie Olympic hopefuls. It's an honored tradition in the country to be included. But Jackson's seven artistic photos, including a topless cover shot, sparked American national debate, mention in a syndicated cartoon, and more publicity than when she was named the league's 2003 Most Valuable Player.

With such coverage, it seems that the WNBA would be less averse to a player being lesbian than nude. While a big stink may erupt over such "bad behavior" as posing nude for a magazine, the WNBA remains rather quiet in regard to its lesbian players and audience members. One *could* attribute this silence to an acceptance of homosexuality in the sport; if stereotypes make it seem like everyone associated with the sport is a lesbian, then incorporating lesbian-themed advertising and promotional campaigns would seem unnecessary. The WNBA could reasonably raise such a defense, that is, if it weren't for all the attention granted to the personal lives of its straight players, who seem to be praised for their heterosexuality.

Rebecca Lobo's wedding pictures, baby stories, and overt "male approved" sexuality gushes from the WNBA's Web site year-round. Employees say some of the images, especially during the off-season, are simply fluffy fillers to give fans something new to keep their interest in the league. Still, the league would not do the same if Van Gorp or Swoopes wanted to make their civil union public fodder. In an era when President Bush was re-elected based on moral values and a wave of public support to change the Constitution to include specific wording that marriage is between one man and one woman, the WNBA's stance is understandable. During the 2004 election, 12 states moved to ban gay marriages and Texans voted to strengthen the state's position against homosexual rights in 2005 the same month Swoopes came out.

The WNBA needs a $12 million stipend from the NBA to function. Ackerman expects the WNBA to generate a small profit in 2007, and satisfying the wants of conservative sponsors is still the primary goal. Names like Proctor & Gamble, Toyota, McDonald's, and Coca-Cola aren't synonymous with gay rights. And while some places, such as Seattle, San Francisco, Massachusetts, and Vermont, may have made headway in equal rights for homosexuals, the WNBA does not have to look far into its past to know how the public stance could implode.

Various reasons are given for why charter teams in Salt Lake City and Cleveland and franchises in Miami and Orlando did not last. Analysts have looked at the mind-set of the demographic that in the summertime would rather cruise the beach or hit the theme parks in Florida. And ownership interest in Cleveland. And the already poor reception women's basketball receives in the college ranks in Utah— the University of Utah and Brigham Young only getting an average of 2,500 to attend their games despite having quality teams.

Coincidentally, these failed (Cleveland Rockers and Miami Sol) and relocated (Utah Starzz to San Antonio and Orlando Miracle to Connecticut) franchises were also located in places deemed "red states" during the 2004 election. Utah, a predominately Mormon community, couldn't get behind the idea of supporting women's sports, with its stigma of being a lesbian haven, according to some former players. "You couldn't even say the 'L' word," said Kate Starbird, who played for the Starzz prior to joining the Storm in 2002. The Sol and Miracle, nestled in Florida's deep south, also had problems finding support, even though Miami is one of the hottest locations for gay vacationing. And Ohio recently banned rights for homosexuals to marry, tying into its unwillingness to offer equal rights to gays and lesbians.

Currently the WNBA is economically successful in Washington, the 16th most liberal state in the country; New York City, another gay metropolis that can draw from a dense population on the East Coast; Detroit, an intense sports town in a widely Democratic state; and Washington, D.C., which draws a large black population to games and has led the league in attendance since its team's inception in 1998. But baseball's Washington Nationals are starting to tug at the Mystics' sports-going public.

The areas have several common ties such as women in power positions. The state of Washington has a female governor and two women senators. King County (which includes Seattle) even has a woman sheriff. Across the country, hordes of political leaders are female, walking the steps of Capitol Hill while pregnant, showing the change of times. The areas are also highly educated and are located in bigger cities that contain several individual mind-sets. Maybe the majority doesn't like women's pro ball, but there's still enough to support a team.

In cities where the WNBA isn't working, the reasons range from losing teams, such as Houston and San Antonio, to closed-mindedness, such as Minnesota and Charlotte.

"A lot of times it's just educating people," Campbell said. "And that's across the board. Educating people on what women are capable of, what blacks are capable of—you know, not having biases and restricting people in their little box of what you think should be and shouldn't be. In America, we bred people into maintaining stereotypes. It's passed down and it has to stop."

The WNBA could be viewed as taking a stance if it spoke in support of some of its players' and fans' plights. Its "family-friendly" image would be attacked, regardless of the fact that lesbians come from and form families too. Players, many of whom dread playing overseas without the love and support of family, seem willing to sacrifice part of their identity in a unified effort to drag the league to stable financial ground. They probably realize that if the WNBA doesn't work with the billion-dollar backing of the well-established NBA, no professional women's league ever will.

So, the WNBA and its fans form a massive pink triangle that no one dares to mention. And it's depressing. Women have long infiltrated male-dominated worlds and climbed their way to the top of numerous corporate ladders. WNBA games give businesswomen a comfortable environment to gather, have social meetings, or relax—the same luxury men have relished since the invention of sport.

The WNBA attracted 1.8 million fans last season, down from its height of 2 million with 16 teams in 2000. Do sponsors really think all 2 million, some of whom are lesbians or had to know they were seated next to one, would really dump the league if 40 percent (as some have suggested) of its players willingly stepped from beneath the veil of secrecy?

CHAPTER SEVEN

Lauren Jackson

Tears dripped on the green carpeted floor. On the computer screen were images of colorful flowers, family seated in pews, and a beautifully adorned casket. As Storm teammates streamed into the training facility for practice before one of the biggest games of their WNBA careers, power forward Lauren Jackson sat motionless on a cushioned metal chair in a makeshift cubicle watching her grandmother's funeral via the Internet.

Her father had set up the technology, filming the October 2004 service in Albury, Australia. The video was choppy at times, but it was the only thing keeping Jackson sane. Nan Irene's home was where young Jackson would go anytime her parents traveled for their respective basketball teams. At the time, Jackson bickered too much with brother Ross, who was 14 months younger, and they had to be separated. He went to Sydney to stay with their father's parents, and Lauren stayed with her maternal grandmother.

Nan Irene, a seamstress, had made all of Jackson's clothing and practically raised her as Jackson's mother Maree rose to basketball acclaim, playing for the country's national team from 1974–82. Now Ross, a handsome 6-foot-8 young man, was standing reciting his sister's last public words to their grandmother, a sweet poem written in the midst of the Storm winning their first playoff series against the Minnesota Lynx. Then the somber lyrics of British musician Robbie Williams's emotional tracks "Angel" and "Nan's Song" flowed through the speakers.

Jackson felt guilty for not being there personally, especially for her mother. Maree, who stands 6-foot-1, had quit her job managing a mill in 2001 to be on call for her only daughter. With a simple emergency phone call, Jackson could enlist her dad to help sweet-talk Maree into an 18-hour flight to be with her. Her arrival always spiked Lauren's spirits. She'd announce countdowns to her mother's arrival to anyone who'd listen. Once Maree arrived, the two would clasp hands as they walked or sat, talking for hours about Lauren's life, basketball, or politics.

Maree didn't ask the same of Lauren. She, along with the rest of the family, understood when Jackson wanted to return to Seattle after the Olympics, not fully grasping the gravity of her grandmother's health. The spirited elderly woman had loved to watch Jackson play basketball, last seeing her win a silver medal at the Sydney Olympic Games in 2000, shedding tears in the stands. And no one wanted Lauren to miss this opportunity—to win a WNBA championship or, possibly, a Most Valuable Player award. All of which felt like meaningless, selfish goals with every tear shed while watching the funeral.

"I was numb," Jackson said. "I don't think I've ever felt like that in my life. I have never gone through anything as hard as that in my life. It was difficult not having my mother with me. It was really, really hard. But I felt like I wasn't there for my mum."

After viewing the ceremony, Jackson composed herself and joined her teammates on the court. They were distant, none knowing exactly how to approach her. Jackson, then 23, was the silly one, always ready to party or laugh. Try to get mushy with a sentimental good-bye speech, and she'd be the one in the back giggling because she was unsure how to respond. Tears, she says, are saved for serious times. And this was one.

Because of newspaper articles, television segments, radio interviews from stations back home, and Jackson's openness, everyone knew about her situation. Storm fans wrote thoughtful messages on Internet sites, and bouquets of fragrant flowers were shipped to the team's training facility, sprouting an array of blooms from the locker room to the facility entranceway, for the suffering All-Star. They had watched her grow on the KeyArena court, from a pimple-faced teen who banked on her talent too much, to a towering young blond woman who sought perfection. Their hearts ached for one of the hardest-working players they'd seen.

"It was emotionally draining watching her," Storm coach Anne Donovan said. "Just at 23, trying to handle all of these different pieces in and of themselves is huge. To throw them all together in a short period of time, it was really a challenge for her."

Jackson entered the league in 2001. The Storm's door prize for a brutal tumble through its inaugural season was the No. 1 draft pick, and the early buzz was that the Australian post was considering playing in the WNBA. But Dunn, the shark, would never throw a game to secure a pick, would she?

"I'm not going to say anything," said Dunn, whose team's 6-26 record was worst among the four expansion teams. Miami was 13-19, Portland finished 10-22, and Indiana was 9-23. "But, you never want to win too many too quick, and you never want to lose too long. Don't think I haven't had conversations with [Portland coach] Linda Hargrove and [Indiana coach] Nell Fortner. The difference in them winning one more game, let's say they win 10 and we win nine, the difference between one or two games is the difference between Lauren Jackson and someone else."

Jackson was just 19 when the Storm finished its season, but she had played professionally for two years for the Canberra Capitals in the WNBL and had Olympic experience as the leading scorer of the

Storm forward Lauren Jackson lays in the basketball against Connecticut. The Aussie is one of 29 international players in the WNBA. (LATRENA SMITH PHOTOGRAPHY)

Opals, her country's national team, making her eligible to enter the WNBA draft. Adding to her cachet was the Sydney Olympic Games incident in the gold medal match with Team USA, where Jackson overshadowed her own 20-point, 13-rebound night by pulling out the nine-inch ponytail hair-weave of center Lisa Leslie.

Leslie, the proud daughter of a truck driver, is nine years Jackson's senior, and you simply didn't mess with the American star. Leslie's lean stature, captured globally in numerous modeling shoots, and her vicious attitude on the court had made her an idol to Jackson as an emerging teen player. Jackson studied every twist and stretch Leslie made in the paint, adding the tricks of the WNBA first-teamer to the foundation of talent Jackson's parents had already instilled.

In the Olympic Games, though, Jackson just wanted to beat Leslie. Jackson's mellow blue eyes flicked with an aura of blazing fire at the opening tip. And her mouth spewed flames as she tried to will her team to the country's first gold medal. Her skill erupted on the court, but by the second half, the matchup wasn't competitive, with the Aussies down nearly 20 points. Still, there was the comedic moment when Jackson tangled her body with Leslie's as they positioned themselves for a rebound. Jackson's thick fingers dug deep in Leslie's ponytail, and when both jumped, Jackson landed with what she called a "dead rat in my hand."

Changing back into teenage mode, she immediately flung it to the court and yelped. Leslie immediately tossed the piece into the photo gallery. Later Jackson discovered it was a hair extension, Leslie's beauty secret, that she often adorned with bows in her team's colors.

"I swear I had no idea," Jackson said. "We were laughing in the huddle about it."

After a time-out as the crowd erupted, Team USA members Sheryl Swoopes, Yolanda Griffith, and Dawn Staley joined a clipped Leslie in calling Jackson a "punk" and telling the first-time Olympian to "watch out!"

"I was thinking, 'If I come to the WNBA, I won't have any friends for sure,'" Jackson said with innocence. "They all hated me!"

Her mother knew different. Maree still holds the career scoring (26.4) and rebounding (14.7) records in the Southeastern Conference from her 70-game stint playing at Louisiana State University from 1977–78. She was the first from her country to earn a full college scholarship. The bayou had a different mentality from her native Australian countryside. There was a frigid, segregated, oppressive nature. But Maree loved the spicy Cajun cooking, and the people always treated her fairly.

Maree had played with another Australian, which made her collegiate years even more bearable, especially when it snowed in the normally humid region, an abnormal sight for her. She was part of the decade when Nancy Lieberman became "Lady Magic" with her red hair at Old Dominion. Carol Blazejowski was simply "Blaze" for lighting it up in numerous 40-point games at Montclair State. And Ann Meyers stirred interest on the West Coast, shining at UCLA.

Traveling to America later as a newlywed to husband Gary, whom she had met when both played for the Australian national team, made Maree confident in telling Lauren the Americans she met would take care of her.

Not being able to defeat Leslie was one of the driving reasons Jackson decided to leave her comfy Australian home, despite a youthful fear of leaving her native country for five months. The media deemed the WNBA "Leslie's League." Center Rebecca Lobo, the early favorite to challenge Leslie's reign, suffered back-to-back knee injuries in 1999 and 2000 that kept her from corralling her college popularity to boost the league's popularity with her play. After a miserable 1996 Olympics and reaching the WNBA Finals with New York in 1997, she was never the player the media predicted. With Lobo struggling and Swoopes out with a knee injury, Leslie capitalized on the sole spotlight and her team's budding success. She made guest appearances on television shows, was used by the league as a spokesperson, and broadcasters couldn't make a comment about any player without mentioning Leslie in the same sentence. She was the competition, it seemed to Jackson.

Being drafted by the WNBA was the only way Jackson could develop her game to ultimately topple the prized center and become internationally known as the best player in the game.

"It's great basketball; it's the best basketball in the world," Gary Jackson said of the WNBA. "If you want to succeed and want to really raise your profile, the WNBA is the place to play. It's disappointing from a parental point of view because you could see her going to Russia, playing two or three months and making a lot, lot more money than what she can earn in the WNBA. But as far as competition, it's the best."

Dominance was a quiet wish of Jackson's. Australians don't boast, keeping an endearing humble nature about them, yet Jackson couldn't hide her ultracompetitive nature. Plus, her mother missed an opportunity to play in the Olympic Games after her team did not qualify in 1980. Instead, she became pregnant with Lauren in 1981. She gave birth in May and 14 months later was back in the delivery room to give birth to son Ross. Maree Jackson met a goal of making it back to the court to play 10 weeks later, rising at 5 AM for practices, returning home for a quick breakfast, jetting to work, and ending the day with another practice. But she couldn't take the time to make the Olympic team roster in 1984 with two small children. Her life was quickly moving in another direction just as her husband's had years before, skipping his chance to play in the 1980 Games to marry and start a family. The couple didn't regret their decision, but when they were told later that the boycott of the 1984 Games due to the Russian invasion of Afghanistan would open a spot for the Aussies, depression crept in about what could have been.

"It was a very tearful moment in the Jackson household," Gary said. "Maree realized what she could have done and it just wasn't meant to be."

The children were always around during the winter days of Maree's playing career, except when she traveled. Gary had gone into coaching and running a business to support the family. Jackson's grandmother stitched a toddler-sized jersey out of Maree's old green and gold national team warm-up, and Lauren would have to be tricked into taking it off.

Going to work with her mom was Jackson's favorite. She'd wave a tiny Australian flag on the bench during games and ask for autographs from her mother's teammates afterward. Sick with the beginnings of chicken pox once, she slept under the bleachers at practice. Healthy and full of energy most days, and wanting to join the older players, she'd drive coaches batty.

"Lauren, get off the court! Get off the court!" she remembers hearing as a lanky youngster. "Go make five baskets on the other end!"

She'd quickly return with a bright smile, having achieved the task.

"Well, go make 150!" the busy coaches would demand.

"Even as a kid, I just couldn't get off the court," she said.

Typical troubling teen years ensued during which Jackson went through a Goth stage, dressing like music idol Marilyn Manson to freak out people at the local pub. Drinking and being what Jackson flatly calls "a little shit" forced her early exit from the family home. Later, with a mature mind-set, basketball became the gift of joy she wanted to give back to her parents. A gold medal for the sacrifices they had made, even though neither parent had pushed her to play. Both describe themselves as quiet observers who were more analytical because of their rich knowledge of the game. Dad wondered when she'd develop a mid-range jump shot. Mom sighed at her taking an hour to finally meet them for postgame dinners.

"They weren't a huge influence on me, but they were the ones at the back of the stairs watching," said Jackson, whose 12-and-under team was coached by her mother. "Early on, they never talked about basketball."

As she grew up, there were roundtable discussions about the game between the whole family. Gary, Maree, and Lauren all say Ross would have been the best—an Andrew Bogut before Bogut, who became the first male Australian selected No. 1 overall (by

Milwaukee) in the NBA draft in 2005, making $4.3 million his first season. But Ross was more interested in trains and entered that field of work. Lauren had to make a living, too. Although she fills leather-bound books with morbid poetry, paints colorful landscapes, and is an excellent chef—gutting freshly caught octopus while her mother squeals on the family boat, then turning the catch into a tasty dish—basketball is what she feels she was destined to do.

And to make a living at it, she'd have to go to America. Though she carried the moniker of "professional athlete" in Australia, the WNBL was hardly "professional." Teammates held full-time jobs, forcing practice to be held at 5 PM, and their schedules only allowed for weekend games. Gyms were tin sheds or sawed-off high school gymnasiums with a seating capacity for a few hundred. Competition was scarce. Jackson had to leave.

Aside from the Olympics, Seattle fans first saw her on the television screen hugging her mother and walking to the podium to greet president Val Ackerman as the league's third international player selected with the top pick. Sporting cropped auburn hair, wearing a black leather jacket and jeans, and holding her new green-and-gold jersey, Jackson still had puffy eyes from crying in a hotel bathroom the night before. Her mother had stayed up with her all night playing cards and comforting her daughter, who would be leaving her native country for the first time.

She roomed with Storm center Suzy Batkovic at the Institute in Canberra when they were teenagers. Jackson plastered INXS and Tina Turner posters on her side of the concrete walls and sneaked out of the dormitory with friends after practice to hustle their way into concerts, only to get tossed out by security while Tina Turner wailed away on stage. But the lush, cosmopolitan city was just 121 miles from her parent's home in Albury. Seattle, however, was a world Jackson couldn't even imagine on draft day. And if it was anything like New York, with its honking yellow cabs, musty air, and abrasive people, Jackson wasn't going to report to training camp. Her specificity about location and pay led to Jackson's agent taking five months to negotiate her three-year contract, worth $55,000 the first season without incentives.

"She was just a baby," said Dunn, who questioned whether Jackson would even enter the draft. The self-proclaimed country girl who'd watch kangaroos gallop in her front yard was just starting to prove herself on the basketball court. Jackson won two league titles with the Capitals, was a league leader in rebounds (14.3), and shot three-pointers like a shooting guard.

The battle between the global talents, Jackson and Leslie, was an instant marketing success for Seattle. Tapes of their exploits gave Dunn so many goose bumps she snubbed her nose at potential draft trade offers. The fact that Seattleites already despised Californians, that they believed the transplants were turning the city with its small-town feel into a plastic metropolis cloaked in traffic, made the Storm games against the Los Angeles Sparks even more fun. The Storm was in its second year. Still, the "Beat L.A.!" chants were as passionate as Mariners fans' disgust for the New York Yankees. Seahawks' distaste of the St. Louis Rams. Or the Sonics' rivalry with the Lakers.

During the inaugural 2000 season, the Storm had upset the veteran Sparks once, a 69-59 overtime victory for the first win at KeyArena. But during Jackson's 2001 rookie season, the team had trouble finishing. In the latter half of the season, they pieced together impressive scoring spurts against Los Angeles (7-0), Detroit (15-2), Phoenix (16-2), Houston (7-3), and Utah (18-2), only to lose every game, except for the 74-69 overtime win over Detroit.

Leslie would get the best of Jackson in two of three matchups with the Sparks that summer too. Their first rematch since the Olympics was headlined "The Mane Event" in the *Seattle Times*, making the game an interesting draw. Jackson expected retaliation and remained consistent that the hair incident was purely accidental. Something the Sparks didn't believe. "It wasn't an accident. How are you going to be all up in somebody's hair, trying to get a rebound? I thought it was very immature of her to do that, and, you know, things have a way of coming back around," Olympic and Sparks forward DeLisha

Milton Jones told the newspaper. Leslie scored 16 of her final 22 points in the first half of the 73-60 romp in June. Jackson finished with 19 and no hairballs. It was tough to decipher which was the dirty player as elbows flew and the pinkish skin of Jackson's arms had cat scratches.

The rookie would outscore her nemesis 26-22 in a 19-point August Storm loss, but the Aussie was still adjusting to the American style and her teammates, often standing around on defense with her wrists limp like puppy paws at her waist. Flashes of her potential shined in her stepping back for three-pointers off a high screen and driving right at Leslie to draw a foul on a layup.

"Lauren is crazy," said teammate Charmin Smith, who attended the Storm's draft-day party set up for fans at the practice facility to make sure Dunn picked the Australian. "She's got all this emotion and fire and Lisa's getting after her and Lauren is ready to go to blows. She doesn't even care. You've got to respect that."

Jackson solidified her fiery reputation four games into the season in a 70-57 loss to Miami by getting a record four technical calls against veteran forward Sheri Sam, finishing with 14 techs that summer. She marked the organization's first double-double in scoring (24 points) and rebounds (12) in a record four-overtime loss to Washington in July. By season's end, Jackson led all rookies in scoring (15.2), rebounding (6.7), three-point field goals made (40), steals (1.9), and blocks (2.2), but the team finished 10-22. She was attracting media attention, but the American scribes awarded Portland guard Jackie Stiles the Rookie of the Year by a vote of 32-20. Stiles, whose Fire team finished on a 10-game losing streak, captured the nation's heart by leading her Southwest Missouri State team to the Final Four in April. The Storm's finish was not exactly what many expected with an international star on the roster, but it would again pay off.

The WNBA had initiated a lottery system similar to the NBA's, where all of the teams that didn't advance to the postseason were given Ping-Pong balls to determine the order of the 2002 draft. The last-placed team received the most balls, marked with its logo, giving it a higher percentage chance to secure the No. 1 pick. The lottery team with the best record was given the fewest balls. A law firm conducted the drawing that determined the order of the draft. The Storm tied with the Indiana Fever and the Washington Mystics for the league-worst finishes in a year featuring eight non-playoff teams. Miraculously Seattle won the lottery again.

Across the country was the nation's most notable point guard, Sue Bird, in the throes of leading her University of Connecticut team through an undefeated season (39-0) and NCAA championship. Bird's collegiate record was 136-9. In 18 Storm appearances, she would eclipse the total number of losses she experienced in four years at UConn, despite missing 20 games her freshman season due to a torn anterior cruciate ligament in her left knee. Dunn played coy again about her pick, requesting the world to trade for the top draw, which to WNBA general managers boiled down to their entire roster. Great franchises are built through the draft, and every team needs a formidable post and point guard to solidify its foundation. Dunn knew she'd be able to secure both in back-to-back drafts.

Bird, whose draft-day studio appearance was part of a whirlwind postseason of collecting national awards—from the Wade trophy to Naismith Player of the Year—signed a three-year rookie contract worth $57,500 the first season. The pivotal change was immediate, even if Jackson didn't recognize Bird when they first met.

Back in Australia playing in her WNBL, Jackson didn't hear much about the American college game. She arrived about a week into the 2002 training camp with blurry eyes from the 18-hour flight. She thought the 5-foot-11 Adia Barnes, a free agent with long curly hair and a mixed heritage of black and white, was the notorious Bird, a 5-foot-9 native New Yorker with dimpled cheeks and fair skin accented by dark brown hair. Then the ponytailed sensation whisked the ball inside the paint at a pancake breakfast practice set up for fans at Lake Washington High School, located in the area's affluent Eastside across the 520 bridge.

"Oh. *That's* Bird," Jackson mumbled to herself, perking up at the idea of playing with someone who could get her the ball.

"There's nothing like this," Bird told reporters of the pressure on her and Jackson when she arrived. "I mean, we've known each other for two weeks and we're expected to do all of these great things. I've never been in that type of situation."

The two immediately had to bond, forming a playful rivalry. Bird emphasized to Jackson that the Australian was younger, even though the 21-year-olds were only separated by seven months. They always had to beat each other at practice shooting games, but the evenings often brought a calm mood when they hung out at Jackson's Queen Anne condominium with other teammates.

On the court, the young duo won seven of the Storm's final nine games to sneak into the postseason back door with a 17-15 record. "I don't know how we won, but we did," Bird told the *Seattle Times.* "We were just inconsistent offensively. Some nights we'd play well together, then other nights it was like, 'What the heck is going on?'"

The Sparks swept them 2-0 in a three-game playoff series, the Storm exposed as the inexperienced franchise it was. Although the franchise players joined teammates in laughing at Dunn's quirky antics—"Sometimes you'd stop and say, 'Wait, did she just say that?'" Bird recalled—the coach clashed with her stars at times during the season. Bird and Jackson would feel an on-court rhythm, only to have Dunn jolt the flow with a time-out or jerky substitution with a surrounding player. Bird, a devout student of the game, could even be caught during time-outs fiddling with her shoelaces, superstitious about their placement, appearing as if she weren't listening to Dunn's game plan. At other times the coach and player debated how a possession could have been handled.

Named All-Stars and first-team WNBA players, Jackson and Bird weren't going to develop under Dunn's system at the speed upper management wanted. Fans started campaigning for a change midway through the season when the Storm was 8-10. They could understand not winning with just one star in Jackson, but when their team had one of the league's top guards, too? Unacceptable.

Most disregarded that Bird was a rookie too. Maybe because she had a brash, winning attitude that stemmed from playing in a top college program. Three of the top five draft picks were Bird's former Husky teammates. But Bird was second in the league in assists (6.0) and first in free-throw percentage (91.1). She scored a franchise-record 33 points in an 83-74 win over the Portland Fire and helped Jackson improve her shooting accuracy from 36.7 percent in 2001 to 40.3 in 2002, averaging 17.2 points—fourth best in the 16-team league.

"It's very cut-throat," said Maree Jackson of the intense pressure in the WNBA. "It's like a game of chess where players are moved around and teams do all of this stuff to be the best that they can quickly, not looking toward the future. Everything is for right now."

Hemorrhaging an average of $1 million in losses each season, the organization wanted a championship and instant progress, not steady growth. Depending on who is telling the story, Dunn picked the conclusion of the 2002 season to take a sabbatical. Or she was told her contract wasn't going to be renewed. Or she was told she wasn't going to get the big money she was asking for after doing so much for the Storm.

In any case, the setup inside the training facility on Tuesday, September 3, 2002, was unusual. At most press conferences there's a table atop a makeshift stage with a few chairs, a couple of microphones, and some bottled water for the speakers. The announcement or reason for the gathering is provided before a logo backdrop, and time is allotted for a question-and-answer session.

The arrangement that day, however, was less sterile and more personal, like the job had been for Dunn the past three seasons. Instead of rows of chairs facing a stage, the media was gathered in a semicircle. There weren't any microphones or water to sip. Dunn, casually dressed, walked into the room tucked inside the training facility with a face already flushed. She had obviously been crying and, before her speech was done, she'd shed a few more tears. Lin Dunn was retiring. She was the only coach and general manager the Storm had known, but now, at age 55, she was strained emotionally and professionally. For three years she had whizzed around the state making appearances at Rotary club meetings and high school assemblies and on talk radio shows. She was drained.

Aside from her stress, fans were tired of her actions on the court. The intoxicating southern drawl couldn't soothe fans watching a team with All-Stars Sue Bird and Lauren Jackson that couldn't make more of an impact in the WNBA. Or explain why Dunn would yank players around in her rotations, using an average of 13 starting lineups as the team grew in three seasons. She stated her mother's health and her own as concerns, but really she just wanted some Dunn time. "Everybody says, 'Why quit now?' and I say, 'Why not?'" Dunn told the *Seattle Times* at the press conference. "I've been thinking about it for a long time, maybe even before the third season. There's not one definite moment. It's time for me to take some time for myself and see what my next step is going to be."

Dunn had compiled a 33-63 record with the Storm, the only organization she left with a losing record in 31 years of coaching. After picking up other teams' so-called scraps through the expansion draft, she had just two players—centers Simone Edwards and Kamila Vodichkova—from her 2000 roster.

Karen Bryant, who wasn't going to renew Dunn's contract, wasted no time picking up the phone with another short list of replacements for Dunn. This time the hot name was current Charlotte Sting coach Anne Donovan. Bryant called the WNBA, who handled the Sting organization in a brief absence of ownership, to ask if Donovan was available for interviewing. But Bryant allowed Billy McKinney, the team's general manager, to handle the interview. He added former NBA coach Mike Thibault to the serious list of candidates. They were longtime friends, and Thibault had family roots in the Pacific Northwest. Donovan, a three-time Olympic center who had starred at Old Dominion, was relatively unproven on the professional level. She had coached the Indiana Fever to a 9-23 record their inaugural season, standing in for Olympic coach Nell Fortner, and had turned a 1-10 start with the Sting in 2001 into a trip to the WNBA Finals. But she had only three and a half seasons of professional experience, if you counted the 14 games before the ABL folded. She began her career as an assistant coach for her alma mater, then landed a head coaching gig at East Carolina University, compiling a 33-51 record in three seasons (1995–98).

What McKinney was impressed with, as an afternoon talking at his Bellevue home morphed into dinner at the Palisades restaurant overlooking Seattle's Elliott Bay, was Donovan's basketball mind. She had in-depth knowledge of the team, and her experience as a 6-foot-8 center would do wonders for Jackson, McKinney immediately thought. On December 18, 2002, she was named the franchise's second coach.

"Mike is a close friend, but he would have been the safe pick," McKinney said. "I wanted to step out of the box. I felt the team needed to go in an original direction."

Back in Australia, Jackson received the news via e-mail. She was steadily leading the Capitals to their second consecutive championship, but playing year-round since age 16 and not really taking care of herself with late nights and such was beginning to wear on her young frame. Shin splints prevented her from practicing, so she only played on weekends. She still won the league's Most Valuable Player honors, averaging 27.6 points and 11.2 rebounds. She wouldn't report to her first training camp under Donovan until May 6, however, breaking for two months at her beach home with her parents.

Jackson was sort of intimidated at her first meeting with Donovan. But in typical fashion, Donovan quickly made the power forward feel at ease. Donovan had been teased as a youth for her height, like Jackson, choosing to scurry away from the public eye with her older sister rather than face ogling peers. Jackson had

Storm fans show support for All-Star forward Lauren Jackson and her Aussie teammate Suzy Batkovic. (LATRENA SMITH PHOTOGRAPHY)

whitewashed her face and used it as an artistic palette, or dyed her hair funny colors, creating a hardened exterior that hid the pain of unwillingly standing out. For both, basketball had been a refuge.

Immediately after Jackson passed her physical, she went through private drills with Donovan, a ritual they'd continue until Donovan told Jackson to go home some nights, believing rest was the best lesson of the day.

Jackson blossomed under Donovan's tutelage, with the coach constantly telling the player how good she could be and showing her moves that could better rival Leslie. Jackson was the league leader in scoring (21.2), becoming the youngest player in WNBA history to reach 1,000 points. On a roster with two other Aussies in guards Sandy Brondello from Queensland and Tully Bevilaqua from Western Australia, and with the Olympics on the horizon, Jackson was named MVP of the WNBA. She was the first international player to win the honor, but as she waved from the black Chevrolet Trailblazer given to the award winner, Jackson's smile wasn't tinged with its usual giddiness.

The presentation was at the WNBA Finals in Detroit, and Jackson's Storm was not part of postseason play, finishing with a franchise-record 18-16, but losing a tiebreaker to Minnesota for the fourth and final playoff spot in the Western Conference. The Lynx, with Olympian Katie Smith, defeated the Storm 3-1 in head-to-head play, edging Seattle out. Injuries had plagued the Storm throughout the season. Making matters worse was a *Seattle Times* article in which Lisa Leslie stated MVPs should be playing in the postseason, not sitting at home, as a last-ditch effort to win the award. On the court when Jackson won the award was Leslie, trying to win a third consecutive title.

Jackson was shocked she won. She's always felt like an outsider in the bubble-gum league that pushes "family values." Jackson speaks her mind, although she claims now of half the daggers shot at Leslie: "I wouldn't own them, I was young." Jackson curses so much, when Leslie was fitted for a microphone for a televised game, guys in the truck blushed at some of the exchanges between the players. "It was bad. A whole lotta 'fuck yous' and everything. They were going at it," a public relations representative said at the time. And Jackson is notorious for her drinking, brushed off as the "Aussie way." She's a regular customer at the only Australian pub on the West Coast, the Kangaroo & Kiwi in Seattle's Green Lake neighborhood.

The wood-accented place reminds Jackson of watering holes in Albury, minus the busy highway out front. She's hosted Storm after-parties there where Bevilaqua has hopped on a tabletop to twirl around to blaring INXS or Men at Work music pumping from a jukebox. Brad Howe, the owner, regularly stocks the place with Australian foods like Vegimite, Jackson's favorite Violet Crumble candy bars, and meat pies. Jackson has free rein of the bar, and Storm fans mingle with the Aussies, marking up the old bathroom stall with messages for the players.

"Lauren is something that's out of the mold of what the WNBA has liked to market because of whatever their slogans have been," Donovan said. "But I think that's what makes it so neat, that you can be diverse. Just like all professional careers, there's only certain amounts of diversity that are accepted. But I think Lauren has shown that you don't have to be in the mold. That you can step outside that mold, and people can get to know and love you for who you really are."

Jackson constantly tests American ideals or limits. In June 2004, when news broke that the MVP had posed nude in a special edition of the Australian publication *Black + White*, Bevilaqua chuckled at trying to get Jackson to understand its potential impact. Even Bird being raked over the coals for making a pouty face in an Allen Iverson jersey for *Dime* magazine didn't make Jackson grasp some pockets of conservative America.

Syndicated L.A. radio personality Tom Leykis used about 40 minutes of a Wednesday program dubbed "radio for guys" to talk about the topic, playing a musical score normally heard in the background of pornographic movies while reading the *Seattle Times* article first talking about the spread in America. Then calls from across the nation trickled in critiquing Jackson, either saying she was cheaply exploiting herself to sell tickets or not acting like a role model.

"It's nothing new in Australia. You could go down to the beach and see more than you could in the photos," her father said. "They were very tasteful. I don't know anyone in Australia that thought of them being anything but that. It surprised me a little bit that America reacted the way that it did. We were walking down the streets of Las Vegas and this guy was handing out [postcards] of naked women. I mean, what's the standard? I don't know. In Australia we know what the standard is."

On the Internet, various chat rooms were alive with debates for and against the pictures, too. But when Jackson held a book signing for the $40 keepsake once the team returned home from the Houston road game, where the news broke, a line of guys waited outside for tickets to see her play and only a few people raised a judgmental eyebrow. The crowd of 8,265, as the Storm lost to Houston again, 63-57 at KeyArena, was the largest since playing Los Angeles in the second game of the season.

"Call me stupid, I was thinking, 'It's not going to make that big of a deal,'" said Jackson, whose WNBA Web page, after the magazine came out, set a record for most hits and whose little splash in the nude was depicted in *Tank McNamara*, a syndicated cartoon. "Anne knew and I was a little bit worried. She pulled me aside before I spoke to the media and asked if I was ready for this. I didn't know what the media were going to say, what people were going to do, whether I'd be booed out of the stadium or what. But it was fine."

Seattleites had already welcomed their rebel child into their hearts, chanting the country's cheer "Aussie! Aussie! Aussie! Oi! Oi! Oi!" in unison as Jackson made three-pointers or before she shot free throws. The sound from an average of 8,000 people always brought a tiny smile to the warrior's face.

"Seattle is so liberal, more liberal than other places in America," Jackson said. "I'm proud that it's my adopted home. It's the only place I can see myself living outside of Australia."

CHAPTER EIGHT

Lattes and Layups: Howard Schultz Purchases the Storm

What's not widely known about Seattle rain is how it makes the city look at night. Buildings and streets washed with a day's worth of water sparkle like glitter beneath a disco ball in the moonlit darkness. A sight Anne Donovan didn't expect to see when the pilot announced his "Welcome to Seattle" to the passengers, notifying them it was raining—but what else is new?

Donovan had fidgeted the entire flight. She was the leading candidate to replace Lin Dunn for the Storm's head coaching position and knew it was a dream job. Her older sister Mary had even said it was the perfect location for "Annie" to expand her blossoming career, but Donovan remained incredulous. Billy McKinney waited eagerly at the airport to begin the interviewing process. He could rattle off Donovan's statistics—1983 Naismith Player of the Year and one of the first five women inducted in the Basketball Hall of Fame—and now the former NBA guard wanted to talk to the person behind the stats. He wondered if Donovan could strip the organization of its "expansion" mind-set. McKinney had had long talks with players about not seeing themselves as the "three-year-olds playing six-year-olds" that Dunn liked to call them in postgame interviews to surmise why the Storm lost. To McKinney, in order for the team to improve, they were going to have to see themselves on the same level as the other established teams.

Donovan wasn't one for making excuses, and never has been. She could find the proverbial "silver lining" but always spoke from the heart in telling you exactly how she felt. It was why players immediately trusted her. She was honest, straightforward, and knowledgeable.

She walked hesitantly into the two-day interview, however. She hadn't exactly had a positive experience with owners in the WNBA or defunct ABL, coaching the Philadelphia Rage in 1998. The Charlotte Hornets ditched the Sting in 2001 when the NBA team relocated to New Orleans. The WNBA operated the Sting in the 2002 season, which felt like punishment. Donovan was able to do her job, but with Charlotte being a league afterthought, marketing and connecting to the community to drum up ticket sales was difficult. Robert L. Johnson, former owner of Black Entertainment Network, was stepping in as the new owner of the NBA expansion team coming to the city, but Donovan was already sour. Plus, word was that Johnson had been forced to take on the WNBA team or not be awarded the franchise.

Quality owners are essential to a team's success, evident in the Cleveland Rockers and Portland Fire folding behind management who had other plans, rather than from failing attendance or disinterest from their respective cities. When money and commitment are poured into a team from the top, it shows in a quality product on the court. There's gifted coaching, innovative marketing, tangible connections with fans, and visibility at games. The Maloof brothers, Joe and Gavin, often sat courtside at Sacramento Monarchs home and road games in jeans and button-down printed shirts, hollering at officials and escalating the decibel of rowdiness. The colorful Johnny Buss carries his wild antics over to the Los Angeles Sparks side, traveling with the team and unabashedly getting into verbal fights with opponents if needed. Washington Mystics owner Sheila Johnson, who divorced Robert, was pictured on the Jumbotron dancing in her suite, gave pep talks before games, and invited players to her celebrity-studded second wedding in 2005.

Other owners may not be as visible, but their touch is felt. When Detroit owner Bill Davidson agreed to rename the street leading up to The Palace of Auburn Hills, where the Pistons and Shock play, Three Championship Drive in honor of the two NBA titles and the 2003 WNBA title, the gesture made the Shock players truly feel part of the organization. The street has since been named Four Championship Drive after Davidson's Tampa Bay Lightning won an NHL title. Los Angeles, which changes its stance about the WNBA quicker than Hollywood stars change spouses, is an exception. But there's an ease in Sacramento, Washington, DC, and Detroit that an effort will be made toward longevity.

In the WNBA, an owner's mark is really made with coaching, since players' salaries are limited by hard salary cap that's basically the taxes of what's doled out for NBA players (the 2006 salary cap is $700,000). Arenas with posh locker rooms are already established in most cities, and owned by the respective NBA franchise. Travel is limited to commercial flights and merchandise is minimal. If an owner or organization thinks highly of its women's team, it actually has a separate staff dedicated to ticket sales and has its general manager spend time searching for a quality leader. Otherwise, a local NBA face is thrown in the position, and the organization hopes the name will muster ticket sales and the past playing experience will translate into the ability to coach.

Not that all coaches with ties to the NBA aren't competent. Detroit coach Bill Laimbeer, a key face on the Pistons "Bad Boy" teams, was a successful personality his first full season in 2003, finishing 25-9 with a roster full of All-Stars, whose masterful team play masked his ability. Former Los Angeles coach Michael Cooper, who won championships with the Lakers and won four Western

Conference titles and two league titles with the Sparks, also had questionable skill. But former NBA coaches Ron Rothstein (Miami), Richie Adubato (Washington), Brian Winters (Indiana), and Mike Thibault (Connecticut) have all found respect with their talent in the women's league.

The Phoenix Mercury was a comedy show after Cheryl Miller left in 2000, hiring Cynthia Cooper and John Shumate, both of whom had no coaching experience and were exposed on the sideline. At least Miller knew what she was wailing about when she flapped her arms on the sideline. Cooper and Shumate simply cussed and slammed scoreboard tables for appearances. Washington, which has had eight coaches in as many seasons, allowed Michael Adams, another former NBA player, to use its team as a stepping stone to a men's college assistant position in 2004. And in 2005, coaches working hard to gain credibility were livid at the hiring of Henry Bibby and Joe "Jellybean" Bryant in Los Angeles and Mugsy Bogues, a former guard for the NBA's Hornets, in Charlotte. The trio reportedly stated they didn't know anything about the WNBA prior to being hired and tried to make jokes about their coaching experiences with women, referring to youth leagues as past knowledge. "They're an embarrassment," one coach commented, requesting anonymity. It appeared as if management felt that any warm body would suffice and fans would actually buy a ticket because of the coach's name recognition, not the play they would see on the court.

That philosophy doesn't fly far in Seattle. The importance of coaching isn't lost on Seattle women's basketball fans. Pockets of University of Washington followers have bickered about June Daugherty and her recruiting and coaching styles for years, questioning everything from player development to substitution patterns. For the Storm, Dunn was a fabulous "first face" of the team that didn't have players, uniforms, or a name. Yet one of the biggest fears was that the Storm would be relegated to some sort of a sideshow under new ownership in 2001, not given the resources to be a successful team, especially as fans started to grow wary of

Chairman Howard Schultz (right) and president Wally Walker joined to purchase the Sonics and Storm in 2001 as part of The Basketball Club of Seattle LLC.

(LATRENA SMITH PHOTOGRAPHY)

Dunn's methods on the court. Unlike NBA fans, who have grown passive over the years, the WNBA fanatics are a vocal, united group willing to put in work to support their team.

Scott Englehardt and his wife started the Web site stormfans. org following the team's inaugural season as a way to connect with other avid fans. They had never attended an ABL game, not having heard much about the Reign, but couldn't escape the mass marketing appeal of the Storm. Despite a 6-26 season, the couple was hooked and wanted to talk Storm with others practically 24/7. The site was modest at first, taking over a year to accumulate 100,000 hits, but the incessant typing about players, coaches, media coverage, and ways to drum up interest in the team added zeal to monotonous workdays for some or a connection to the team for others in Australia, Europe, and the Philippines.

Internet chat rooms were already active in January 2001 because of a rumored sale of the Sonics and what that would mean for the WNBA team. Fear always seems to be the first emotion when you're

Anne Donovan (middle) argues her case with an official during a Storm home game versus Detroit. Donovan is the first woman, fourth coach overall, in the WNBA to have won 100 career games. (LATRENA SMITH PHOTOGRAPHY)

a fan of a niche sport that's losing its founder. But while Barry and Ginger Ackerley were pivotal in Seattle obtaining a WNBA team, fans felt an immediate dedication to the Storm once Starbucks guru Howard Schultz put together an assembly of 50 local businesspeople to form The Basketball Club of Seattle, LLC. The private group of investors purchased the Sonics and Storm from the Ackerleys for $200 million in April 2001, declaring they would bring back the magic of the old-school Sonics days.

"When Barry Ackerley told me that he was interested in selling, I said, 'Go no further, I have exactly the person who can put together a group to buy the team,'" said David Stern at the Sonics' 2004–05 inaugural tip-off luncheon at the Seattle Exhibition Center. "I had been meeting with Howard Schultz over a period of time, talking about what a team might be as a community asset."

Barry Ackerley, with Wally Walker as his point person, had strained relationships with some Sonics players and worn ties with fans, especially after changing the team colors to a hated brick red and forest green and making a bundle of disliked business moves. Guard Gary Payton seemed to be the only thing fans and ownership could agree on, Ackerley making Payton virtually untouchable with a seven-year, $85 million contract. Yet, as sales talk swirled, rumors about Payton being traded were tossed in the mix. G.P. not playing in Seattle was like the region sans rain. If that could happen, surely the Storm could be absolved, one Internet blogger wrote.

Schultz, a young, inventive mind, immediately launched a campaign claiming the "green and gold" was back, anointing his team in its original colors and displaying a logo with a touch of yesteryear blended with futuristic impressions, thus reconnecting the dented chain of basketball history in the city.

Schultz, who joined the Starbucks company in 1982, was an NBA fanatic. A native New Yorker, he was raised loving the Knicks and felt a connection to the Sonics to the extent of being called a "cheerleader" by media when spotted at games, leaping high from his seat after powerful dunks or blown calls.

"He's a real committed fan. He has a lot of energy on the sidelines, very involved in the game," Nate McMillan, who was dubbed "Mr. Sonic" after two decades with the franchise as a player and coach, told the *Seattle Times*. "Looking at his face during big plays, he has a passion for the game. I visualize him as a guy who will be very involved with the team. He just seems to really enjoy the games when you see him on the sidelines."

Schultz—father of a teenage daughter who often accompanied him to games—knew little about the Storm, however. And after a function at Green Lake that spring, he wondered about his joint investment.

"There was no one there; it was the mascot and 10 people," he said of the kick-off where fans had an opportunity to meet players before the 2001 season. "I looked around and thought, 'God, what a disaster this is. What are we doing?'"

Then he questioned the public relations staff to see if season ticket holders had been notified.

"We told everyone, Howard, but no one came," was the response.

After calming down, Schultz wouldn't be deterred. He was a successful businessman who had hypnotized the world into justifying paying $4 for a cup of coffee, giving new meaning to the term daily grind. Certainly he could tackle this project.

"I can't believe the Storm has not ever made any money," Schultz said. "From a business perspective, one could dismiss it as a disappointing business, but it has been far from that for me personally and the organization. It has added tremendous value to the organization; it has added tremendous value to the community. Everybody wants instant gratification and instant rewards. Professional sports are not that way."

A value Schultz had to experience firsthand. In a courtside conversation with NBA legend Bill Russell at a Sonics game, Schultz was schooled on what to expect from the women's game. Russell, a frequent attendee of Storm games, said, "The best basketball in the world is being played here by the women in the WNBA. Fundamentally, the women play a game that is below the rim, and the fundamentals are true and authentic. The Michael Jordan era produced so much athleticism above the rim that the fundamentals suffered; that's not the case with the women."

Schultz witnessed a raw Lauren Jackson, who could shoot like a guard and had the body to own the paint. Then a sparkling tandem between the Aussie and Sue Bird, who could thread the ball inside with the zip of a whip, motivated Schultz in 2002 to do even more with the organization. Separate staff was hired to focus on ticket sales year-round, giving Karen Bryant more leeway to attract the Storm's still ambiguous fan base. A bigger budget was formed for television and print ads, in addition to marketing across public transportation and flapping signs from flagpoles—although some fan events suffered cutbacks, like open practices and meet-and-greets, which became solely for season ticket holders and not the general public.

At the Storm training facility, the team had its own entrance with its logo stenciled on the door. A walkway to the locker room adorned with past team photos and the logo painted on a massive white wall gave the Storm its own identity separate from the Sonics. Storm travel was always organized, and the players used connections from the Sonics to stay in the finest hotels for half the price. Suddenly, Seattle was the underground destination spot of the league, a place players begged their agents to land them a contract.

Coaching was another way Schultz could show he was serious about building a successful basketball organization, developing the young product on the floor. He didn't know the names of the top leaders, so he left the details to Karen Bryant, McKinney, and minority owner Jack Rodgers, who had invested his own money into Schultz's coffee venture in the 1980s, forming an everlasting bond.

Rodgers dove into the women's game after the sale. Dressed in black Storm practice shorts and a cotton polo, he strolled into practice one day and shocked Dunn, who had never heard of an owner getting involved on a personal level. The women, however, meant something to Rodgers, 74. His two daughters are in their mid-40s but had played athletics prior to Title IX. Neither were diehard athletes like their dad, who had been a quarterback at Kansas and had also won a 1952 NCAA championship with the legendary Dean Smith, but Rodgers never missed a competition. Nancy, his wife of 52 years, would simply smile at his dedication.

"She'd say, 'When I want you to be home you can never arrange your schedule, but how come your [traveling] schedule always manages to be fixed, and you always manage to be home for one of the kids' athletic events?'" remembered Rodgers, who also has two sons. "And that's true, they were high priorities in our life and family. Nancy was right there with me—I didn't go alone."

Retired from IBM, making a living off ownership of a few fast food chains, Rodgers just wanted to be involved in basketball again. Especially since Smith had nixed his idea to volunteer-coach the University of North Carolina Tar Heels back in 1998. Dunn was much more welcoming. Rodgers would shag balls while players shot free throws or offer up 20 bucks to made half-court shots after practice was over. With snow-white hair and a delicate voice, he was a grandfather type for the players, who referred to him as "Mr. Storm" and celebrated his August birthday with balloons, cake, and singing and listened to his encouragement during rough losing skids.

At quarterly board meetings, Rodgers reported back to president and CEO Wally Walker and Schultz about the team. How forward Adia Barnes, a University of Arizona alum, was gaining confidence offensively but still was one of the team's strongest rebounders. How Jackson didn't back down from Sparks center Lisa Leslie, scoring 21 points in a win at KeyArena. Or how Bird was acting as if the WNBA was an extension of the college season, hardly playing like a rookie as she led the team to win seven of its last nine games to slip into the 2002 postseason as the fourth and final seed in the West.

"Most of the time it's [the presentation] on the Sonics because the Sonics represent the majority of the commitment, financial and what have you," Rodgers said. "But at every meeting I find something to discuss about the Storm. And then I'd answer any questions. This never became a dominant part of any board meeting. I always do what I can to keep the Storm on the front burner."

Rodgers was one of those saddened to lose Dunn. He had played golf with her, Bryant, and McKinney at Overlake Country Club in the postseason, listening to what they needed to improve everything from ticket sales to wins. But understanding the reasons for change, he stayed active in finding a replacement. Rodgers dropped in on McKinney's interview with Donovan, not wanting to be too involved since he was modest about his authority, but wanting to share some thoughts. Donovan, taken aback at the interest, instantly felt the little touches she believed would make her job a breeze upon arrival. "Jack just epitomizes women's basketball [fans]. Fans and supporters of women's basketball that are a little bit older that really relate to the girls as their daughters," Donovan said. "It was a very comfortable situation for me to see this owner that took that much care, that had that much passion about the women's team. That was not my experience [in the past]." Not that coaching the Storm would be easy.

For Schultz, a man who purchased the six-store, Seattle-based Starbucks Company in 1987 and turned it into a global brand synonymous with the morning wake-up call, the women's team shouldn't be mistaken for a charity case. With anointed superstars in Jackson and Bird, Schultz wanted championships. Community service was a distant reason for pouring resources into the organization. Schultz, 52, immediately saw the Storm as a way to build community relations while making an added profit for the NBA franchise.

The question was whether he'd have enough patience to see a return. Did anyone in the WNBA? It's one thing to be part of a grassroots organization like the ABL, staying in midlevel hotels, traveling coach, and making concessions on a per diem basis because you own 10 percent stock in your livelihood. But playing under the umbrella of the NBA, staying at the Four Seasons and Ritz Carlton while still traveling coach and having your salary stipulated by a cap not even worth the value of two minimum-waged NBA players was harsh.

Fans' desires didn't change because the players made less, either. They wanted the same championship dream, especially after the team reached the playoffs in its third season, only to be embarrassingly swept by Los Angeles in the first-round by an average of 13.5 points per game.

A New Jersey native, Donovan knew she could deliver after meeting with McKinney and Rodgers. And she was surprised about the area. She likened Seattle to a "jeans and T-shirt" kind of city where she could easily blend. Plus, who wouldn't want to coach Jackson and Bird?

"The diversity here is very welcoming for someone who's a little out of the box," Donovan said. "This [Seattle] is the only place I've lived where I don't get stared at constantly because I'm 6-foot-8. It's just this feeling of acceptance of people of all different kinds of beliefs and being."

Ridgewood, New Jersey, Donovan's birthplace, is an affluent, quaint neighborhood about 24 miles outside of New York. Donovan, born in November 1961, would call her block ritzy, but her family wasn't wallowing in wealth. Her father died when she was a child, and her mother worked two jobs to provide for the eight children.

They called her Anne, Andy, or Annie and cared for her like most families do the baby child. All understanding the struggles of being tall, ranging from 7 feet to 5-foot-11, they protected her from gawking eyes and kept her focused on basketball and academics since it was the only way to pay for college. Maybe it was her strict Irish Catholic upbringing, but Donovan will always be more reserved than Dunn. Schultz didn't care about that, though, upon meeting her. There was an attitude she exuded that radiated winning.

Dunn was a model mother to the Storm concept. Her personality was bigger than Mount Rainier and her creativity more vast than the population of the artsy Fremont neighborhood. She was the face of the organization, featured on the cover of the 2001 media guide, and regularly made radio and television appearances to whoop it up about the new team. It all perfectly covered the fact that the talent in the league hadn't reached its level of hype.

Even with the merger of ABL players, the WNBA was riding on past triumphs from most of its players when the pro class of 2004 began to hone its talent as freshmen on college campuses. Guard Teresa Weatherspoon nailed a spectacular half-court shot in the league's early years and was adored by her New York Liberty fans but was hardly the player who had won a 1988 NCAA championship with Louisiana Tech. Guard Ruthie Bolton, a scoring highlight on the 1996 Olympic team, went south after her first season in Sacramento. And Rebecca Lobo, the most recognized face in Connecticut, never reached her anticipated potential in the WNBA. They were the players carrying the league, however. Others in the same age bracket, like Sheryl Swoopes (Houston), Yolanda Griffith (Sacramento), Katie Smith (Detroit), or Taj McWilliams-Franklin (Connecticut) worked hard to alter their playing style to stay ahead of the young crop the league salivated over, eager to promote as its new face.

"I'll have to admit the women's game was at times painful to watch a few years ago," said Billy McKinney, who served as the Storm's executive vice president in 2001. "The skill level has increased tremendously."

In Seattle, that was Jackson and Bird. Both twenty-something phenoms that needed their own platform to shine. Dunn's health prompting her to resign or covering for not having her contract renewed at the price she wanted was a prime opportunity for the Storm to head in a different direction.

The WNBA started to shift too. No longer were Houston and Los Angeles, winners of the first six titles, dominating with alternating dynasties. The bubbling talent boom by 2002 made every season open to every team (except San Antonio, which never seemed to escape the cellar), putting more of an importance on coaching and scouting. Dunn could spot rough talent—Kamila Vodichkova remains an underrated center at age 33—but Dunn didn't adjust to coaching on the professional level, despite her previous successes in the ABL. "Players were so hesitant out there," former center Danielle McCulley told the *Seattle Times* of playing under Dunn. "Everybody knows the top two guns are Sue and LJ. Everyone else didn't know if it was OK to take a shot or make a move, so they just sat around and watched, thinking, 'If I mess up, I'm getting snatched out of the game.'" Donovan seemed to be a better fit for the Storm's future, and McKinney wasted no time in offering her the position.

"I think she [Anne] brought a level of professionalism and maturity and guidance to the organization," Schultz said. "It's no knock against Lin, it's just a different style, and it was just the appropriate person at the right time."

To Donovan's surprise women's basketball fans in the area were receptive. After weeks fretting over the possibility of the organization becoming another team to throw an NBA name in the head coaching slot, message board junkies were ecstatic to learn Donovan was the choice, even posting rumors of her hiring before the news officially broke in the *Seattle Times*. Donovan, one of five women coaches in 2003, made it clear she wasn't going to fry chicken or bet on coloring her hair any shade if she didn't win, like Dunn had done in her nonstop campaign to promote the team. But Donovan was confident she could get the team to start thinking like champions.

The tone was more businesslike upon Donovan's arrival. The players weren't allowed to wear jeans when they traveled. There were stiff fines for being late or not following directions. Every moment was to be taken seriously. Donovan worked hard, spending hours at her office in the training facility, only breaking to feed her epileptic gray cat Romeo. Her staff was just as dedicated, often changing clothes at the facility to make it out for evening plans after long days. Donovan started to thaw her personality, showing more of a comical side to the media than she did in Charlotte as she grew more confident in the position. As long as it remained off the record, she'd share tales of her imperfections that would end up being sidesplitting stories, making pregame interviews more entertaining.

"I know people will always love Lin Dunn and what she brought to the city," Donovan said. "She brought the Storm with all of its fans initially into KeyArena and gave them an identity. So, I knew it was going to take a while to win some of those people over because our personalities are so different. And yet, never ever did I feel unwelcome or that people were skeptical. People were really educated, they knew what I had done in Charlotte, they knew what I had done with the expansion team in Indiana, so they were willing to give me a shot. Just like all fans—you better win or else that trust goes away. When I first got here, I felt that trust."

The Storm was Seattle's second chance at women's professional basketball. A chance the players were reminded of almost daily by nonfollowers curious about the longevity of the league. Former Storm guard Michelle Marciniak, a fan favorite, would often say while playing in Seattle that if the NBA can't make a women's league work, they should probably stop trying, because the public obviously wasn't ever going to be ready. A dedicated few hundred were. The team was like an investment. They'd attend every fan function with new items for the players to sign. Players and coaches knew them by first name. They'd charge their credit cards with airline tickets to road games or stuff themselves into a van and alternate driving to close destinations like Sacramento or Portland, when it had a team, just to watch a road game. One young fan named Michele Oliver even tattooed the Storm logo on her lower back and purchased season tickets to both Storm and Fire home games.

Seattle fans relished the fact that the players were so accessible, just like in the ABL, but could sense changes every season. And it wasn't just rising ticket prices. Donovan did have the public relations staff pull back on appearances, needing her players to rest or focus on basketball a little more in pursuit of winning, instead of constantly promoting the team. The increased exposure through marketing also meant less one-on-one time for fanatics as functions at downtown restaurants or arcade spots were packed with people wanting to give shout-outs to Bird or center Simone Edwards. Even the gates where the players entered KeyArena to park their cars were becoming overpopulated by 2003, as little girls nudged their way in between grown men trying to get an autograph. What the league had always contended was coming to fruition—if tempted inside the building to catch one game, fans would be drawn to come back.

It was true after the 2002 season when the Storm made its inaugural playoff appearance. A winner was brewing, and Donovan added a new flavor, even though around the league prognosticators brushed the postseason berth off as a fluke. But by July, the Storm was second in the Western Conference, winning four of the six games heading into the All-Star break. Jackson was the league's leading scorer, averaging 19.7 points for the 9-6 overall Storm. Instead of sulking or allowing opponents to fiddle with her mentally during games with cheap shots and trash talk, she was learning from Donovan how to ignore the personal jabs and respond with strong defense and wins. Once Jackson returned from the All-Star game with Bird, who was voted a starter, she tore through the league's interior defenses, being named Player of the Week three times and averaging 21.2 points on 48.3 percent shooting to win the MVP award after placing 10th in voting in 2002. She was Seattle's third pro athlete to win an MVP award, joining the Mariners' Ken Griffey Jr. (1997) and Ichiro Suzuki (2001).

"She's by far the best coach I've ever had," Jackson said of Donovan. "I don't think I'd be the player I am without her."

As attendance swelled to an average 7,109, however, the team stumbled toward season's end and was booted from playoff contention with two games remaining. Kamila Vodichkova sprained her left foot with six games remaining, while Barnes tore her anterior cruciate ligament 16 games into the season, so two starters were knocked from the team's lineup. Jackson fought to carry the team, tallying nine double-doubles in the second half of the season, but the Storm lost five of its final seven games, dropping out of the playoff race.

Donovan was the most disappointed. She didn't have the pieces she wanted to win with and, used to veteran leadership with her Charlotte teams, her stars in Seattle were a little more carefree than the coach would had liked, laughing and joking when Donovan felt they should be stewing and contemplating how to stop losing winnable games. The Storm was already swirling through a cloud of uncertainty prior to the 2003 season when Bryant started hunting around for a more affordable place for the team to play. The Storm's KeyArena lease had expired, and as a cost-cutting measure, Bryant researched moving the team to other cities in Washington, such as Everett, Spokane, Yakima, or Tacoma. The cities were delighted to woo the organization, but about 65 percent of the fan base was from either King, Pierce, or Snohomish counties in the greater Seattle metro area, making a move unfeasible regardless of the Storm losing about $3 million in its first three seasons. Add to the battle the collective bargaining agreement, where ratification was mired because of player demands for salary increases, and two franchises folding, and Donovan hoped for more of a determined approach from her young leaders.

Donovan sat in a quiet room at the training facility and discussed the upsetting finish with members of the media. You can't fault injuries, but it wasn't what she'd planned for her first season in Seattle. Suddenly she transformed into a kid making out a holiday wish list, detailing exactly what she wanted for next season to catapult the team deep into the playoffs: "a big veteran perimeter player who can score." The first season with true free agency was approaching, and fans across message boards on the Internet were already starting to sift through possible names that Donovan could pick up to fill the void. With Donovan's motion offense that honestly had "motion," the continued development of Jackson, and Bird deciding to undergo surgery to clear out gunk in her left knee that slowed her play that season, fans could feel something stirring. About 200 of them filled in one section of Jillian's Billiard Club in Seattle to honor Jackson winning the MVP and to watch Detroit break the West Coast dominance and win the championship. Letting out a sheepish squeal, Jackson couldn't believe the people were there for her, giving her a standing ovation as she walked in and chanting "M-V-P" during halftime.

People wanted to soak themselves in the moment because it didn't last long. Unlike baseball or even football, the WNBA season is only five months, if you count training camp and the playoffs. Once the first dried brown leaf hits a windshield or crushes underfoot, it knocks out the breezy summertime trance. Fall is coming.

The team shows its off-court personal style at a gathering at Gasworks Park along Lake Union in Seattle. (LATRENA SMITH PHOTOGRAPHY)

Around Seattle, that means the last trail of tourists will shuffle out of the city in time for the icy rain to trickle in. Time to snuggle in layers of fleece, grab a cup of java to warm the insides, and look forward to the weekend's football game. For the WNBA, the lights simply fade to black like a Broadway play. Players, adopted by each city, suddenly disappear for eight months to either play overseas or blend into daily life stateside, practically unheard of until spring. Only the impersonal postings on message boards keep the beat alive until another season unveils another level of excitement.

CHAPTER NINE

Betty Lennox

I t felt like an inescapable punch line. Betty Lennox would return home during the WNBA off-season, sit down at the dinner table with family, and mumble, "Pass the potatoes and my team just folded."

In September 2003, it was her Cleveland Rockers that became part of the league's collection of franchises past. Rumors circulated throughout the season of the possibility, but players were under the assumption that if they advanced to the playoffs, which they did with a 17-17 record, the organization would be saved. It wasn't. Even a modest "Save the Rockers" campaign initiated by fans could do nothing for the charter team. Soon Lennox was on a teleconference call, hearing how her team no longer existed. "That was our early Thanksgiving Day present," she scoffed. Weary of the downside of a new league, Lennox accepted a position with the General Motors plant in Kansas City. Her thoughts as she walked the office floors often drifted back to 2000 when she was part of a high-scoring duo with Olympic guard Katie Smith in Minnesota. Lennox averaged 16.9 points on 42.7 percent shooting from the field while Smith led the team with a 20.2 point average.

The Lynx weren't successful, finishing 13 games back from the Western Conference–leading Los Angeles Sparks with a 15-17 record, but all Lennox could remember were the magical moments. Being the only rookie selected for the WNBA All-Star game played in Phoenix. Screams from an adoring Target Center crowd. Being named Rookie of the Year. It all seemed so distant as she drove in her black Yukon Denali from her stylish home in Independence, Missouri, to arrive at work at 5:30 in the morning. Lennox, a manager's assistant, was hardly recognizable in a neutral-colored business suit, her dark chestnut hair pressed straight, softly curled at the ends, looking more like her own twin of the player who strutted on the court in a headband and cornrows with tattoos etched into a muscular build.

A former star at Fort Osage High School in Independence, Lennox used to roam the same Midwestern streets visualizing what it would be like to be a professional women's basketball player. The Kansas City Mustangs had played in the National Conference of the Women's Basketball Association (1993–95), a 12-team league that disbanded when Fox bought its supporting television station, Liberty Sports. Lennox never heard of the undefeated 1995 Mustangs (15-0) as she grew more interested in the sport. By the time she was looking for professional role models, the league had folded. But for some reason, she believed there would be a new league coming and she'd stand atop a podium as its star.

Reality was harsh. Injuries she could handle, it was part of the game. The first came in June 2001 on the road against Detroit. Lennox, the leading rebounder among guards at the time, had to leave the game with 15:39 remaining in the second half because of a strained left hip capsule. She finished with 10 boards in the Lynx's win but missed 20 games, then reaggravated the injury the final game of the season, needing surgery. Her comeback was painful, hours spent in deserted gyms working out with trainers or alone, but it was almost incomparable to the cold greeting of the business side of pro ball.

Minnesota had needs and Lennox, trying to retain her old form, couldn't become something new simultaneously. Coach Brian Agler had no time to wait. The Lynx were 4-3 and desperate for a point guard to start the 2002 season, and if he didn't find one, he'd lose his position. Agler looked to Lennox to handle the ball but felt she failed at the position. Pressured from upper management, he dealt his second-most-prized player, Lennox, to Miami along with a first-round draft pick for guard Tamara Moore and a second-round pick. The Lynx also had to ship about 5,000 promotional Lennox bobblehead dolls to the Miami team.

Being expendable stung. "I put trust in this man, not only as a friend, but as a father figure and this is what I get in return," a steamed Lennox told the *Palm Beach Post* at the time. Lennox planned to retire in Minnesota. Instead she became a personification of how the WNBA was still sedimentary soil in a vast sports landscape. At every shift in the WNBA's groundbreaking growth, there seemed to be Lennox, a 5-foot-8 apple-cheeked face of change. Except adjusting seemed to put more shields around the guard.

Agler was fired behind a 6-13 record in July 2002 while Lennox was busy helping Miami with its playoff push, adding enough instant offense off the bench to be dubbed "The Microwave" by Sol fans. Differences between the teams were deeper than the Spanish-inspired jersey she now wore. The league improved its average attendance by 2 percent (9,228) for its biggest improvement since 1999, after the ABL folded. New television deals with ESPN and ABC were in the works to boost the WNBA's visibility, and with more sponsors joining in, the NBA board of governors wanted to move the sister league toward self-reliance. The group of 29 owners, who financially backed the women's league regardless of personal possession of a franchise, voted to reconstruct the WNBA to have the individual teams be financially responsible for themselves instead of the front office handling the paperwork.

It was also a gut-check moment when the 16 individual WNBA owners decided if they were going to continue or opt out. The board lifted a restriction for non-NBA owners to purchase teams for about $10 million, playing in non-NBA cities. So, if an owner wanted out, it could find a seller to relieve it of the team. Four teams wanted out. Only two were relocated, one to a private owner.

The Utah Starzz, which had struggled internally and externally to draw support, relocated to San Antonio, becoming the Silver Stars. The Orlando Miracle was purchased by the Mohegan Tribe and moved to its casino in Connecticut with forward Nykesha Sales, a Bloomfield native and former University of Connecticut star, as its headlining player.

Portland and Miami also used the loophole to wrestle loose of their WNBA obligations. Billionaire Paul Allen, owner of the Trail Blazers and also the NFL Seattle Seahawks, never showed much interest and couldn't find a taker in the city. Heat Group owner Mickey Arison plainly stated the organization couldn't cope with the financial hit. After three seasons, the expansion team had already reported losses of $7.5 million and, according to Arison, it would escalate before breaking even. Some teams were padding their stats anyway: the Starzz gave away 3,000 comp tickets a game; others hid costs under their NBA team to show a better bottom line. Sustaining a new venture halfheartedly didn't seem feasible.

Regardless, players like Lennox were out on the court doggedly trying to entertain fans, smiling at every public appearance and signing every autograph to make a connection. Hearing that the Sol was to be disbanded that fall was a blow Lennox wasn't ready for, especially after just arriving and learning to shift to a reserve role after having starred in Minnesota.

The hiatus was the worst feeling. A powerless void where future desires were determined by external factors. Lennox waded in the mood following the rush of an exhilarating and frustrating season packed with emotion. Suddenly, her future was in doubt as the WNBA decided what to do. Sol coach Ron Rothstein openly cried when he spoke of the surprising end to his WNBA career. A former NBA head coach, he enjoyed the experience of coaching women, leading Miami to the playoffs in 2001. Fans wrote letters of disgust to local papers, commenting on how they upgraded their seats to season ticket packages worth $800 for two seats, so how could the team be in financial ruin? The Sol's attendance was seventh-best at the time

Storm guard Betty Lennox shoots an acrobatic jumper against Sacramento. Lennox finished second in Most Improved award voting in 2004. (LATRENA SMITH PHOTOGRAPHY)

(8,828), but the Heat Group said competition to grab corporate sponsorship in Miami would be troublesome. The situation left fans with refunds and reunion parties to say good-bye. The same happened 3,000 miles away in Portland, where the team was widely successful, averaging 8,037 fans that summer, but couldn't find an owner to replace Allen even after pleas from loyal fans.

Also swirling in the league's winds of uncertainty was the collective bargaining agreement, which was originally signed by the Players' Association and the WNBA in 1999 and expired on September 15, 2002. Since the league was moving toward independence, the players wanted flexibility, mainly the chance to test their market value through free agency, freedom with endorsement deals, and more pay along with some benefits. The WNBA, learning a lesson with escalating salaries from the NBA, and still wanting to control development of the fledgling league, was stubborn in its negotiations. According to former Storm player Sonja Henning, then president of the union, the league rarely responded to proposals it sent and wouldn't meet until late in the negotiating process. By April 8, with training camp scheduled to start at the end of the month, commissioner David Stern issued a deadline for a deal because of stalled talks. If an agreement wasn't reached by the 18th, he said he would cancel the WNBA's seventh season.

In stuffy boardrooms in downtown Manhattan, the union met with WNBA officials along a mahogany conference table that seemingly stretched the length of a football field. It was nearly impossible for those seated on the ends to hear each other speak, but not much compromising happened anyway. While the NBA agreed to subsidize the women's league by $12 million, the union and league were about $900,000 apart on terms like salary cap and increased pay for the players.

The union wanted a $750,000 salary cap with a veteran minimum salary of $48,000 and increased rookie salary of $30,000. It also sought unrestricted free agency after a player's fifth season and restricted free agency, where teams have an opportunity to match any offer a player received from an opposing team, after the fourth season.

The league was prudent. It wanted a five-year contract with a $616,000 salary cap. Rookie salaries would drop to $25,000 and veteran minimums would raise $1,200 to $41,200. Plus, the league wanted to halt free agency until a player's 10th season, a move many players laughed at, seeing how the distant 2012 date meant none would ever experience free agency. Those players weren't even born yet, some joked.

Approaching the final hour of negotiations, the WNBA wavered on a few fringe issues to reach an agreement. The eventual four-year CBA with a league option for a fifth increased veteran minimum salaries to $42,000 but kept the rookie minimum pay at $30,000. The salary cap was set at $622,000 the first season while players' marketing restrictions decreased from 18 to six. Restricted free agency was granted in a player's seventh season in 2003, sixth in 2004, and fifth in 2005.

Wanting to play, the players reluctantly voted to ratify the new CBA.

"They said if we didn't accept those terms, they would cancel the season at 5 o'clock," union spokesman Dan Wasserman told media at the time.

Word came days later there would be a dispersal draft of the combined Portland and Miami rosters on April 24, 2003, a day before the league's college/international draft. The top three picks were from Miami, Lennox being the third overall selection to the Cleveland Rockers.

In the industrial Ohio city, things worsened for Lennox. She felt trapped in a system where her talents weren't used. She withered away on the bench under coach Dan Hughes, waiting to prove her worth. A highlight was in Game 2 of the Rockers' Eastern Conference first-round playoff matchup against Detroit, where Lennox scored 14 points on 6-for-9 shooting to help Cleveland force a deciding Game 3. But the Shock won the best-of-three series, ending the Rockers' season. The shroud of doubt crept back again. Lennox felt she rode a roller coaster, often pouting on the end of the bench, averaging a career-low 7.6 points in 34 games. A former All-Star, she started only once that season.

"Betty creates a certain drama and portrayal of things, she paints it like she's had all of these situations that were really difficult for her, and I've talked to all those coaches and they all say good things about Betty," Hughes said. "I have good feelings for Betty. Betty helped me win some games in Cleveland. It wasn't a smooth ride, but we would not have been in the playoffs and we would not have gotten a win in Detroit without Betty.

"But, I think Betty uses that as a means of motivation. People love Betty a lot more than she thinks they do. But in some way that motivates her to work."

The presumed disrespect is an old-school mind-set. One honed early when going up against the odds and needing to keep your edge. Names. Put one rubber-soled sneaker on a basketball court, and a barrage of disses will swoop around you like a gust of wind after a ferocious dunk. There's the "you ain't got nothin'" dig and the infamous "you got took to school" while onlookers coo about a sick crossover dribble that leaves a defender in a puff of dusty asphalt or a wicked jump shot that makes the nylon net snap like a whip.

If that shoe is a size seven belonging to a girl? Oh, it's on.

Before Lennox had received her first driver's license as a teenager, she'd heard it all. She was too puny to play basketball, standing at just 4-foot-11 when she finally mustered up the nerve to follow her older brothers onto the basketball court. The sound of what was to come for her and this game she felt compelled to play was muffled by the parched dirt that seemed endless in her native town of Hugo, Oklahoma. Situated in the southeastern part of the state, about 120 miles north of Dallas, the town of 5,536 didn't offer many visual dreams.

The Oklahoma sun would sprinkle an amber light over the family's white three-bedroom trailer home in the country, and Lennox would awake thinking about basketball as she fought internally with herself to get out of bed and complete a host of chores before heading off to elementary school. There was hay to help haul and corn to pick, along with cleaning up around the house. Motivation was the precious hours she was allowed to play basketball on the balding court in the backyard with a rusted bicycle wheel nailed to a splintered wooden post as a makeshift hoop. She played against her brothers and area boys, needing to steal the ball and shoot quickly, otherwise she'd "never touch it" because no one would pass to a girl.

"I was an outdoor person," said Lennox, the youngest of nine. "My sisters would put dresses on, nails and makeup. They'd want to go in there and cook all together and I just wasn't into that. I can't wear a dress and play basketball! When we went to church, yeah I had a dress. But I'm not fond of dresses too much. I liked to be active."

Three-on-three basketball, where 12 players were on the court at once and none could cross the half-court line, was the only organized version of the game provided in schools, Oklahoma being the last state to convert to the traditional game for girls. That was fine, then. Lennox would grow comfortable with scoring at her end of the court at school and learn how to create a shot at home against the boys, playing until her mother screamed for them to come into the house.

When Lennox enrolled at Fort Osage High after moving to Missouri, she froze basketball practice, not moving across the court to play defense because of the rules she'd become accustomed to. Her coach had to lead Lennox into modern times, telling her to cross the half-court line and play defense or be cut from the team. After three days on the freshman team, she became a varsity starter, moving on to win a junior college national championship at Trinity Valley Community College and being named Sun Belt Conference Player of the Year at Louisiana Tech in 2000. She averaged 13.7 points and 5 rebounds under legendary coach Leon Barmore. Each season moving closer to her goal of playing for professional leagues.

"She is awesome," said Storm forward Alicia Thompson, who ran across Lennox at a USA basketball tryout in 1998. Neither would make the team, which was preparing to play in the Jones Cup in Taiwan. "I was like, who is that girl? And she didn't make the team. We could not believe it, she did so well. She was takin' people to the hole. She was showing people up. I mean, she stood out enough to where everybody was talking about her."

As a youth, the only image Lennox had of a woman advancing in basketball was through coaching. Professional leagues seemed the stuff of Hollywood, like in the 1994 sitcom "Living Single," when Olympian Cheryl Miller guest-starred as a former high school rival of Queen Latifah's character, Khadijah.

On the show, the characters dunked, blocked shots, and used deft crossover dribbles in a one-on-one game to wow a cheering crowd inside a high school gym—Khadijah telling Miller's character, "Basketball is your life." Outside the set, there weren't any stable American leagues for Miller to play in, so she missed her opportunity to be a role model for Lennox, who "didn't know of any great women basketball players until college" and didn't have cable to catch any of Barmore's famed 1980s teams. Or even Miller's feats at USC.

Still, she continued to train to reach the top level. Lennox was always in the gym. And if she wasn't there, she was on her couch watching her favorite CBS daytime soap operas.

"I can't even put into words how hard I worked," said Lennox of her youth. "It's hard for someone to continue to work at something knowing that it wasn't even existing yet. When it did exist, I'm that . . . I'm that crazy athlete that always wants to work out 24/7 just because I want to be better. Not better than everybody, but better at my job, at what I do. And I want to compete to the fullest . . . I work so hard and everybody wants to call me a gym rat or that I'm boring because I don't want to do anything but play basketball. Those people I can kind of look at and smile—not laugh—smile and be like, 'All the things you said about me and all those times you doubted me, now look at where I'm at.'"

Lennox was knocked back, again, when former Cleveland Cavaliers owner Gordon Gund put the WNBA team up for sale in the first phase of preparing to sell the NBA franchise. Gund, who lost money the entire seven years as one of the women's league's charter teams, dissolved the team in September 2003, despite having phenom NBA rookie LeBron James jolt the organization's worth by about $34 million, according to *Forbes* magazine. The sweet-natured Ohio native, who had unprecedented high school games aired on ESPN before he made the leap from prep to pros as "the next Michael Jordan" garnered sold-out attendance, merchandise sales, and television ratings for Gund. James, who knew he was headed to

Cleveland when it won the draft lottery in May 2003, was paid the NBA-regulated three-year rookie contract of $12.9 million, but also signed a $90 million contract with Nike and with other sponsors, making him worth about $200 million before playing one NBA game. The following year, Gund sold the Cavaliers to Dan Gilbert, founder of an online mortgage company, for $375 million after originally purchasing the organization for $20 million in 1983.

The Rockers, meanwhile, were 10th in the 14-team league in attendance and a playoff contender, but a weight in Gund's plans.

"I can't speak to the money being generated, but attendance-wise it was well supported. It was a good franchise in terms of fan involvement," said Hughes, reflecting back on his four seasons in Cleveland. "Sometimes when you see franchises fold, it's for various reasons and not always for a lack of attendance. If you watch what happened in Cleveland, Gund was a good owner, but we were the first step in selling the team [Cavaliers]. He was moving out of the business of basketball. Of all the franchises that folded, though, that one shocked people a little bit because they not only saw a successful franchise, but they saw the involvement with the fan base."

The Rockers had just returned from a disappointing playoff loss when they received word of Gund's plans. Hughes was called into management's office two hours before the announcement went public. Experiencing the loss of a team for the second consecutive season, Lennox began to look past basketball for the first time in her life. The league had a program with a sponsor, General Motors, and Lennox signed up for a position with the company. That off-season she'd work toward building a career while keeping in shape with a personal trainer.

Lennox's outer shell hardened even more, however. NBA players making more money was understandable—the WNBA was new and still budding. But the 27-year-old had hoped to be an established player in a city gravitating toward the new league. She didn't want to move for the third time in as many seasons, adjusting again to a new coach, players, and location.

"I was raised with little or nothing," Lennox said. "In one of those families that we couldn't get what we wanted for Christmas or anything like that. I knew I had the talent from God, and I knew I could go to college with my ability on scholarship because my mom couldn't afford it. Having an opportunity like that made me feel like I could be somebody someday. . . . My start already has been . . . not good. Four teams and stuff like that. Everybody's dream or purpose is to be part of one team and do the things [Indiana Pacers forward] Reggie Miller has done. But Reggie is part of the NBA, and we're part of the WNBA. When we have an opportunity to retire, it would be good if we had three or four years for a team. That means a lot to us just because our league is so young. I would love for something like that to happen."

The thought remained a fantasy, though, as Lennox focused on work at the GM plant, playing pickup games with guys. It was a solid gig that she actually enjoyed, in addition to weight lifting. Maybe she'd become a professional bodybuilder? Both kept her mind from worrying about the WNBA. Lennox was in line for another expansion draft and didn't know what to expect after rifts with Hughes and playing as a reserve player. She was at home when the draft was held by teleconference on January 6, 2004. Selected with the sixth overall pick, though, she was exactly what new Storm coach Anne Donovan was looking for to fill out a youthful roster. Lennox wasn't big, but she was versatile and electric. If Storm fans gave her a chance and Donovan was correct about her evaluation, Lennox would draw fans to KeyArena as the third prong in Seattle's foundation.

By 2003, women's basketball on the elite level was back in Seattle. Too bad it came from opposing teams and not the majority of the talent on the Storm roster. Needing to act quickly in a "prove it" society, the Storm sought to unearth that sparkling player who would make the city show up to see them play whether it was in a cramped gym or spacious arena. Not that No. 1 overall draft picks Lauren Jackson and guard Sue Bird were slouches. But, compiling a 35-31 record in their two seasons together, they had an inside-out game

Storm guard Betty Lennox (third from right) poses with her brothers, sisters, and other relatives, most of whom played basketball. Lennox learned the game from her brothers, though, following them to the court. (COURTESY OF BETTY LENNOX)

that was too easy for teams to defend, combining to lead the team in scoring in 59 of those 66 games. To spread the defense out, the Storm needed more consistent offensive fire. Yet fans were willing to suffer through the growing pains. It's what made the region unique.

The Portland Fire and the Storm enjoyed rowdy, basketball-educated crowds that showed up for anything their teams hosted to give support. The Northwest expansion teams organized chartered buses when they played each other to pack their respective arenas with a cross-section of fans, and people would wait at the airport, practice facility, or arena parking gates in rain or sunshine, on the road or at home, just to get autographs. Seeing familiar hardcore fans pop up in New York for Storm road games or Australia to catch Jackson during the off-season startled the players at times but demonstrated the shared passion for the game.

Outside the Pacific Northwest, other teams weren't feeling the love to the same extent. Empty seats, failed promotions, and disinterest by owners were signs Lennox had seen too often. The possibility of it happening again made her apprehensive. But the lure of 2000 and the threat of not achieving her goal of being the league's top player ignited her solitary workouts.

She wouldn't walk into Seattle with an open heart, though. Lennox was slightly guarded when she first spoke to her new coach, wondering what reputation had preceded her. A positive was assistant coach Jenny Boucek, who knew Lennox from their days at Miami, where Boucek served as an assistant coach. Lennox had given herself to God after her father passed away when she was a teenager, and Boucek was a devout Christian herself, peering through Lennox's perceived hard exterior into the gentle-natured person she was inside.

As Lennox listened to Donovan in that first telephone conversation, the shooting guard began to think Seattle might be the place for a rebirth. She'd give it a try, arriving in March before the May training camp opened, working out alone with a chair as an opponent in the team's training facility, and rediscovering her smiling face for various community appearances to introduce herself to the city.

"My goal was to become the most improved player," Lennox said. "When Anne drafted me she told me what she wanted me to do: 'I want you to play behind Sue Bird and Lauren Jackson.' When there was a spot that needed to be plugged in, I was the person to plug it up. Just to kind of take up their slack. Whatever they needed from me, I did it."

Lennox was changing. The league forced her to do so. The eight tattoos inked into her skin no longer symbolized her completely. If she could, she'd at least wash the tangled barbed wire and "duce duce" tats off her brown skin because of their assumed gang ties to unveil the new woman she now strived to be. She snarled on the court, but that was just her baller's style. Off the court, she melted the trash talk into comical ribbing and was very giving, especially to young fans, who flocked to her magnetic charms and related to her diminutive stature.

Whether she liked it or not, Lennox would be pulled into the vortex of Seattle's women's basketball bubble.

CHAPTER TEN

That Championship Season

Every season starts the same. Lights flicker on in a stale gym, with racks of freshly pumped basketballs along the baseline of a newly waxed court dotted with hoops measured precisely. Faint memories of seasons past drift through as the sound of light bulbs warming to their brightness buzz above. On that first day, carpets bear witness to where vacuums recently grazed their surfaces, and everything from chairs to name tags in the locker rooms stand guard, positioned to take on a new challenge.

Across the WNBA, players trickle into a similar spring setting, some still stumbling over NBA remnants as their brethren teams head deeper into their postseason. Others only acknowledge their counterparts through whiffs of their dried sweat in the stale air. The chatter is usually an extended conversation from the night before, when most returned to their summer homes. There are details to be worked out like housing accommodations, the fit of practice jerseys, or which players are sharing rental cars. Once the first practice begins, every team in every city says the same thing—this is the year we win a championship.

For some it's not a joke. The Houston Comets won the four initial WNBA championships. The Los Angeles Sparks have been in the conference finals six consecutive times and the WNBA Finals three times, winning the championship twice. The New York Liberty has always been the Eastern Conference playoff representative, while the Detroit Shock made the Cinderella turnaround of cellar dweller to champion in 2003. Other teams boast bold proclamations and ignore the snickers from those who would judge the future on the past. The Connecticut Sun winning the championship, for example, seemed as likely as Paris Hilton winning an Emmy, especially since the Sun started the 2004 season with six new faces, including five rookies.

And the Storm players? They bopped around with chests proud like puffer fish and attitudes equal to the species' deadly poison. From their three-time Olympic coach to the starting lineup featuring four past All-Stars, their talent and capability were apparent. But the team didn't even make the playoffs in 2003 and was neatly swept in two games by the Sparks in the first round of the 2002 postseason. Seattle was an expansion team with a pair of youthful stars barely old enough to mosey up to an American bar and order a cocktail. (Although in Australia, Lauren Jackson has no problem playing the part of Tom Cruise in *Cocktail*, getting patrons sloshed at friends' bars.)

Winning a championship is why they were brought together. And winning a championship is all they talked about the first day the players started getting to know each other on the freshly waxed court.

Lennox was the first to arrive, making appearances around the Puget Sound. On the court, she's brash and tough, but in the weeks waiting for her new teammates to arrive, she was nervous, eager for someone to appear. Finally, after working out on her own, she saw Sue Bird walk through the parking lot one day, packing boxes into her car.

"Hey, ya need help?" Lennox asked her new point guard.

"That's not what I was expecting at all from Betty. Not that I wasn't expecting it, but she doesn't know me from a hole in the wall and yet she was very eager to be helping me and go out of her way," said Bird, who was thankful the Storm drafted Lennox so she didn't have to guard the shooting guard anymore. "She wanted to make it work and saw that this could be a good place for her. The only thing I knew about her was that she was really tough to guard and that she spoke in the third person."

Bird was Lennox's first chance to show her changed approach to her profession. But the sharpshooter with the supposed sharp tongue knew it was going to be more than lifting boxes. There was still practice and trying to blend in on a team with two well-established stars and six new faces. At least those faces weren't completely unfamiliar. The day before the WNBA's college/international draft in April, Anne Donovan, in her new role as director of player personnel, traded her sixth draft choice to Minnesota for veteran small forward Sheri Sam and emerging center Janell Burse. Both were former teammates of Lennox's, Sam in Miami (2002) and Burse in Minnesota (2001). Burse and Lennox had initiated a close friendship, calling each other to vent or offer encouragement long after they were teammates.

The trade was stunning, especially since the Storm had had a high pick in the league's deepest draft since the merger of ABL players in 1999. The 2004 list included names like Diana Taurasi and Nicole Powell. Plus, Minnesota had edged Seattle for the playoffs in 2003 partly due to the play of Sam and Burse, beating Seattle 3-1 in the regular season series to break a tied 18-16 overall finish. But the Lynx, with slumping attendance, was desperate to draft point guard Lindsay Whalen, who had built the fan base for the University of Minnesota as a state native with a frank charisma as on-point as her no-look passes. The Lynx didn't want to let go of Burse, but Donovan wouldn't budge without her being part of the deal. A New Orleans native, Burse had started the final 14 games of the 2003 season, averaging 11.9 points and 6.2 rebounds to help Minnesota secure the fourth and final playoff seed. By the end of the business day on Thursday, April 15, the Lynx had its draft pick and forward Amanda Lassiter, while Donovan received what she believed to be the final pieces to her championship puzzle. The only thing left was practice.

"When I first got here it was difficult because we didn't know each other," Lennox said. "I knew what Lauren could do, I knew what Sue could do, and I guess they didn't put the thought and effort into seeing what I could do in the past. But it's kind of hard to see what I've done in the past when, as people say, I was inconsistent and jerked around—just haven't had that opportunity. But I always knew, I always trusted my heart that once I got that opportunity, I could just let my ability show for itself."

Lennox may have entered training camp as a teammate who had played a minor reserve role for the past two WNBA seasons, but she immediately jumped out as the Storm's starting shooting guard with athletic capabilities. Alongside Bird, she was able to exploit her talent, but the trick was playing within Donovan's system, which the coach was strict about. Lennox also had to understand that she wasn't the No. 1 option. The Storm was still going to run its pick-and-roll with Jackson and Bird. Lennox and Sam, who ranked among the game's top five scorers, needed to create off that scheme.

Still, Donovan tried to keep her starting lineup under wraps the first week of training. One glance and it was clear. Media began to peg the starting five as Lennox and Sam with Bird, the steady maestro; Jackson, the gifted MVP; and Vodichkova, the sturdy veteran banger inside. Off the bench were five former starters and two little-used rookies in Michelle Greco and Trina Frierson, who underwent knee surgery and sat out the majority of the season.

"Playing off a strong point guard is very advantageous to Betty," said San Antonio coach Dan Hughes, who coached Lennox in Cleveland. "Sue is an absolute key to Betty. That Sue is an outstanding point guard gives Betty the right vehicle to be successful."

Of the other reserves, gritty Australian guard Tully Bevilaqua, Bird's backup, had the potential to make the most impact because of her improved offensive capabilities that she had worked to hone in the off-season and her signature style of aggressive defense. A chance for the title seemed possible.

Storm fans were quick to idolize guard **Betty Lennox**, the team's second leading scorer since arriving in 2004. (LATRENA SMITH PHOTOGRAPHY)

The Storm front office helped propel the lofty championship goal by running its "Bring It" marketing campaign, designed by the Seattle-based firm Sedgwick Rd., for a second year. The Storm plastered Metro buses and bought newspaper ads showing a tunnel with Jackson and Bird silhouetted before a beaming white glow. From that first day, Bird and Jackson would comment that something felt different. A confidence was engulfing them. "Everywhere I went, people shouted 'Bring It' or asked 'Are you gonna Bring It?' It was really catching on," said Bird.

Then Seattle traveled to Phoenix for its debut exhibition game and was encircled by a plucky team led by Taurasi, the hyped No. 1 overall draft pick.

The Mercury, who had won only eight games the previous season and featured five players with two or less years' experience in the WNBA, used athleticism to hand the Storm its worst loss in franchise history: 83-44. Although exhibition games don't count toward official records, Phoenix players Tamara Moore and Shereka Wright bounced through America West Arena's lower corridor barking with pride. Taurasi, winner of three NCAA championships, followed behind and after giving former University of Connecticut teammate Bird a noogie, Taurasi reminded her team that the Storm didn't have Lauren Jackson. Jackson, the 2003 MVP, chomped bubble gum on the bench, sidelined due to a groin injury. Alicia Thompson, who had returned to the league after a one-year absence from being cut in Indiana, replaced her in the lineup. Donovan also was forced to play five inexperienced training camp invitees because of foul trouble and a missing Vodichkova, who hadn't arrived to camp after completing her Russian season.

The coach was more inclined to side with Moore and Wright's animated smugness following the defeat. Donovan never looked so befuddled in her entire life. Her team had executed its offense flawlessly in a scrimmage against the Chinese national team. They were quickly picking up her schemes in training camp and were creating a chemistry unimaginable even in the simulated reality of video games. Donovan watched the tape of the exhibition game three times and still couldn't believe the magnitude of ineptness. The Storm players were immediately shuffled back to the training facility after landing in Seattle around 1 PM the next day and were forced into the locker room for a viewing. They winced at the missed shots. Sighed at the blown defensive coverage. Shook their heads at the 39-point conclusion. Donovan snapped. Then she briskly walked to the practice court and snapped at the men's practice players brought on board as volunteers to give the Storm stronger opponents to build strength against.

"You're responsible for this loss too," she said, towering over the men gathered in a semicircle around her. They looked right back at her, absorbing their lashing. The men, an assembled collection of varying talent from college to former high school stars, were a crucial part of Donovan's plan to keep her team healthy by not having to practice against each other, which could lead to injury, and improving competition. The guys, led by Mike Lawson, who trains athletes through the Redmond Athletic Club, picked up their intensity. Wearing green mesh jerseys, they viewed themselves as part of the Storm, wanting the women to succeed as an extension of their work.

"Some guys were going through the motions, a little awestruck because you see the players on billboards and buses," Lawson, 38, told the *Seattle Times*. "But after that, everybody understood."

Practices became feisty. Donovan, a marvel center during her playing days, clamped down on the post players to juice every drop of talent from their veins. She'd spend 10-hour days at the facility, working one-on-one with Jackson and preparing scouting reports for the upcoming season. The "fellas," as Donovan called the group of male practice players, would leave the facility soaked in sweat as if they'd just ran out of a shower, exhausted from bodying-up against the strong women.

At times tempers flared, but 12 days later the Storm opened the season at KeyArena. Before the game Howard Schultz gave a speech to the promising team. "He pulled us all aside and told us we've got to make something happen," Jackson remembered. The Storm responded by beating Minnesota 88-85. This time Jackson was on the court, scoring 31 points. After the game she folded her body like the Dalai Lama and pondered on the future. She had seen it in Minnesota center Nicole Ohlde, who mirrors Jackson's build and at 22 was only one year younger, but lagged three years behind in WNBA experience. Nicole didn't play like it that night. The No. 6 draft pick out of Kansas State, whom the Storm could've selected if it hadn't made the trade, posted a double-double in her debut with 16 points and 10 rebounds, forcing Jackson to admit she needed more conditioning. Two days later Jackson scored 16 points in a 93-67 rout at home against Los Angeles and was backed up offensively by Lennox's team-high 20 points. Nine Storm players scored in double figures as they handed the Sparks their first season-opening loss since their inaugural season in 1997.

It was a glimpse of how the pieces of Donovan's championship tableau could fit together. Still, positive vibes were chased again by negatives as the Storm players packed their duffel bags and headed on the road for two away games.

Seattle promptly lost both, again to Phoenix with its matrix defense, and to Los Angeles, who was bitter from the 26-point loss six days earlier. Seattle is notoriously incompetent on the road, as are the majority of the WNBA teams. In 2003, only Los Angeles (13-4) and Detroit (12-5) had winning records outside the comforts of their home arena. The rest of the league played villain in the sport's subplot of good versus evil, losing in often heroic efforts to the home team. The Storm compiled a 5-12 road record in 2003, one of the main reasons it didn't advance to the postseason.

It's not like the Storm is a wild crew on the road. There are groupies, but nothing like the NBA, whose players actually have road phones to keep up with the action. WNBA players typically hang with their opponents on nights before games, like when UConn alumnae Bird and Taurasi are spotted eating dinner at Marjle's in Phoenix. Otherwise bundles of team friends like Vodichkova and Simone Edwards will lug takeout back to their hotel rooms and chill while watching silly movies on television.

On June 4 the team checked into the Hyatt Regency in Sacramento. The procedure would be a hectic one if it weren't for director of operations Missy Bequette, who's been with the team since its inception. She takes a cab to beat the team to the airport to pre-check in the players and staff, so when they arrive on a chartered bus about an hour later, all they have to do is grab their tickets and stand in the security checkpoint line. Once the team lands, Bequette again boogies ahead of the pack to the hotel to make sure the rooms are ready, organize the keys, and prepare any special instructions for the team. Players, sometimes droopy-eyed from early flights, grab their bags and shuffle to their rooms to freshen up.

"Traveling with the team for away games gives me an appreciation for the players' commitment to and love of the game," said Jack Rodgers, who schedules a few road games into his itinerary every summer. "Getting up at 5 AM, killing time in airports, navigating long security lines, and oftentimes sitting in coach middle seats. Ugh! That was no fun."

In Sacramento, there are always people for the Storm players to see, since Sam's off-season home in San Jose is about two hours away and Adia Barnes, a San Diego native, has friends in the city. The Hyatt also is located at the foot of the state capitol, which is surrounded by a park, the perfect setting for assistant coach Jenny Boucek and trainer Annmarie Henkel to go on a quick run while warming their rain-soaked bones under the California sunrays.

The point of the trip is the game. And in Sacramento, that's always been a point of frustration. The Storm had lost seven consecutive games at Arco Arena, an oddly placed facility just outside of downtown. The Monarchs, one of the eight WNBA charter teams, seemed to enjoy reminding the Storm it still hadn't fully kicked off its "expansion franchise" dress.

Storm newcomers like Lennox and Sam didn't particularly care about their new team's past or road curse, however. They were successful players who were going to finish their careers on top, and this was the team that was going to take them there.

"I remember reading some of [Lennox's] quotes early on and [she was] like, 'Yeah, I know this is Sue and Lauren's team and I'm just here to help in any way I can,'" Bird said. "That definitely downplays how important she is. She just hits big shots. When she was drafted, I thought, 'Thank God, I never have to guard that girl again,' you know? She's had a little bit of a tough career before she got to Seattle, being bounced around and every team she ended up on ended up folding. It's hard because part of being able to play to your full potential is being comfortable. Regardless, though, she's really hard to guard and can score over anybody. It's pretty impressive when you see it."

The Storm needed oomph—especially on the road. Jackson was candid with a tinge of duplicity. She'd crack on how her body felt like she was 42 and tease that after five years in the league, she was still not much older than the college rookies on her team, who were 22. The 24-year-old Aussie had no problem getting in her teammates'

Players gather in a pregame huddle, where Sue Bird often does a freestyle rap to pump up the team. (LATRENA SMITH PHOTOGRAPHY)

faces to tell them to get in gear or get her the ball because she's feeling that player's zone where the basket is the size of a wading pool. But at times her humility quelled her will. Jackson, as the star everyone looked to, needed someone to show her how to bring that leadership to the team. Lennox and Sam were perfect candidates.

Lennox, the 5-foot-8 guard who's really closer to 5-foot-5 sans Nikes, oozed attitude with a growling accent on her face. It was a defense mechanism from years of playing with boys and dealing with coaches who didn't understand her playground style. Lennox was tenacious. When she went to work on the court guys in the stands would say, practically in unison, "Now *that's* a baller," after a look at her jump shot.

But it was Sam, a 6-foot forward, who was able to relate that strong-willed attitude to Jackson. Only Sam, then 30, exuded a Rasta coolness, with dreadlocks and a Bob Marley tattoo. Her socks pulled high and a headband made her look like a flashback player, but her game was modern—exuding the expected small forward's role to make contributions on defense and offense. She'd put Jackson in her place if needed, but she also helped the Aussie become a leader, much like former guard Sonja Henning had helped Jackson learn when she first entered the league in 2001.

"I have to remind her who's older sometimes," Sam said.

Neither Lennox nor Sam liked to lose. Unlike Jackson, who had a tendency to turn bitter in her youth if the opposition pulled away point-wise, the veterans fought nastiness with aggressiveness. The Storm began to understand this trick in Sacramento.

Shootaround was its usual lively affair that concluded with the players taking half-court shots for 50 bucks of coach Anne Donovan's money. No one made the shot, but Sam was determined. "Save it up for the game," Donovan shouted to her starter. Sam flung up one more attempt, then headed to the bus. In the game Sam scored nine points as Seattle built a 32-11 lead. The Monarchs don't back down that easily, though. Sacramento started three players who are 6-foot-4 and had the flashiest point guard in the league in Ticha Penicheiro, the WNBA's career leader in assists (1,591). With 1.4 seconds remaining, the score was tied at 63 points, and the crowd of 7,094 was screaming with nervous excitement. Seattle was on a nine-game road losing streak, dating back to an ugly nationally televised loss in Detroit on July 18, 2003. Plus, the Storm was the last of the 13 teams to collect a road win that summer.

The fate of the season seemed to be balled up in Lennox's palm as she drove to the basket, stopped, and flung an awkward shot, leaping off her back foot over the outstretched 6-foot-4 body of Sacramento forward DeMya Walker. The basketball dropped through the hoop, and Lennox tipped her head back to roar at the upper rafters. After Sacramento center Yolanda Griffith's attempt rimmed out of the basket, Seattle, stealing a 65-63 victory, celebrated its new road-winning attitude. The moxie continued with convincing wins in New York, where the Storm embarrassed the Liberty 86-62 on their famed Madison Square Garden court, proclaiming themselves a defensive force, and in Houston, where they beat the four-time champion Comets 69-63. By the time the Storm defeated San Antonio 74-61 at the SBC Center, Seattle had pieced together a franchise-record six-game win streak and won for the first time in four different arenas. The Storm had the WNBA's best record at 8-2, the team's best start in franchise history.

The delighted atmosphere extended away from the training facility and KeyArena. A tad cliquish, the Storm had formed deep-rooted bonds of friendship. Co-captains Jackson and Bird, known to everyone as LJ and Birdy, became closer as the season progressed, along with Bevilaqua, Barnes, Sam, and Alicia Thompson, who was dubbed Chelle.

When LJ traded her MVP-prize SUV for a sporty silver Jeep, Birdy was the first to get a call about the new ride. "They're so competitive with each other, it's funny," said Barnes that season. One of the more humorous times to witness the pair was at the end of practice, when Donovan had each pick teams for a shooting drill/competition. The intensity was as big as Game 3 in the WNBA Finals as they tried to get teammates to make shots to beat each other. Whoever won got to pick the punishment, Jackson often going for the throat with push-ups or running. Bird often picked jumping jacks, not wanting teammates to hate her.

The duo sat behind each other on bus rides to and from road practices or games, constantly text-messaging the other on their cell phones. The only thing they couldn't share was their iPods, Birdy preferring the rapping beats of her East Coast roots, and LJ listening to everything but.

"I do like Usher because of her," said Jackson of the touch of hip-hop flavor she grew to appreciate. Otherwise it was Basement Jaxx and Nine Inch Nails thumping in her ears.

Basketball definitely opened up the relationship. All Bird could think about prior to arriving in Seattle when drafted in 2002 was how Hawaii was the only thing farther from her New York home in the quaint Long Island suburb of Syosset. She grew up in a Norman Rockwell painting, where streets named after flowers depicted the same beauty. Her mother, Nancy, still owned the childhood home where Bird would play basketball at the neighborhood park and walk to elementary school with her older sister. Cinnamon toast and hot chocolate awaited the neighborhood kids upon return at the end of snowy days, a refreshing aboveground pool and lemonade in the sticky summers.

The painting altered as Bird entered high school, her parents divorced, and she started grabbing more press as a highly acclaimed point guard. The starting five from her AAU team received Division I scholarships, Bird choosing the UConn Huskies, where she won two national titles. The home became a museum, with Bird's bedroom cluttered with trophies, the living room full of photos of the daughters with presidents (Bird's sister, Jennifer, interned on Capitol Hill), and the basement walls adorned with plaques and framed newspaper articles.

Relocating to Seattle was a change. The light shining on Bird was bright, but the magnitude a little dimmer. The crowds weren't sold out like in college, and friends, knowing which buttons to push, teased her for making a living as a professional ball player. Then there was the losing.

Bird, needing time to settle into her new environment, eventually looked to Jackson for companionship, especially since the Aussie had experience being the sole focus of a team. Now, there were two elite talents on a formidable roster.

"I had really come to appreciate Lauren," said Bird, who has been named to the WNBA's first team five times. "I didn't realize how good of a situation I was walking into. She's ridiculously good, no other players in the league do what she does, and we became best friends. We started to realize what we could do together."

"The first year was difficult because we were both so young getting to know each other and I'm sort of out there, I've never been a person to not say what I've felt," Jackson said. "Whether you like it or not, you're going to hear my opinion. Sue is completely opposite, and that's why it was really tough the first year for us to figure each other out. We did want to and we've talked about it since. But in the third year we got to know each other better and found we had a lot more in common than we knew. So, we became quite good friends and started hanging out more."

As the teammates gathered at Jack Rodgers's Mercer Island home for their annual barbecue, they were all an uncanny bunch of friends. There were all-night karaoke parties to celebrate birthdays and homemade dinners cooked by Chelle, LJ, or Simone Edwards.

At the barbecue, a catered affair begun when Dunn coached the Storm, the players loosened up with each other through water sports, volleyball, and good food. LJ commandeered one of the Seattle Police boats, getting them to take her for a ride, and Catrina Frierson serenaded Lennox and Thompson with her gospel voice while Rodgers took Donovan for a spin on a wave runner.

"As soon as I'd take some tight turns she'd yell, 'Ahhh! Don't dump me!'" said Rodgers. "The temptation was great, but then she has eight inches on me. I don't know why she didn't want me to dump her, you know that's part of the fun—go ahead and make some fast turns and dump the damn thing over." The breezy midseason picnic was a nice getaway from some injuries and complications chasing the team.

While Bird was returning to her rookie form, having successfully recovered from off-season knee surgery, Lennox suffered a broken nose in a loss to Houston in June. She missed two games due to realignment surgery and suffered from migraines that dipped her scoring average from 13.6 to 11.2 by season's end.

In July, Burse injured her right hip in practice and was diagnosed with bursitis. She also received word from her family in New Orleans that her sister had been shot in the head while sleeping in her home.

Despite breaking her nose in Game 2 of the Storm's first-round playoff series against Minnesota, All-Star guard Sue Bird averaged 8.5 points and 5.3 assists in eight games. (LATRENA SMITH PHOTOGRAPHY)

She was rushed to the hospital, and Burse immediately flew home to tend to the matter.

Burse leaned on Lennox during this dark time and the guard felt the pain as deeply as if it were her own family. She rushed to Burse's side after receiving the 2 AM call, and both relied on their faith to make sense of the situation.

"That's what best friends are for," Lennox said. "I didn't want her to take it as deep as she did because it was out of her control. It was in God's hands. It brought her closer to God and how to deal with reality. But our relationship is one of those that people should try to find—someone you can always call on no matter what."

Jackson, meanwhile, was beginning to feel her inflamed shins flare and had a minor back sprain by July. Still, she was on a roll, showing a defensive proficiency against the league's top forwards. Jackson was named Player of the Week, averaging a league-best 21.2 points after a 67-63 win against Houston at KeyArena on July 24. That game was part of a five-game winning streak, and Jackson's team-high 26 points marked her 11th game of scoring 20 points or more, including three 30-point nights.

For all the excitement inside WNBA arenas, the league was still on shaky ground. Women's sports overall receive about 10 percent of the coverage that men's do, and the *Seattle Times* was the only remaining newspaper in the country budgeting a full-time traveling beat reporter for the WNBA. The WNBA's biggest challenge in 2004 was how to handle the Summer Olympics, which landed right when the WNBA normally closes its regular season and prepares for the postseason. After off-season deliberation, the front office decided to form its schedule around the Games in Athens, Greece, giving a month-long hiatus to its 30 Olympians, including Team USA. The decision kept most players from having to skip the entire season for a chance to represent their countries at the Games, but it meant the league would resume in September, a time reserved for football and major league baseball playoffs. Olympian Dawn Staley felt Team USA had to bring home the gold medal in order for the league, having never experienced "going dark," to survive its 30-day absence from the public's eye.

Playing-wise, the Storm would have preferred to go without the hiatus. Seattle defeated Staley's Charlotte Sting 87-55 in its final game before the break, delighting the crowd of 8,338 at KeyArena with 11-for-18 shooting from the three-point line and building a 36-point lead at one time in the second half. Jackson beamed on the court, making three of five three-point attempts. The massive lead allowed Donovan to play Edwards, a crowd favorite, who grabbed eight rebounds to balance out Vodichkova, who was struggling inside. It was the Storm's largest margin of victory in the season and capped a 17-8 first stanza of play that placed them second behind Los Angeles in the conference.

Realistically, the team needed the break. Donovan was selected to be one of Houston coach Van Chancellor's assistant coaches for the national team, while Bird backed up Staley on the roster. Jackson represented the Australian national team, meaning the three critical components of the Storm would have been missing if the league hadn't halted play. The break also gave the reserves and remaining starters time to work together under the leadership of assistant coaches Jessie Kenlaw and Jenny Boucek. Lennox especially looked forward to the time, as she needed to regain her shooting confidence after breaking her nose. She'd drive to Rainier Community Center or stay late after practice to perfect her game.

For Bevilaqua and Vodichkova the Games were tainted with ill feelings for their national federations. Both were told that returning to the WNBA would eliminate them from Olympic eligibility, yet both disregarded the threat that became reality. Vodichkova felt she owed Storm fans after suffering a sprained left ankle in 2003 and hearing the crowd's appreciation for her play.

"I felt it was my duty to get back and play," Vodichkova told the *Seattle Times*. "They [the Czech Republic] didn't believe my injury was real and blamed Anne. It wasn't a smart decision, and if their decisions are going to be like this, I don't want to play with them."

The Australian Opals were tangled in a thick political web, too. Coach Jan Stirling was unpopular with players, making questionable decisions, and used the Olympic year to exert her power. She couldn't control Jackson, the country's top player, but she could stifle "bubble" players like Bevilaqua, who was told her chances of making the team would be nil if she played the WNBA season instead of training with the national team. But Bevilaqua was never given any guarantees she'd make the team if she had stayed. She left, and despite her improved play wasn't named to the Olympic roster.

"I made the decision a while ago because I had so much fun last season and thought my best chances to make a team would be here," Bevilaqua told the *Seattle Times* in training camp. "I'm trying to keep my feet on the ground."

Sam didn't join in the bonding extra workouts. She decided to travel to Athens to see her close friends, Jackson and guard Shannon Johnson (San Antonio), compete in the gold medal game, a decision that would later disturb Donovan.

While the players were in Greece, they were dubbed pitchmen for the women's game, an antithesis to Team USA's men's team. Although both teams stayed on the *Queen Mary*, a yacht that would normally cost $5,000 a night, the women spread goodwill, answering every question and arriving for every interview because they knew how the grand stage of the Olympics played a part for a woman athlete in everything from marketing deals to the pure visibility of the WNBA. The men, on the other hand, noticeably complained about playing time and practice, and eventually lost the gold for the first time since using professional players.

Jackson, taking cortisone shots to play on an injured left ankle, was a beacon in the Greek setting, steamrolling her country to the gold medal match as the Olympic Games' leading scorer (22.9 points). Bird, however, was relegated to junk minutes and did more cheering than playing. Team USA averaged 84 points while holding opponents to 60.3 as it tore through its bracket. Three-time Olympian Lisa Leslie was the leading scorer (15.6) and rebounder (8.0) as the Americans prepared for a rematch against the Australians for gold.

But Jackson didn't perform as she'd dreamed about so many times leading up to the Games. She had promised herself she'd win the gold for her mother, who hadn't competed as an Olympian because of the decision to have children. The daughter wanted retribution, but the Americans were the best opponents the Opals faced, and Jackson was ineffective offensively. The ball didn't move her way and frustration began to consume her. Still the Aussies led 38-34 with 5:44 remaining in the third quarter. Forward Penny Taylor (who played for the Phoenix Mercury) was leading the Opals offensively while Jackson was working underneath the hoop, grabbing rebounds. But by the fourth quarter, the American roster proved to be too loaded with talent. Forward Tina Thompson was breaking away from the

Aussie defense for open looks, scoring a game-high 18 points. Her dish inside to Leslie with 2:08 remaining pushed the Americans' lead to nine points, and Team USA simply held on for a 74-63 win. The final buzzer brought tears to both teams. Jackson managed to turn hers into joy, doing cartwheels and jumping around with fans to try to celebrate the silver medal.

It was the last time her heart beat with pure innocence. Before returning to Seattle to resume the WNBA season, Jackson was told by her mother that her grandmother was ill and had been admitted into a hospital. Donovan encouraged Jackson to go home to Australia, but Jackson's mind swirled with thoughts. She didn't fully comprehend the severity of her maternal grandmother's illness, how much time she had, or whether her teammates would understand her absence as they headed into the playoffs.

Jackson returned to Seattle for one day and couldn't stay. Her ankle was unbearable from the all-out Olympic play, and her mind was thinking about Nan Irene, the 83-year-old grandmother who had practically raised her. Jackson changed plans, hopping another flight to return to her birthplace in Albury.

While she spent time with her family, consoling her mother and trying to make her nana feel comfortable, the Storm started a decline. Donovan benched Sam, disappointed in her decision not to train during the hiatus and wanting to reward Thompson for improving. Regardless of the change, the team was not the same without Jackson. Bird had a fire burning in her eyes after being around veteran Olympians Staley, Leslie, and Swoopes, averaging 19.5 points in Seattle's four post-Olympic games. But the team that she was now in sole control of lost three games following the break.

One of the consecutive losses was on the road at Los Angeles, where Sparks guard Tamecka Dixon elevated her trash talking into pushing Lennox with the score tied at 81 points late in the second half. Dixon, who scored 20 points in the win, popped her jersey to show off her electric scoring night, hitting a nerve with Lennox. Once the guard shoved Lennox in the face to gain control of the ball, Lennox responded, and a scuffle occurred in front of the Storm bench. The two had to be separated by teammates, Thompson leaping from her seat to do so. The emotion wasn't just normal spite for the rivals. The Storm, who had won seven of eight games entering the Olympic break, had a chance to overtake the Sparks to win the regular-season conference title. Los Angeles started two rookies in place of veterans Mwadi Mabika, the team's second-leading scorer, and DeLisha Milton-Jones, making the goal more realistic. Despite leading in most important statistical categories, Seattle lost 82-81. Lennox and Thompson were fined $500 apiece for fighting, Thompson also getting a one-game suspension for leaving the bench. Dixon, who was ejected from the game, was also fined $500. Jackson, halfheartedly keeping up with the team through stories posted on the Internet and some phone calls, returned for the Storm's game against Detroit, but her mood was heavy. In addition to her grandmother's condition, she had to adjust to playing with Bird and Donovan again, post-Olympics.

"The first couple of practices I was thinking, 'Shit. I hate you,' because we really wanted to win the gold," Jackson said. "We worked so hard and there they are with it."

Jackson had traveled to three continents in the span of nine days, saying she was "dazed and confused" upon arriving in Seattle. Her teammates had to rely on their own energy to climb out of an 18-5 deficit against the Shock, mostly inspired by Lennox's improved offense, using her creativity to knock the defense off balance. Bird clicked after halftime, shooting 8-for-9 from the field, finishing with a game-high 23 points in a 86-67 win at KeyArena. The Storm clung to its second-place standing in the Western Conference as it traveled to play Minnesota, who closely trailed them at the time. But the team showed its youth and laziness, watching for Jackson to make something happen and losing 64-61.

Donovan, noticing a trend, separated herself from the team following a 71-64 loss in Connecticut on national television. She was calm even though Sun guard Katie Douglas was the second player in as many games to have a sparkling performance against

Seattle's defense, finishing with 21 points. Sure, the Storm had had a harsh traveling schedule, waking at 5 AM to depart Minneapolis and practicing after an hour's bus ride from the airport in Hartford, Connecticut, to the Sun's location on the Mohegan Indian reservation. The 2 PM matchup hadn't allowed time for a shootaround, but that was standard procedure for the WNBA. If the Storm, who had still clinched a playoff berth, couldn't find a way to pull themselves together, Donovan knew she certainly couldn't. The Storm ended the three-game trip with a 76-70 win at Indiana. Jackson scored a game-high 20 points, supported by Bird's seven assists, and had nine rebounds. But the problems didn't disappear.

Owner Howard Schultz awaited his Storm when they returned to Seattle. Practically jumping the players as they filed off the bus at the training facility Tuesday afternoon, he started rambling to Donovan about the sense of urgency, the magnitude of losing, and the implications of recognizing where and who they were. He paused for a breath. Donovan cut in.

"Howard, you know you're preaching to the choir," she said.

He stopped talking.

"I think they would really like to hear that from you," she continued, pointing to the players' locker room. The team was dropping their stuff and assembling to review game tape. Donovan had already cancelled practice, giving the players a break since they had to host Phoenix at KeyArena the following day.

Schultz, nattily dressed in slacks and a sweater, walked in. He motioned for the women to gather around, stood before them, and started to speak. "The power is yours," he implored.

"It was about somebody who personally knows what success is," Donovan said of listening to Schultz speak to her team. "Not as the owner that has taken on the Storm as his pet project. Not as a fan. Just as somebody who saw great potential and didn't want these people to let that potential pass."

The talk resonated with the players, especially the reserves. On September 15, Simone Edwards and Bevilaqua helped to outscore the Mercury bench 21-15 in a second rally to win 73-58 before 7,855 fans.

The Storm still slipped, which wasn't the way they wanted to enter the postseason. When Lennox's possible tying three-point shot at the buzzer of a home game against Los Angeles rimmed out of the hoop, sealing an 83-80 loss to end the regular season, the Storm had won only three of its nine games after the Olympic break. The record crowd of 14,884 belted its chant of "Beat L-A" and "M-V-P" for Jackson, but the chemistry built before the Games had evaporated on the court. There were too many off-court circumstances consuming the team. Burse's sister was in a coma and still needed medical treatment. Hurricane Ivan was cutting a swath through Edwards's native Jamaica home. Jackson's grandmother's condition was deteriorating. The players wanted to shed their collective skin and start anew.

"In the second half of the season, there's been a lot of hardships, tears, and a lot of hugging," Jackson told the *Seattle Times.* "We'll have some time to regroup as a team and get back to where we were before the break, playing awesome again. It's all character building."

Daylight hit her eyes and a groggy Jackson reached for her ringing cell. It was her mother, who was sobbing, wanting to complete a sentence but unable to. Jackson, confused, didn't know what to think. In a blur, she heard something about her "Nan Irene" and "that morning" and "died." Jackson threw the telephone. "I've got to hang up," she told her mother.

"That sort of freaked me out a little bit, I just broke down and that was it. I was gone for the rest of the day. I wanted to go home, but I couldn't because . . ." Jackson's voice trails off. It's too superficial to say you prefer a WNBA championship over being with your family after a death. And that wasn't really the case, but it's how it looked to anyone outside the family. The Jacksons encouraged Lauren to return to Seattle to vie for the WNBA title. Her mother even had an agreement with Donovan that she would call the coach first with the news of the death so Donovan could be in the room with Jackson as her mother told her.

It didn't happen that way. Jackson's eyes started to fill with tears. Then there was a knock at her door. It was Donovan.

On the road the eve before Game 1 of the first-round playoff series against the third-seeded Minnesota Lynx, Donovan was a split-second late due to waiting for the elevator to ride down to Jackson's room at the Radisson Hotel. On that windy Friday in September, Maree couldn't wait. She called her daughter back and softly said her grandmother had died of natural causes.

"She was a complete mess," Donovan said of Jackson's condition. The two left the hotel and walked around the corner to Starbucks. With jazz playing in the background and patrons fluttering about, ordering their morning fix, Jackson and Donovan talked. "I don't think there was much coffee drank," Donovan said.

Jackson's agony was hardest to watch. Donovan was swallowing her own pain that season, losing her mother to a heart attack in January. Her mother was Donovan's biggest fan, keeping up with her coaching career and holding on to dated pictures, including high school photos in which Donovan played in yellow bloomers and first realized she could succeed at the sport.

Donovan didn't allow herself to give much thought to memories of her mother's smile, kind words, or quirky ways until seated across from Jackson, who wept about everything for her grandmother. She hid behind basketball. Donovan again told Jackson, however, that she could go home to be with her family, that everyone would understand, but the Jacksons had already agreed that when Lauren returned, she'd stay until the end of the playoffs. At the time, they didn't think her grandmother would pass so quickly.

"[Jackson] didn't miss a practice, didn't miss a shootaround, she was right there every step of the way," Donovan said. "Out of it, very much out of it. Very professional, going through the motions on the court, trying to lose herself in the moment of basketball."

The Storm's championship season attracted several local athletes. Sonics All-Star Rashard Lewis and forward Reggie Evans caught a game along with NBA legend Bill Russell, a Storm regular. (LATRENA SMITH PHOTOGRAPHY)

The Minnesota game was a noon tip-off at the Target Center just a few blocks down the street, practically visible from a few of the players' rooms. Jackson didn't sleep, feeling even more alone inside the room miles from her Seattle condo and worlds away from her heartbroken family in Australia.

Puffy-eyed with a reddened nose, she started the game strong, barreling down for the opening tip against Ohlde with her blond hair in a tangled, messy bun and pale blue eyes directed at the basketball. Around Jackson's left bicep was a strip of black electrical tape, a tradition for Australian players who've lost a loved one. Jackson, feeling isolated, expected to be the only one wearing the symbol but was surprised when her teammates also grabbed the tape and wrapped it around their jerseys, wrists, forearms, and biceps in solidarity. Jackson was playing for her grandmother, and the only way being separated from her family would feel right was if the team won the championship. Her teammates understood, wanting to win for their own reasons too, but when the point was brought up in a pregame huddle, Jackson broke down in tears. Quickly, she wiped them away and tried to drown herself in the game.

Four minutes after play started, she was back on the bench with three fouls. She sat hunched over, trying not to think about anything but basketball. It was hard. As much as playoff fever may hit the players, sometimes it doesn't carry over to the general public. The official attendance was announced as 4,277, but the arena, which seats 19,000, looked empty. And with the Storm dominating 9-1 at the time she left the game, it was deafeningly quiet, not enough to distract her from the thoughts in her head.

By the second half, Jackson was determined to stay on the court. She was part of the Storm's 55.6 percent shooting from the field to collect the franchise's first playoff win, 70-58. Jackson scored a team-high 14 points, but Seattle was paced by Sam, who had 11 points, 10 rebounds, and seven assists. Everyone scored in the game, even Lennox, who suffered a minor concussion and was replaced by Thompson in the second half. The Lynx, who were less experienced and not as deep as the Storm, were simply overpowered, even if Jackson wasn't playing to her full potential.

"There was a glaze over her eyes," Donovan said.

Jackson remained professional, however, walking to the podium to answer questions before a WNBA playoffs backdrop. In the best-of-three series, her team had the chance to sweep the Lynx with a win at KeyArena on Monday, September 27. After mumbling a few replies about the game, she crumbled again into tears in the Target Center corridors.

"Talking about it makes it real and makes you have to deal with your emotions in front of other people," said Donovan, who stood a few feet from the power forward as she tried to keep her cool in front of media while telling little anecdotes about her nana. "She definitely was not the same kid."

Feeling confident, the Storm was struck with a different blow in Game 2 of the series. A hyper crowd of 7,261 collectively stopped breathing when Bird plopped on the court after Lynx guard Teresa Edwards smacked into her face, breaking Bird's nose neatly across the bridge three minutes into the game. Edwards was crushed. Although the incident had been completely accidental, she expressed extreme guilt after the game and wanted Bird to know she had meant no harm.

After a moment sitting on the court, Bird made a beeline to the locker room, cupping blood in her palms. Trainer Annmarie Henkel quickly followed, and two white towels filled with blood as they tried to stop the bleeding. Bird whizzed past the bench and Bevilaqua, but her backup didn't click that it was time to replace Bird.

"Tully! Tully! Tully, let's go!" Donovan yelled to snap the guard out of her trance.

Bevilaqua rose and had to play a season-high 27 minutes, running the team in place of Bird. The Australian, still wearing electrical tape around her biceps to support Jackson, had the crowd rocking with her nine points, including one three-pointer, four assists, and four steals. In fact, it was the Storm's bench, including Thompson and Burse, who guided the team to a 64-54 win. The reserves outscored the Lynx bench 27-16 and Burse highlighted a 14-1 Storm run to close the game with a strong layup at the 2:51 mark, ensuring the first-round sweep.

The KeyArena audience, beginning to catch on to the magical moment, started to chant "Send them home!" as Burse and Thompson displayed a smooth inside-out game during a 14-4 run. Bird, able to stop the bleeding, returned to the bench and covered her nose with cotton pads with one hand while putting a fist of supremacy in the air with the other. She shooed cameras away from filming her "broken beak," as it was called in the press, but assured everyone it wouldn't stop her from competing in the playoffs. Unlike Lennox, who had to wear a teammate's mask when she broke her nose, Bird was seeing a specialist the following day and would be fitted with a mask immediately. Donovan was doubtful, but when the Storm headed to Sacramento for Game 1 of the Western Conference finals against the Monarchs, Bird was in the starting lineup, fidgeting with an acrylic facemask.

"That's a target for any team," Lennox told the *Seattle Times*. "People don't understand how sensitive your nose is. It depends on how tough you are. You get hit, it can bring tears to your eyes. But you step back and you'll be OK, but you may not want to go inside again. It depends on how tough you are."

With dueling black eyes and swollen cheeks, Bird patted her face three times to be sure the protective mask was on correctly and started the game with a determined look. She drove her small frame inside the paint filled with 6-foot-4 bodies and still spotted clear paths to zip the ball to open teammates, helping the Storm build a 14-point first-half lead. The crowd of 10,662, wearing metallic purple wigs and rattling everything from ThunderStix to cowbells, had their spirits dampened. One woman behind the press row even sighed, "This is so depressing," as Jackson showcased her untouchable turnaround jump shot, scoring over forward Tangela Smith. "I didn't do a great job on Lauren tonight, she's a challenge," Smith said of Jackson finishing with a playoff-first 31 points and 13 rebounds. But it wasn't Seattle celebrating after the final buzzer in overtime.

Perhaps overly confident, the Storm stopped playing defense in the second half, allowing the veteran Monarchs to come back after the break. Forward DeMya Walker slithered past Burse to make a game-winning 8-foot hook shot. Ecstatic, she high-stepped marching band–style to the other end of the court, crowded by elated teammates. The purple party was in front of Seattle's bench and lasted so long, most of the players didn't even shake hands following the win. Stunned, Seattle was quiet in the locker room. Bird had missed a jump shot that could've won it in regulation. The posts were outplayed 39-20 in the second half and overtime. Sacramento had 12 steals, forcing the Storm into 16 turnovers. It wasn't the type of basketball that was going to advance them to the WNBA Finals.

Luckily, the following two games of the series were at KeyArena, since the Storm had the better regular-season record. The Monarchs had advanced to the conference finals by defeating the league's top team in Los Angeles 2-1 in the first round. The Sparks' loss meant this time it was Leslie sitting at home when she learned she had won the league's MVP award, topping Jackson by a vote of 425-351 among a panel of 48 national broadcasters and sportswriters. Although Jackson had won the regular-season scoring title, Leslie had averaged 22.9 points in eight post-Olympic games to lead the Sparks to a 25-9 finish. The scoring figure included one 31-point night and a triple-double in points (29), rebounds (15), and blocks (10) against Detroit. Leslie averaged 11.3 points and 8.7 rebounds in the three-game playoff series against Sacramento.

Jackson learned of Leslie's win in between games. The snub motivated her as she played on the playoff's grand stage before a nationally televised audience. Game 2 against Sacramento was her rebuttal, scoring 11 of her final 23 points in the first half to help the Storm build a 32-14 lead with 5:49 remaining. The Monarchs, who spoke of the game being a "war" prior to tip-off, were 1-for-7 shooting from the field to open the game, falling behind by 14 points early. Still, they laughed at intermission. Guards Ticha Penicheiro, Ruthie Bolton, and Edna Campbell, plus center Yolanda Griffith had been around the game so long they felt as if they invented it. Campbell and Griffith played in the ABL together, and Bolton was a Monarch original. Comebacks were as much a part of their style as Penicheiro's sassy no-look passes. Sure enough, they rallied to pull within 58-54 after Sheri Sam's seventh turnover led to two made free throws by DeMya Walker. But the Monarchs' 11-2 run would end there. Bird, who was aiming to win a championship on every level from high school to the Olympics and pros, showed her competitive spirit—the one that prevents her from losing even a "friendly" bowling match or cards. Bird made three of the Storm's closing five free throws and picked off a bad pass by forward Tangela Smith to give the Storm a 66-54 win. Seattle's finish was capped by an open three-pointer by Chelle Thompson at the buzzer, a move Donovan didn't particularly like because it felt a little showy. And the last thing her team needed to do was try to show up a bunch of veterans. The Storm had history on its side, however. The home team was 16-6 all-time in Game 3s of the WNBA playoffs.

"I'm so wired right now," said Jackson to the *Seattle Times.* Her offensive rebound with 36.9 seconds left set up Bird's heroics. Bird finished with 12 points and five assists. "I want to play now. It [Game 2] feels so far away and we have too much to get done in that period of time in terms of being ready."

The Monarchs, who had had their season ended in the conference finals twice by the Sparks in the past, seemed to have expended all of their energy on getting past their in-state rivals. A growing following of 8,826 fans was delirious inside KeyArena as the Storm made 12 of 18 three-pointers to defeat the Monarchs 82-62 in the decisive Game 3. Bird, who'd had realignment nose surgery two days earlier and coughed up blood during practice, orchestrated a playoff-record 14 assists as her team shot a sizzling 54.7 percent from the field. Jackson squealed "Oh, my God!" after every made three-pointer, not believing herself. The bench, again, played a critical role as Thompson came into the game with the Storm clinging to a 44-43 lead with 14:45 left, scoring seven consecutive points in a 20-0 run to help prevent a Sacramento comeback in the second half.

"Chelle won the game for us, I can't even tell you," said Jackson, who made all five of her three-point attempts in the second half, a playoff record, and led the team with 27 points. "She just brought that confidence that we needed. Without what she did, I don't know if we would have won. No, we would have won, but I don't think we would have won like that."

Confetti littered the court, and Lennox was one of the first to whip on an oversized conference championship shirt and cap, but the Storm knew there was more to come. Donovan became the first coach to lead teams in both conferences to the WNBA Finals and now she could become the first woman to win the league championship while bringing Seattle its first major sports title, men's or women's, since 1979. The lure of a title possibly coming to the Emerald City started to pique interest in the team outside of the loyal legion of followers who logged onto stormfans.org daily. Karen Bryant commented that in the past she'd had to call the other professional teams and beg them to check out a Storm game.

"They're calling me now and we barely have the tickets!" she said as Mariners outfielder Randy Winn joined members of the Seahawks, who were undefeated at the time, former Sonics forward Shawn Kemp, and Garfield High coach Joyce Walker in the stands. The WNBA Finals also brought Sonics legends Slick Watts, Fred Brown, and NBA legend Bill Russell, who were already regulars at the games.

Brown was on the Sonics roster that had won a title 25 years earlier. The city hadn't been swept with this kind of surprise since the Sonics lost 4-3 to the then Washington Bullets in the seven-game Finals series in 1978. The Sonics were expected to return to the elite stage the next year, this time defeating the Bullets 4-1. Guard Gus Williams, dubbed "The Whiz," tossed the basketball high into the Washington rafters as the Sonics sealed the championship 97-93 on the road. The team returned home to a June parade, with fans packing the downtown streets, popping shotguns in the air, and draping themselves from light posts or peeking from office windows just to get a glimpse of the champions.

Winning put a happy perk in Seattle that lasted longer than coffee, but not long enough to stretch two decades. Over time football and baseball would tease the town with that feeling, but normally it would fade fast with a loss, and people succumbed to a losing mentality. The fall of 2004 was no different. Teachers in Marysville were recouping from a 49-day strike; Boeing, having uprooted its headquarters to Chicago, had dispersed 24,000 workers since the 9/11 attacks; and national outsourcing of jobs had caused Seattle to become one of the nation's leaders in unemployment that summer.

Toss in the city's collective liberal view that the war in Iraq was unjust, and something positive to cheer about was welcomed, even the new and different women's basketball team. The Storm had just three days to sell its championship tickets, worrying the front office, but new pockets of fans clamored for the high-priced seats, ranging from $16 to $90, moving the team to open the curtain-draped upper bowl.

Three thousand miles away from the budding euphoria, Lennox couldn't sleep. Game 1 was in Connecticut, after the Eastern Conference champion Sun (18-16) swept New York to advance. The Mohegan Sun arena is located inside a smoke-filled casino with front doors steps away from slot machines. The players' rooms were also connected to the facility, meaning you'd have to step out on the pool's solarium to breathe natural air. Lennox tossed in her fluffy bed, then woke up Burse, her roommate.

"Getting that close, it's nerve-wracking. You can't sleep. You've got butterflies all in your stomach," Lennox said. "You know you should lay in bed no matter what and at least try to get off your feet for the game, but no. Me and JB, our instincts tell us to go!"

The players hustled downstairs and walked past a massive blue glass sculpture, designed by Tacoma native Dale Chihuly, where ESPN2 had decided to set up its makeshift studio. The animated noise of the slot machines is where Lennox and JB stopped. After blowing about $100 apiece, the two made their way back upstairs to talk themselves to sleep.

"Betty thought the slot machines would be warmed up by then, ready for a win," Burse said. "So, we're up at 3 AM and didn't win anything. She's funny sometimes."

What happened hours later in Game 1 was not funny. Sun coach Mike Thibault had his defensive scheme ready for Seattle's signature pick-and-roll play. He put an early end to the move between Jackson and Bird by putting 6-foot Katie Douglas on the Storm's smaller point guard. Then Connecticut double-teamed Jackson. After viewing a season's worth of tape on how to defend the three-point-loving Storm, the Sun knew exactly how to dissect its opponent. Seattle missed 10 of 16 three-point attempts and turned the ball over

17 times as Connecticut built a 14-point lead. Lennox seemed to be the only player capable of adjusting her game, leading Seattle with 17 points. But as rookie Lindsay Whalen left Bird on her butt on the final possession of the game, the Sun won the matchup 68-64 to make the top-seeded Storm look like chumps.

Bird, who's normally reserved with her emotions, screamed "Fuck!" as she tore off her green jersey and flung her face mask into her visitor's locker. Since she'd graduated from Connecticut, the state hadn't been friendly to her. Fans held hostile signs like "Give Seattle the Bird" or "Cage the Bird." A golf clap was all she received during player introductions, and even her mother admitted her youngest daughter "never played well' in the Constitution State, as if the glass structure along the bank of the Thames River were lined with kryptonite. Donovan was just as tight as her superstar, however. Jackson, who played all 40 minutes, was noticeably worn from the double coverage defense, but the coaching staff didn't move for a substitution inside until the final eight minutes of the game. Edwards entered the game then and helped the team chop a 16-point lead to two points with 17.4 seconds remaining. It was too late; the bench that had lifted the starters up until the Finals whittled away under the coaching scheme.

"Thank God there's a Game 2!" belted Bird to the press after turning the ball over six times.

Movies were the selected distraction in between games and practices to keep Jackson's mind busy with anything but home. She spoke to her mother often, wishing her a happy 50th birthday on October 11, but tried to spend more time watching DVDs. Ironically, Jackson and Sun guard Katie Douglas watched horror flicks in between playoff games, though Douglas hated scary movies. She sat in her team's hotel plugging her ears and blabbing "lalalalala" as her fiancé watched the creepy parts prior to Game 2 in Seattle. Jackson,

Storm guard Betty Lennox drives past Connecticut forward Nykesha Sales. In the WNBA
Finals, both displayed shooting fireworks in Game 2 at KeyArena. (LATRENA SMITH PHOTOGRAPHY)

meanwhile, reveled in them. The fright took her mind off things as
she laughed at how special effects could startle her.

For the decisive game, she taped three small Marilyn Manson
photos to the side panel of her KeyArena locker and took the court
with a changed attitude. Douglas had yet to witness scary.

An amazing sight awaited Jackson on the court. The crowd had
doubled to 17,072, a sellout, and homemade posters were as high
up as the rafters, proclaiming everything from "Sun Don't Shine in
Seattle" to "You may have [Nykesha] Sales, but we've got the Money
[Betty Lennox, who was dubbed B-Money]." The bowl-shaped
concrete facility seemed to contain sound well, which would affect
Douglas's team, making them understand the importance of home-
court advantage in the Finals.

After the Sun closed the first half ahead 35-30, forward Nykesha

Sales and Lennox were in the midst of an offensive duel. Lennox was guarded by Whalen, who had suffered from food poisoning the night before and tried to use a bruising game to knock Lennox off balance. It was a mistake. The shoves that ended in no calls from the officials simply made Lennox tougher to defend. With dizzying baseline layups and wicked jump shots, Lennox was in her element, filling the void for smothered Bird and Jackson. But Sales, a streaky shooter, also felt "it" that night. She responded to every shot with her own mix of showtime baskets, getting away from Sam's soft defense. The score was tied at the 5:43 mark, but Lennox outscored Sales 8-5 to close out the game. Lennox also set up Vodichkova with a kick-out dish to the free-throw line, which the Czech easily drained 10 feet from the hoop.

Sales, who scored 21 of her Finals-record 32 points in the second half, had a chance to win it all with a three-pointer at the buzzer. The play was directly after a time-out on the Storm's end of the court. Sam blew her defensive assignment, getting lost in the paint as Sales hustled out to the corner. Sales was open in the right pocket when she retrieved the basketball. Sam watched as Sales hoisted a rushed shot, thinking there was less time on the clock, seeing it clank off the side of the backboard. Another second ticked off the clock before the buzzer sounded. Seattle even had a foul to give that could have masked the blown defensive assignment, but it would go unused. Sales later claimed she didn't know it was a potential game winner, losing a chance to sweep the Storm behind a 67-65 loss. Lennox was serenaded to chants of her name, making 11 of 16 shots for a season-high 27 points.

"That shot should have gone," Jackson said. "It was my nana up there looking over me."

The two days in between games were a blur. Both teams had practices, but also had to meet with ESPN2 broadcasters for packaged Q&As

about their lives, winning the championship, and tales about their teammates. The starters for both teams also filmed clips of them kissing and dancing around the silver WNBA trophy. Lennox wore her hair in its curly natural state and flexed her arms as she looked at the hardware adoringly.

Game 3 was a pure nightmare for the Sun as another sellout crowd packed KeyArena, screaming at a pitch louder than a jet engine for an hour before the game started. It was a clear night as dusk settled on Seattle for the 7 PM tip-off. Even more homemade signs rippled in the air, like "5 years for this game, thank-you Storm" and "Bird's beak may be broke, but she can still fly past the Sun." Donovan took a moment to spin around, looking at every nook of the arena filled with poster-waving fans. Tickets had sold out in three hours as people gravitated to the reality of a championship coming to Seattle.

Her team was warming up as Lennox stopped to give ESPN2 sideline reporter Heather Cox a pregame interview. Smiling widely ever since her shootout with Sales, Lennox replied, "I never have pressure at all. That [Game 2's heroics] is why Anne brought me to Seattle," in response to one of Cox's questions. Lennox mouthed "Hi Mom!" as Cox sent the telecast over to co-reporter Doris Burke standing across the court with Sales.

"We all were screaming when we saw Betty on the screen," her older sister, Victoria, said of the Finals party at her house. Lennox often called to talk to Victoria's husband about the game, although Victoria insists Lennox got some of her moves from her former playing days, too. "Betty sent a box of Storm things when she joined the team and we all would wear it on her game days."

Burke also inquired about an encore to Game 2 when she spoke to Sales during the pregame warmup. "The opportunities were there for me," she said. "If they're not there today, I'm not going to force anything." The visiting team had never won the championship on the road in the league's eight-year history. But no one on either team or staff had ever experienced a Finals before, so anything could happen in the decisive match-up.

Footage of Jackson and Lennox on the KeyArena Jumbotron helped get the fans ready shortly before player introductions. "And now for my favorite cheer, Aussie! Aussie! Aussie!" Jackson was shown saying. The crowd belted "Oi! Oi! Oi!" Jackson repeated the cheer, then Lennox's image appeared on the screen, "You're almost ready to bring it, Storm fans," she beamed to the crowd. "I just need one more thing . . . Everybody, as loud as you can, make some NOOOISSSSE!" To a backdrop of techno music, the place erupted. Hardly anyone would sit down for the next three hours.

Bird controlled the tip and the Storm would play a perfect opening five minutes. The New Yorker hooked a pass over Douglas to the big Aussie inside and she turned to score the game's first points on a short jumper over six-year veteran center Taj McWilliams-Franklin. Whalen, a rookie, would drive past Jackson two minutes into the game to score on a reverse lay-in, but Jackson dominated early on. With the help of Vodichkova, the duo posts would score 17 of their team's opening points to give the Storm an early 20-11 lead.

Sales made the crowd whisper, "Ooooh!" with a three-pointer over Sam, but by the nine-minute mark, she was seated on the bench with two fouls and a dejected look at her 1-for-4 shooting from the field. Lennox wasn't stellar, either. Her first made basket was off a high screen from Jackson to get a wide-open look at a 15-footer with 11:47 remaining in the half. Bird also struggled offensively, not attempting her first basket until five minutes before halftime. Still, the Storm opened the game shooting 60 percent. But after Burse's shot dribbled over the backboard, prompting her to shout "Fuck! Shit!" to the rafters, Seattle missed 14 straight shots from the field.

The crowd was nervous. Lennox was 2-for-9 from the field, making horrible decisions with the ball. Jackson barely touched the ball because the Storm's offense had stopped passing. Bench players Simone Edwards and Tully Bevilaqua had to keep the team together with their performances.

Seattle took a mere 37-36 lead into halftime. Inside the locker room, Donovan didn't stress offense, however. She emphasized defense. Jackson brushed her hair into a new ponytail, this time braiding the blond locks as Donovan said, "We gotta get it together!" Donovan told her shooter Lennox not to push too hard, but really wanted her to stay on Douglas, who had yet to make a field goal. "Even though she was known a lot for her offense, she stopped a lot of people," Thompson said. "Donovan was like, 'Betty you have to do this. You have to stop Katie.' And she did. Betty went out there and she really worked hard on stopping those players. She's a very emotional player and brought a lot of intensity to the game."

Vodichkova led the team with 12 first-half points, 11 in the opening seven minutes. Lennox was concerned about her offense, however. "I stunk it up for the first seven shots," Lennox said. "It was terrible."

Thompson was one of the first players in Lennox's ear to make sure the strong shooter didn't take the start too harshly on the grand stage. Lennox had improved her play in every round, averaging a series-leading 22 points on 54 percent shooting in the Finals. Her ability to create from years of playing against guys helped her stand out in the Storm offense. Lennox was angry at herself, but not enough to get down. She had worked too hard and too long for this moment. After experiencing two teams fold beneath her and a reputation shattered by misperception, she was going to win the title.

"She always just kind of regroups," Thompson said. "Betty is the type that, you know, she's always hard on herself. She'll get angry and then go out in the second half and just kill people."

Lennox exited the locker room with a fire burning in her eyes and an inspirational biblical verse written in black ink along the crease of her white sneakers. She was ready to play. But her offense still hadn't clicked 14 minutes into the second half. A burst by Bird saved the Storm from ever trailing in the game. She made a jumper and converted a turnover into a lay-in to quickly help give Seattle a 43-36 lead.

Lennox, meanwhile, was knocked flat on her back after running into a textbook screen by Connecticut forward Asjha Jones, a former college teammate of Bird's. When Lennox missed her 12th shot, she backpedaled to play defense, tapping her chest as she said "My bad." Any thoughts of winning the Finals MVP trophy seemed in doubt. She was taken out of the game with 12:22 remaining.

The Sun's lack of a strong post presence and their shooting woes kept them from capitalizing on the Storm's miscues. McWilliams-Franklin was a three-time All-Star, but she played out of position during the Finals. Douglas, who averaged 16.0 points in the previous games, was hounded by Lennox. Even the Storm guard's brief absence on the bench couldn't spark Douglas's game.

Lennox returned with 10:37 remaining in the game and her team leading 56-46, although the game didn't feel as if it was in Seattle's control. The explosive guard, though, would secure the MVP award over the following six minutes. She dribbled the ball through her legs then led Whalen, her defender, to the corner like a puppy and flickered a jumper into the net as she was fouled, yelling, "That's what I'm talkin' 'bout!" to the crowd. Then she dribbled around the corner of another high screen and hit a fadeaway over Whalen. Sales tried to answer as she did in Game 2, but when her three-pointer at the tip of the arch bricked, you knew Lennox was the only one starring in this show. She drove on Whalen for a basket. She hit a soft floater over Whalen, burning the point guard so much on one-on-one coverage, you wondered where the triage unit was. Instead, the Storm wheeled out the celebratory champagne chilling on ice. The crowd went nuts. Four minutes remained in the game. Douglas hung her head in a huddle during a timeout. She was 0-for-11 from the field, scoring all six of her points from the free-throw line.

Donovan told her team to finish it, knowing it would be the longest four minutes of their lives. Sales could still get hot, so Donovan focused the short huddle on Sam, telling her she had to play better "D." Sam wouldn't, but the Storm already led by 16 points. Lennox had scored 14 of her game-high 23 points in the second half, helping the Storm stretch its lead. The crowd did its job, becoming a constant gust of wind in the Storm's sails, drowning out the coaching staff during time-outs, scaring the Sun with blaring noise. They chanted

"BET-TY! BET-TY! BET-TY!" as she stepped to the free-throw line with 2:35 remaining, sinking her final points. Fans, even those who were attending their first WNBA game, counted down the final 25 seconds, symbolically marking the years on the calendar since Seattle had last celebrated a professional championship.

"I started getting chills over on the bench," said Kenlaw, who wrapped every player in bear hugs and vigorously rocked them as they were substituted out of the game so the deep reserves could log minutes.

Once the final buzzer sounded a 74-60 win, the players rushed onto the court in a heap as mounds of colorful metallic gold, red, and green confetti poured from the rafters. Though celebrated by a metropolitan area of about 1 million, the moment was intensely private. The silver Tiffany trophy was suddenly murky from lip gloss, fingerprints, and tears. Jackson kissed the emblazoned basketball design for her grandmother. Donovan and Thompson embraced on the winner's podium and both gave it kisses for their lost mothers. And Lennox kissed it for her cousin, who had committed suicide before the season began.

"I remember the confetti," Donovan said. "I think that's your sign, whether it's rice at a wedding or confetti at a parade, it's that 'raining down on you' feeling that, yeah, this is real."

For Lennox, the defining moment was holding the Finals MVP trophy atop the makeshift stage at center court, tagging her as the game's top player. She had averaged 22.3 points.

In a postgame interview, chairman Howard Schultz took the microphone from Burke and gave his own speech about the title. He thanked the thousands of "founding fans" sprinkled throughout the arena who had supported the team since its inception. He thanked the players. And he congratulated Donovan, who'll most likely become the first woman to be in the Basketball Hall of Fame as a player and coach, joining the prestige of rare men like John Wooden and former Sonics coach Lenny Wilkens, who already were there as both. The Storm players chanted "Big Sexy! Big Sexy! Big Sexy!"

after Schultz made his remarks. Blushing, Donovan flapped her championship cap at her team, telling them to "stop it," not wanting her underground nickname to be shouted to everyone.

The majority of the team then joined Sonics and Storm employees at an invitation-only party at the Seattle Center. It only took one sip of champagne to blitz the euphoric players and coaches, who were already on a high. Jackson, who ran around the locker room halls with a bottle of champagne, drizzling some on teammates and drinking the rest, made her way home by midnight. Everything she'd experienced the past year was crashing down. She lay in bed, drifting in and out of tears and sleep.

"The whole year just hit me right then," Jackson said. "I was completely numb."

At 2 AM, her phone rang. It was her teammates. They were crashing her spot to celebrate with her. Jackson, still in her pajamas and laying in bed, welcomed Bird, Barnes, Thompson, Bevilaqua, Sam, and their friends into her one-bedroom apartment. They stayed until dawn, returning later that day to clean up their mess. It was like a campfire gathering as they reflected on the game.

"Were you scared?" they asked each other of the small, one-point lead at halftime.

"Nah, I never doubted that we wouldn't win," Jackson deadpanned.

The city partied, too. The Wildrose, the city's only lesbian bar on Capitol Hill, was jammed with elated patrons and the Kangaroo & Kiwi was overflowing, too. While some broadcasters on KJR, the city's only sports radio station, tried to belittle the title as not really being the city's first since 1979 because they didn't consider the WNBA anything more than a niche sport on the level of local semi-professional teams, most people couldn't care less that the league had only been around for five years in Seattle. Or that players were paid as much as the average American worker. What they had seen was competitive basketball, and about 200 had already signed up for 2005 season tickets during the Finals series.

By Friday, the Storm had organized a parade through downtown, which was broadcast live on Northwest Cable News. Players rode atop donated convertible Saabs and about 5,000 people squeezed into the Westlake Center plaza in the heart of the city at noon to see the champions. The players, after weaving through the crowd upon arrival, were taken to an upstairs balcony to greet their fans. "All you could see were people. I just got chills again. My body . . . it was indescribable what I was feeling during that time. It was like we had finally arrived. It was an awesome feeling," said Kenlaw, who won a WBL title in 1979.

Jackson told Seattle she was happy this was her second home. Lennox, who had never allowed herself to feel comfortable, made herself vulnerable by admitting the fans' adoration was making Seattle "feel like home."

"This is needed; it'll put a lot into the city in terms of revenue and something fun to get excited about," longtime fan Shevy Bridges told the *Seattle Times* at the parade. "We haven't had anything good for 25 years. Well, other than Microsoft."

CHAPTER ELEVEN

Hoopin' for a Future

Reality hit quickly for Betty Lennox. Despite Storm coach Anne Donovan advising her to stick around and enjoy the afterglow of winning, Lennox had a contract to play in Caserta, Italy. She hustled around the training facility after the post-championship parade, trying to accommodate the throng of cameras and reporters who wanted some final words from the Finals MVP, while handling business side details, paperwork, moving out of her team-issued apartment, turning in her keys to the team-issued rental car, and filming farewell clips for season ticket holders. The following morning, Lennox returned home to Missouri to spend about three days with her family then was off to Italy for off-season play. The majority of the league's players were making the trek to Europe, Asia, and Australia to keep in shape during an eight-month off-season and to make money while they could. All-Star Sue Bird was making her first trip, but she wouldn't begin play with her Moscow Dynamo team until January, enjoying the title win as long as possible.

The guard joined teammates Alicia Thompson, Lauren Jackson, Adia Barnes, Tully Bevilaqua, and Sheri Sam in soaking up the championship euphoria in a city thirsty for something to celebrate. Bottles of Cristal champagne were sent over to the players' reserved dinner tables. Lavish meals at the elegant steakhouse, the Metropolitan Grill, a regular team supporter, were comped. Ovations were given at musician Jill Scott's concert. Endless autographs were signed. And a chorus of "GO STORM!" was belted everywhere the champions went—on the street from passing cars while shopping or in restrooms while partying at nightclubs.

"I swear to God, for the next two weeks I did not pay for a meal, none of my teammates did," Jackson said. "We were . . . *the* Seattle Storm! Everywhere we went, people were screaming out of windows . . . it was crazy!"

Lennox wouldn't share the feeling. She walked around the postgame locker room in soggy socks and a drenched oversized Storm championship T-shirt, wet from sprayed champagne, as if it were home, but she remained hesitant to allow herself to get too comfortable anywhere. Except between the familiar lines of the 94-foot basketball court. Lennox made $60,000 for the 2004 regular season, received a bonus $10,000 along with each teammate for playing in the title game, and another $25,000 for winning the MVP award. But the grand total of $95,000 was far from NBA players of her caliber. She had to honor her international contract for training and for economic reasons.

"I have bills to pay," Lennox said.

Jet-lagged from the transatlantic flight, Lennox fell under different rules in Italy. The team wanted her to practice right then, paying her top dollar as the American scoring threat. Facing tackling defense more physical than in the WNBA, Lennox managed to score 16 points in a sleepy fog her first game. The small gyms of about 500 fans tried to make her feel at ease, shouting "Bettina! Bettina!" which loosely translated to "little Betty," and adorning the walls with signs like "Dr. B is in da house," but Lennox, dressed in an orange and blue uniform, missed out on the championship glitz.

Her living quarters made the experience worse. The tiny, team-issued apartment looked tossed over because so many people had filtered through it. The city seemingly reeked of urine when it rained, due to poor plumbing. And Lennox didn't enjoy the never-ending pasta dishes constantly served.

"I was on a high when I left," Lennox said. "But as soon as I left, it stayed in Seattle. I really didn't get to soak it in like I wanted to—enjoy and relax like some people did. You're not going to enjoy it in other states because it happened here with all the people and stuff. People back in Missouri knew, but it's different because we didn't win it in Missouri. When I went home, I had people whisper, 'There's Betty Lennox!' But I didn't get to enjoy it, so that means we just have to do it all over again."

Winds billowed across the Puget Sound and tussled pastel cherry blossoms from tree limbs. Sidewalks were stained from the magenta, pink, and white petals, paving a royal runway for the queens of summer to return to their court.

Reports about the Storm scattered across newspapers and telecasts during the spring of 2005 in the form of free agent signings, trades, and the upcoming April draft. Stars like Jackson and Thompson were spotted at high school state championship games, autograph signings at Eastside grocery stores, and leadership assemblies. Even Sam was spotted dashing through the University of Washington parking lot with Jackson at the NCAA first-round regional hosted at Edmundson Pavilion, though Sam had signed a three-year contract with the Charlotte Sting in February. The sights, like the first flowers of spring, stirred a warmth and excitement inside for women's basketball fans—summer was coming.

But not until the madness ended. March Madness.

Seattle was one of eight first-round sites for the Women's NCAA tournament, giving basketball junkies a two-day fix. Players from Texas Christian, the University of Oregon, Baylor, Illinois State, Vanderbilt, Kansas State, Montana University, and Bowling Green descended upon the facility wearing the requisite swishy team sweat suits. As each squad filed into the 10,000-seat arena, peered out of the lower tunnels, or followed each other upstairs, it was like watching a broken-up Olympic parade of athletes, with colors like hunter green, gold, and royal purple tagging their allegiance.

Although sparse, the crowd was a visual who's who of basketball. Anne Donovan sat inconspicuously scouting a few of the six total games with assistant coach Jenny Boucek. Houston Comets guard Sheila Lambert, who had played prep ball across the water at Chief Sealth High School, floated around to catch up with hometown friends. And Lin Dunn, now an assistant for the Indiana Fever, chatted with old Storm friends while keeping an eye on the court.

Jackson unfurled her frame on the plastic purple seats, flopping her size-12 men's sneakers over a seat in front of her, and soaked in the new sight. Leaving Australia before the frigid winter blew in, Jackson had returned to complete rehabilitation on her surgically repaired right ankle. It was the earliest she'd ever been in what she called her adopted city, normally appearing a week into training camp.

After winning in October 2004 and spending what felt like eternity, but really was just four months, either in bed or on the couch, Jackson decided she needed a change. A candy fiend, she was tired of gobbling indigenous treats like Violet Crumble as if the manufacturer were pulling the plug on the chocolate creations. She was mourning the death of her grandmother and fighting to stay fit for a *Sports Illustrated* Olympic swimsuit edition photo shoot in Miami, where she and her mother would be pampered for three days. Earlier that winter, however, it was Maree Jackson trying her best to stay patient as she pampered a healing Lauren. Her daughter's room at the family's countryside home was just off the kitchen, but Lauren still picked up her cell phone and dialed the house number.

"Hello?" Her mother said into the receiver.

"I want eggs. I want toast. I want coffee," she heard her daughter's demanding voice utter.

Maree walked to the doorway of Lauren's room. "Get it ya self," she deadpanned. Even with her husband, it seemed those cushy, caregiver feelings wore off after about three days.

"I couldn't get out of bed, you bugger," Jackson said while laughing with her mother well after her rehabilitation brought a successful return, not wanting Maree to share any disparaging stories to damage her angelic façade. "I couldn't walk! My foot was the size of a football!"

Jackson needed basketball again. A feeling Donovan and Thompson could understand. They had both lost their mothers, Thompson losing hers during the 2001 season while playing in Indiana. She used to write "M-O-M" on the top part of her sneakers so that she could see the word when she looked down while playing. Patricia Thompson loved basketball—all levels, men and women. She'd talk to her daughter about the game constantly and Chelle would share her frustrations about practice or excitement about games. Chelle would stash her mother's handwritten notes or motivational Bible verses in her locker with tons of pictures of her mother so she could read and look over them before she played. The mother was her daughter's best friend.

Patricia Thompson raised Chelle and two older brothers Thomas and Robert alone in Big Lake, a town of about 3,000 in the heart of Texas that has two spotlights on the main drag through town separating the North-side whites from the South-side blacks and Hispanics, where the Thompson home was. A massive blue sky hung like a Tupperware lid over the oil country, preserving a lost time when the children could run the neighborhood streets and not worry about crime. Patricia, a third generation resident, and Robert, along with a gaggle of cousins and aunts and uncles, were regulars at Chelle's Texas Tech University games, moseying 168 miles north to see her play. The forward averaged 23.2 points her senior season in 1998 and was named to the Associated Press's All-American first team. Chelle was the ninth pick in the draft, selected by New York in the first round, but suffered a knee injury 19 games into the season. Her mother hadn't seen her play live in the WNBA, but in June 2001, Chelle was bubbly at planning her family's arrival.

Her mother was in the midst of a 14-year battle with lupus and diabetes, but Chelle wasn't thinking about the illness when she dialed her brother Robert to finalize their plans. Patricia even had had a candid conversation with Chelle about her possible death before Chelle left for the upcoming season.

"If I passed away and you had a game that same night, I would want you to play the game," Patricia said frankly.

Chelle whipped her head around and looked at her mother.

"Momma! I could never do that!" she said.

"I'll want you to," Patricia repeated.

"I wouldn't even be able to make it out onto the floor, I'm just telling you now," Chelle countered.

"Well, I want you to try," Patricia said, letting the conversation end.

On June 22, the Fever played Detroit at Conseco Fieldhouse, but Chelle wouldn't play. Her mother had died that day at the age of 50. Chelle, who turned 25 on June 30, missed five games, returning home to be with her family. When she rejoined her team in time to play at Houston on July 6, she gave a quick speech in the locker room telling her teammates that she needed their support and that her emotions would swing like a pendulum. Channeling her rage, Chelle scored 10 points in 20 minutes off the bench in a 79-64 loss for the expansion franchise.

"I thought it would be good to get back on the court and just forget all of it," Thompson said. "That was how I escaped everything. When I was out there and I was playing, that was the only time I could not think about my mom. As hard as it was, that was all that I had. I felt so much pain. So many different emotions. I was sad. I was mad. I was lost. My whole world had crumbled. All the frustration, everything I felt, I would just leave on the floor. I played my best basketball during that time."

Jackson didn't make any speeches about her grandmother, but she still used her teammates as a crutch as Thompson had done. And after she made arrangements to train in Seattle in February

After winning the championship, an elated group of players took candid photos with the trophy backstage at KeyArena. Clockwise from bottom left: Sue Bird, Adia Barnes, Lauren Jackson, Tully Bevilaqua, and Sheri Sam. (COURTESY OF LAUREN JACKSON)

2005, pulling the cobwebs off the furniture in her Queen Anne condominium, to settle into the American way of life, she taped a photo of her grandmother in her locker. Nana Irene is pictured seated on a tan couch flanked by her smiling daughter and granddaughter behind her. Thompson and Jackson didn't talk much about their lost maternal figures that off-season, but it formed a bond.

"It doesn't get any easier, you just learn how to cope with it," Thompson said.

Jackson dealt with her loss by playing, too. But first, she'd have to get back in shape, having gained a potbelly after the 2005 season. She had never spent this much time in Seattle and was enjoying learning about the culture. She enjoyed the rain: "It helps me sleep. I've always loved the rain. I wish it could rain every day." She continued to marvel at the sight of high school cheerleaders when she made appearances at state basketball tournament games, and she campaigned for the WNBA team at the state legislature in Olympia, the organization making a presentation for a publicly funded new facility to replace KeyArena. Jackson also filmed many advertising promotions while managing to find time for herself. She wasn't paid for the use of her face, name, or signature. It was her part of the still-pioneering aspect of the game. To provide a future for some of the college players now sprinting on the court before her at the NCAA tournament, like petite Louisiana State University guard Temeka Johnson. Some questioned Johnson's 5-foot height as she led the Tigers to the Final Four. She would later be selected with the sixth overall pick to Washington in the April 2005 draft and win the Rookie of the Year award, starting at point guard, averaging 5.2 assists (second to Bird's league-leading 5.9) for the 16-18 Mystics.

Johnson, a loveable pint-sized figure, is one of the emerging college stars the WNBA hopes to build its fan base from. College women's basketball started reaching its zenith in 2003, when the NCAA final between the University of Connecticut and the University of Tennessee featuring Phoenix guard Diana Taurasi was the most-watched basketball game—men's or women's, college or pro—ever on ESPN. Prior to the season in November, Taurasi was photographed with Huskies men's star Emeka Okafor on the cover of *ESPN The Magazine* and featured with Okafor in *Sports Illustrated*. Both players were lottery picks, Okafor selected No. 2 overall by the NBA Charlotte Bobcats, and were named Rookie of the Year for their respective leagues.

"You had to be a fan of the game to understand that at a certain period of time that would have been unthinkable," said NBA commissioner David Stern of the equal exposure in national magazines.

The women's Final Four rating, 4.3, was still lower than the men's 11.1 championship on the CBS network, but it prompted ESPN to ink a record 11-year, $200 million deal for exclusive rights to air all 63 tournament games. The cable sports giant believed like Stern that women's basketball was growing. In 1993, the station only televised 12 women's games. In 2004, the number jumped to 94. Now, there's a game shown every Monday night during the season, and

Las Vegas has even joined the fray, accepting bets on tournament games. Even noted dunker Candace Parker of Naperville, Illinois, received treatment like the boys, having her commitment to Tennessee broadcast live on ESPN.

"We look at women's basketball as a growth property," said Burke Magnus, ESPN's vice president for sports programming, at the time of the station's tournament broadcasting announcement. "We see the improvement in the quality of play plus the parity, and there is no reason to believe the sport won't continue to grow."

However, the station has yet to pay the WNBA for rights to broadcast its games, instead forming deals through its partnership with the NBA. And the station airs most of the women's pro games on its overflow station, ESPN2, not making a concentrated effort to really promote the league, aside from using WNBA players as analysts for college games.

WNBA games are fun, but the scene in Indianapolis, where the NCAA Final Four was held in 2005, was nuts. A city normally pulsating with the sound of race cars or Indiana Pacers guard Reggie Miller's lethal three-pointers gave way to the women's game at the RCA Dome downtown. Indiana is a basketball state. The epic story of a rural 1954 high school basketball team making it to the state championship buoyed the classic movie *Hoosiers*. Bobby Knight with his signature red sweater and infamous sideline behavior became the face of the men's college game at Indiana University, while Dunn, with her equally loud attire and sideline demeanor, had been a presence in the women's game at Purdue University.

"Basketball in some pockets around America, for both men and women, has always been a way of life," Dunn said. "You talk about baseball being the American pastime, I think basketball has always been a community thing. Everybody went to the basketball games. It was a part of life, part of the community."

But after a paper diploma smacks a palm that once wowed crowds with snazzy dribbling skills or jump shots, many expect those same women to pull out their ponytail, rub on some lipstick, and

Storm forward Lauren Jackson weaves through excited fans with the WNBA trophy during the team's championship celebration in downtown Seattle. (LATRENA SMITH PHOTOGRAPHY)

become a mother to some man's children. Or at least find a "real" career. Meanwhile, men who play the same sport, who often don't earn their degrees, are sympathized with for the loss of the game in their lives or for not having enough talent to play in the pros, or they are eagerly cheered for what they might do on the professional level. It's a status the women continually fight for from the general sports-loving public.

And it's not just in basketball. Olympic softball pitcher Jennie Finch, who starred at the University of Arizona, may be featured in designer handbag ads, wedding magazine shoots, and included in every list of "sexy athletes" because of cascading blond hair and blue eyes, but her sport shares the same struggles of acceptance to

The Storm celebrate atop a mall balcony with about 5,000 fans at their afternoon parade. Governor Gary Locke and mayor Greg Nickels were also part of the festivities. (LATRENA SMITH PHOTOGRAPHY)

support a league as the WNBA. Slowly the tide is changing. More women are taking an ownership or leadership role in sports, women executives are mimicking men in making women's sporting events part of client entertainment, and young people don't view a woman professional hoopster as an oddity. But how patient can the segment of believers be?

"There's still a ways to go. The fact that the WNBA is this lone beacon out there in terms of women's pro teams, that's not a good sign," said Karen Bryant. "We're doing what we can. But it's lonely. It's great to see the continued advancement, whether it's prize money or promotional opportunities, for women tennis and golf players. But it's too bad there aren't more opportunities for team sports. It makes the role, the position of the WNBA so much more important. We need to continue to strive to be successful and grow so we can pave the way."

Epilogue

The picture was surreal. On a lazy, sunny Seattle afternoon in September, Jackson sat talking to her mother on the phone while watching the 2005 WNBA Finals at home. The Sacramento Monarchs, whom the Storm defeated in the Western Conference finals the previous season, were on their way to winning their first championship since becoming one of the league's original teams in 1997. In the newly formatted best-of-five Finals series, the Monarchs defeated the Connecticut Sun in four games featuring buzzer-beating shots and prime-time plays by guard Ticha Penicheiro, who at one point dribbled the ball through the legs of 7-foot-2 Sun center Margo Dydek on a fast break.

While the game thrilled viewers, Jackson was bitter. The Storm finished its season at 20-14 for the second consecutive year, but the team exited the postseason early, losing to the Houston Comets in a best-of-three first round. The playoffs had seemed to start right. The Storm, seeded second, whirled into Houston to the dismay of several Hurricane Katrina sufferers who were attending the game for free, having been evacuated from their homes in New Orleans, and tore through the Comets 75-67. Jackson, who had strained her back while grabbing a rebound in the regular-season finale two days earlier, was a defensive menace. She totaled 19 points, 13 rebounds, and two blocks, helping the team take a 33-28 lead into halftime behind 12 points. Knowing the Comets would focus on Jackson in the final half, Donovan prompted Lennox to be creative offensively. With her left wrist bound in stiff tape to protect partially torn ligaments, Lennox scored 17 of her final 18 points in the second half to preserve the win. She even found teammate Janell Burse inside for an assist that ignited a 12-3 run. Meanwhile, Brazilian forward Iziane Castro Marques continued her defensive work on Comets forward Sheryl Swoopes, holding the league's leading scorer to 6-of-18 shooting from the field (15 points). The team flew home elated, knowing one win at KeyArena, where they had finished the regular season at 13-4, would give them a sweep and a week to prepare for the conference finals. They needed downtime for Jackson and Lennox's injuries.

The air at home was different, almost passive, as the Storm took the court for Game 2. After having won nine consecutive games in the arena, the Storm crumbled with two minutes remaining in the decisive matchup. Houston coach Van Chancellor changed his defensive scheme, taking away Jackson and Bird's comfortable pick-and-roll, and Seattle didn't adjust quickly, squandering a 10-point second-half lead to ultimately lose 67-64 at home. Houston, who had won the league's first four titles, squashed the Storm in Game 3, easily winning 75-58 to advance to the conference finals against Sacramento. Swoopes, who topped Jackson by two points for the league's MVP award, recorded the first triple-double in playoff history with 14 points, 10 rebounds, and 10 assists. KeyArena, which hadn't witnessed a loss since July 13, was silent. With Jackson and Lennox hindered by injuries, the team needed more offense from Bird, but she was 9-for-33 from the field in the series. Her trademark pull-up jumper clanked off the front of the rim. Her league-leading three-point shot only found the hoop twice in three games. And by the end of Game 3, she was playing hot potato with Castro Marques, passing the ball between each other on the perimeter, neither confident enough to take a shot.

Who was this team? It was a question that haunted Seattle

throughout the summer. The WNBA had entered a true free-agency period where talented players could finally test the market to see their value. Olympians like Swoopes and Yolanda Griffith were on the trading block prior to the season, Griffith requesting a trade because of coach John Whisenant's desire to go young and her belief that it would hinder her plans to win a title in the winter of her career. Instead, she was named Finals MVP and he won Coach of the Year honors. Other Olympians like Katie Smith and Dawn Staley were traded by the league's deadline in August.

The Storm, however, was hit the hardest. Wanting to get younger in preparation for the future and looking to turn a profit for the team in its sixth season, Donovan was idle as three of her top six players from the championship season leaped at higher offers from other teams. Sam, 31, was an expected loss because of a strained relationship with Donovan, creeping age, and demands for more money. Her Storm gear was discounted just days after the title win. She signed a three-year contract with Charlotte worth about $70,000 the first season. Bevilaqua wanted to be a starter and was never going to be one with Bird around, so she took a gamble to play for Indiana with Dunn. Indiana offered Bevilaqua about $60,000, and by season's end, she had led the Fever to its first conference finals. Vodichkova, playing overseas with Bird in Moscow, was waiting patiently for the Storm to begin negotiations as a restricted free agent, meaning the Storm had the opportunity to match any offer she received. But by late February her agent grew anxious, and Phoenix was desperate for a post player. General manager Seth Sulka threw a whopping three-year contract exceeding $200,000 total at the 32-year-old and waited the mandatory 10 days for Donovan to respond. Depending on who is telling the tale, she couldn't because of the $673,000 hard salary cap or wouldn't because Vodichkova would be 35 at the end of the deal, which was guaranteed money despite any injuries. The amount was too much for an aging center, especially with word that Burse, 26, was developing her offense in China at the time. Vodichkova signed, and by the start of training camp, the Storm championship roster was pillaged.

"I didn't find out until real late because I was in Italy," said Lennox, who grudgingly signed a one-year contract despite wanting a long-term deal. "I remember trying to get Kamila back—I tried to e-mail her. I also tried to get Tully and Sheri back like, 'Come on, dude. Let's not break up like this.' Just kind of saying at the time, 'Don't sign with Phoenix! Don't sign with Phoenix!' It's going to be difficult with the missing three pieces, but I think that's the nature of the business."

Donovan was already working to bring in replacements. Australian center Suzy Batkovic, her 2003 second-round pick (22nd overall), agreed to report after visiting home following her Spanish League season, arriving in June. Castro Marques, a 23-year-old Olympian, signed as a free agent in April. Donovan picked up a gem through the draft in guard Tanisha Wright (12th overall pick), a three-time Defensive Player of the Year out of Penn State University. And Italian guard Francesca Zara, whose team had won the FIBA Cup, was a last-minute sign after Australian Jessica Bibby couldn't play due to a severe back injury. Russian Olympian Natalia Vodopyanova, 24, was the final new addition, surviving training camp with her promising talent as a young 6-foot-3 small forward. She also had played with Bird in Moscow, giving her a slight edge.

The problem was, of the collection of international stars, only Castro Marques had any WNBA experience, last appearing in 16 games with the Phoenix Mercury in 2003. She also had played 19 with Miami, knowing Lennox and assistant coach Jenny Boucek. If you closed your eyes at practice, the various dialects of the players could make your mind drift to dreamy vacation spots like the beaches of Jamaica, boutiques in Italy, or Russia's Red Square. But the reality was a garbled translation of basketball that took time for the players to adjust to. Donovan sat her stars, Bird and Jackson, down during training camp to explain it was their responsibility to bring the team together. The coach had their backs, but it was truly their team—no veterans were there to step in with guidance, as Bevilaqua and Sam had done in the past. Both Jackson and Bird were reluctant at first. Jackson is fiery and speaks her mind, but was unwilling to alter her style. Bird is more of a "lead by example" type, but after a Sunday practice five days before the opener, Donovan called her out to get a fussy team focused. It wouldn't be the first time. The Storm started the season at 8-10, losing five consecutive games on the road.

"Sue and I were like, 'OK, what do we do? What do we do?'" Jackson said.

Scheduling helped. The WNBA headed into the All-Star break, and while Jackson and Bird shined in Connecticut, starting in the game with Donovan as the acting Western Conference coach, the rest of the team scattered across the nation reevaluating what the season meant to them. They returned united, winning six consecutive games to claw their way back to second in the conference. The playoffs were different. More was needed. And with Lennox suffering her wrist injury on a road loss in Indiana on August 4, missing six games and playing with a joint she couldn't even swivel, the Storm didn't have that extra pizzazz. Inexperience consumed them.

"We settled. We gave it away," said center Simone Edwards, the team's oldest player at 31. "I never assume anything [even when playing at home]. I've been here since the beginning and I always think that you've got to fight hard for every game. Pride is a big thing that we have to have as a team. Pride where you say, 'No one is going to kick my ass at home.' It's just something that when you have it you do everything. It's that thing that keeps you doing everything that you possibly can at the time, and I know my teammates work hard, but we needed a little bit of that sometimes. We lost that sometimes."

Reflecting on the season after her teammates had left for off-season play overseas or vacations, Jackson admitted she'd grown up in the past year, learning a lot about herself. She'd learned about her strength from rehabilitating after a three-hour right ankle surgery in three different places on her foot, to finish second in the league in scoring (17.6) and rebounding (9.2) and fourth in blocks (2.0), co-leading the WNBA with 12 double-doubles. About her desire from forcing herself to become a better leader for her teammates, trying to pull even more out of them. And about her will from spending hours analyzing the season, trying to figure out what the Storm needed in order to repeat its championship—even talking to Donovan for hours in their exit interview, unloading insights on the coach.

Lennox did the same. She'd evolved as a player through the turmoil of her second season in Seattle. In the beginning, when Jackson and Bird were hesitant about leading, Lennox was there with her brash and humorous style, welcoming the new players and trying to get a fire going in close games the Storm should have won. When Bird suffered her second broken nose in eight months—this time from an errant Jackson elbow during a loss in Connecticut on June 7—Lennox helped guide Wright, who was getting more minutes at the backup point guard role. Bird missed four games to be fitted for a new face mask. Lennox again turned tutor when Wright replaced Bird later in the season. The former Finals MVP's game changed too; she started passing more to Burse and taking on more ball-handling responsibilities until tendinitis flared in her right wrist and she suffered an injury to her left after falling on a baseline drive.

Seattle still supported its team, no matter how schizophrenic it had become. The various cultures and personalities on the team continued to reflect the diverse area. The games were like added tourist stops as international fans dropped in waving Brazilian, Italian, Russian, and Jamaican flags in support of the Storm. Stormfans.org helped further grow Seattle's fan base, hooking up with the Theater Off Jackson in Seattle's International District, where an average of 150 fans would gather to watch road games on the big screen. The cluster of diehard fans continued in-arena traditions—standing until the Storm scored and wiggling "spirit fingers" for good luck during free throws. Hot dogs, soda pop, and cookies were the light fare sold to raise money for the free viewing, and former players such as Adia Barnes and Ashley Battle, both cut during training camp, would attend to support the Storm.

Every WNBA franchise experienced an increase in attendance

following a championship season, and the Storm saw an 11 percent hike, averaging 8,868 fans—its best draw since averaging 8,912 during the inaugural season. The 2005 jump was the best among the league's 13 teams too. Overall, the league's attendance dropped slightly from 8,593 in 2004 to 8,173, but the WNBA picked up five new sponsors and increased its viewership 27 percent during the regular season with 92,000 more homes tuning in—a 33 percent increase during the finals aired on ESPN2 and ABC. But those numbers aren't even a blip in TV land. The Storm-Sun series garnered a 0.3 rating in October 2004, while the Monarchs-Sun series played mid-September 2005 drew a 0.4, or about 440,000 viewers.

The Monarchs also surpassed the Storm in ticket sales during the playoffs, averaging 11,975—181 more than Seattle—but Sacramento didn't sell out Arco Arena for the finals like Seattle did in back-to-back games at KeyArena. More than anything, the numbers show the WNBA is still trying to find itself and how it communicates with its fans to unearth new followers.

For one, the WNBA needs to give up its push of sex and use the players' marketability to draw more fans in the future. Sure, it's interesting to know who's balancing motherhood with playing, especially after delivering triplets, but the ads with players gussied up without a basketball in sight border on false advertising, not because the players don't dress up, but because that's not how they look on the court. And the game is still the point, right? Attendance numbers, whether inflated or actual, show the novelty has worn off, and no amount of Botox and lipstick is going to make the league look fresh again. Only play on the court will do that, and after nine seasons, there's finally enough talent to go around—even with the addition of Chicago in the historic 10th season. Marketing the players and rivalries, with actual game footage of who's playing and a thunderous voiceover of why it's significant, would go a lot further than pouty lips for the fan who'll really tune in.

At the same time, the WNBA has to fix its product. As in the NFL, owners or general managers should be forced to look at women for coaching positions, or at least candidates who actually have a background in coaching. Not just playing the part of sperm donor to a successful athlete or having been an athlete themselves, like Los Angeles coach Joe "Jellybean" Bryant (father of Kobe Bryant) and Charlotte coach Mugsy Bogues, who asked if coaching his daughter counted as experience. Women actually listen to their coaches, and the one positive comment about the WNBA is the fact that they play team ball; hiring a coach who can actually implement an offense and defense would mean better talent on the floor, which is what people are paying to see. Again, not the rantings of former NBA jocks on the sideline.

And with coaching comes officiating, which is a tough job. League salaries don't attract the top-name officials, but that doesn't mean the WNBA can't spend some money for off-season training, perhaps taking in questions from coaches. But at the same time, all coaches should be fined or given technical fouls for spending too much time hounding refs. It's distracting and takes them out of the game, turning it into the home arena versus the officials. Officials always screw up; it happens to both teams; move on.

The league's biggest battle is the press itself, however, which is dominated by men. The WNBA will always fight the stigma of women's sports being lesser until editors and producers catch a clue that their purpose is to report the news, not decide the news. Newspapers and television stations give coverage to everything from dog shows to minor league baseball, regardless of crowd size, but claim the WNBA isn't worth equal treatment because of small attendance. It doesn't make sense, especially since some of the WNBA's fans aren't regular sports page readers and could bring in money for a dying newspaper industry grasping at survival. But the argument from some Midwestern newspapers is that their purpose isn't to promote the WNBA. (For your information, guys, you're not promoting when you're doing your job, which is serving your readership.) The league does have modern technology on its side with the ability to reach its audience via the Internet. Already there

Storm players watch their championship banner be placed in the rafters before the 2005 season opener against Los Angeles. The Storm lost the game 68-50, with Lauren Jackson scoring just eight points. (LATRENA SMITH PHOTOGRAPHY)

are chat rooms buzzing about the inner workings of the league. Detroit coach Bill Laimbeer and Phoenix's Seth Sulka even log on to share opinions.

Yet, as the WNBA prepares to celebrate its 10th anniversary, the same tired columns will litter newspapers across the country with the "Who cares?" ink. They'll mention for the millionth time that the WNBA will never be the NBA and that 20,000-seat arenas are one-third full with lesbians watching women who can't dunk for the sake of women's liberation. Which, of course, is ridiculous.

"It's the same article every year, some male or even [commentator] Debbie Schlussel feels they have to put us down," Jackson said. "I read most of those articles. It says a lot about male journalists who don't really want to embrace the game. Why? Why wouldn't you want to? It's obviously something that people are very passionate about. I don't get it. Men can't accept that it's a happening thing. I definitely don't think that we're a charity case. I think a lot of people are passionate about what we do, and it's strange to me that there are no other women's sports that are professional. When you look at things like the Olympics where so many women have achieved so much, and then they come back and there's no professional platform for them to play. So, I'd like to say maybe it's growing, and it is, but is anything getting better for anyone really? Nothing really changes for any kind of minority. It's a very slow process."

New WNBA president Donna Orender, 48, doesn't mind slow processes. The native New Yorker came to the league after 17 years with the PGA Tour, serving most recently as senior vice president of strategic development in the office of the commissioner. Plainly stated, she—coupled with the gift of Tiger Woods—made golf cool. Yes, golf. Remember when it was stodgy and best used as a sort of white-noise sleeping aid on a Sunday afternoon? Well, the kick came from the assertive Orender, joined with intriguing talent.

Her plan is to do the same with the WNBA. Orender likened the league to ostriches who'd bury their heads in the sand and work, work, work, not caring if the masses didn't want to pay attention. The

WNBA would focus on feeding those that did, giving them what they want. After her 2005 self-proclaimed "yes woman" tour, when she familiarized herself with the league, Orender views the 2006 season as her first test to see if her plan can work. The WNBA will play four 10-minute quarters and use a 24-second shot clock. The expansion Chicago Sky, featuring former Storm forward Stacy Lovelace, will boost the league to 14 teams, and David Stern said another two teams could be added in 2007, bringing the league back to its 2000 configuration, when the Storm joined as one of 16 franchises.

Regardless of what happens to the WNBA, however, the players will continue to play. There will always be Europe and the Olympics and pickup games on some playground somewhere. And where there's that, there's another sharp business mind who believes he or she has the copyright to a sound business plan for a women's professional league.

Right now, it belongs to Stern and he is not giving up.

"We are determined to make sure the WNBA doesn't meet the same fate as past leagues," he said.

Acknowledgments

I couldn't have written a word without the help of Amanda Slepski, who helped me set up my faithful digital recorder to download on my computer and happily transcribed hundreds of hours of interviews, listening to my cackling laugh ring in her ear. Photographer Latrena Smith, a close family friend, took most of the wonderful photos in here to illustrate what it's like in the WNBA world, and manicurist Celestine Berrysmith kept my fingers nimble and my nails beautiful, making long days of writing much more pleasant. The Storm's Jennifer Carroll heads a legion of fabulous WNBA media relations employees, who were always willing to help arrange an interview or find a stat. And thanks to the players, coaches, and front office personnel for taking the time to frankly discuss the league and its issues with me. I really appreciate the extra time you gave.

Cheering me on was Karen Rolstad, who was sweet enough to read through sketchy early copy and give pointers. Our "ladies lunch" always filled me with confidence; you're just too cool. Thanks to Meredith Bagley and J. Paul Blake for doing the same. I loved seeing my University of Arizona best friends, Bobcats Leandro Arechederra III and Juan J. Herrera; we truly are family and I love you both. Lisa Seligson, my former college roommate, is a treat to see every summer, too. Thanks for always sticking by my side. All of y'all made Storm road trips a blast.

To my family, from Detroit and Pontiac, and to my Momasita and Dad, thanks for the unconditional love you always showered me with, particularly in my chosen career. I am nothing without your guidance and support. Although I have to do it in my own style, I hope I still make you proud because you make me proud to be your daughter everyday.

And to all my Seattle homeys, you know who y'all are, thanks for only grumbling a little as I skipped out on countless summer soirees, Sunday dinners, weekend getaways and backyard barbecues to write this book. Yes, I can come out and play now . . .

Bibliographic Notes

The majority of the research for this book was conducted through recorded personal interviews by the author of WNBA players, coaches, administrators, fans, and reporters. The author's own press clippings were reviewed along with various league-released materials collected through the Storm's seven seasons. The author also found these books to be useful in her research:

Boyd, Todd. *Young Black Rich & Famous.* New York: Doubleday, 2003.

Corbett, Sara. *Venus to the Hoop.* New York: Doubleday, 1997.

Gogol, Sara. *Playing in a New League.* Indianapolis: Masters Press, 1998.

Griffin, Pat. *Strong Women, Deep Closets.* University of Massachusetts, 1998.

Latrena Smith

About the Author

A proud University of Arizona alum, Jayda Evans has lived in nine states. First, to follow her father, the head men's basketball coach at the University of San Francisco, and second, as a sportswriter. She joined the *Seattle Times* in April 1999, covering preps in Snohomish County. Evans moved on to cover the Seahawks, Mariners, and Sonics plus two Olympics and a Super Bowl. She has covered the Storm since their inception.

Evans currently lives with her partner in the Seattle area.

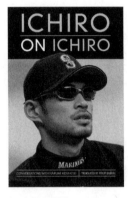